NAVAJO SOVEREIGNTY

Critical Issues in Indigenous Studies

Jeffrey P. Shepherd and Myla Vicenti Carpio
SERIES EDITORS

EDITED BY
LLOYD L. LEE

FOREWORD BY
JENNIFER NEZ DENETDALE

NAVAJO
SOVEREIGNTY

Understandings and Visions of the Diné People

THE UNIVERSITY OF
ARIZONA PRESS
TUCSON

I want to thank Raymond Austin, Bidtah Becker, Manley Begay Jr., Jennifer
Denetdale, Avery Denny, Larry W. Emerson, Colleen Gorman, Michelle Hale,
Michael Lerma, and Leola R. Tsinnajinnie for their commitment and contribution
to this anthology. I also want to thank my NAS at UNM colleagues—Gregory A.
Cajete, Wendy S. Greyeyes, Tiffany S. Lee, Robin S. Minthorn, Catherine
Montoya, and Leola R. Tsinnajinnie—for their support and their heartfelt
commitment to building Native nations and communities.

The University of Arizona Press
www.uapress.arizona.edu

Printed in the United States of America
22 21 20 19 18 17   6 5 4 3 2 1

ISBN-13: 978-0-8165-3408-1 (paper)

Cover design by Carrie House, HOUSEdesign LLC
Cover art: *dine'tah rising* by Venaya Yazzie

Publication of this book is made possible in part by the proceeds of a permanent endowment
created with the assistance of a Challenge Grant from the National Endowment for the Humanities,
a federal agency.

Library of Congress Cataloging-in-Publication Data
Names: Lee, Lloyd L., 1971– editor. | Denetdale, Jennifer, writer of foreword.
Title: Navajo sovereignty : understandings and visions of the Diné people / edited by Lloyd L. Lee ;
    foreword by Jennifer Nez Denetdale.
Other titles: Critical issues in indigenous studies.
Description: Tucson : The University of Arizona Press, 2017. | Series: Critical issues in indigenous
    studies | Includes bibliographical references.
Identifiers: LCCN 2016039130 | ISBN 9780816534081 (pbk. : alk. paper)
Subjects: LCSH: Navajo Indians. | Sovereignty.
Classification: LCC E99.N3 N358 2017 | DDC 979.1004/9726—dc23 LC record available at
    https://lccn.loc.gov/2016039130

♾ This paper meets the requirements of ANSI/NISO Z39.48-1992 (Permanence of Paper).

CONTENTS

CREATIVITY AND VISION

FOREWORD

JENNIFER DENETDALE

T HE TOPIC OF Navajo sovereignty and self-determination has been the
center of vigorous discussion in Diné studies and, in particular, as the
Navajo Nation and its leaders address the state of the nation and, often,
criticism about the numerous issues that leaders face on a daily basis. At the
heart of concerns about Navajo nation building are questions about the extent
to which the nation has been able to exert its powers and independence as sovereign. Many of the contributors acknowledge that the Navajo Nation's history
is deeply connected to that of the United States, which continues to exert its
authority over the Navajo Nation as its trustee and within a "domestic dependent" relationship. This relationship is implicated in the state of the Navajo
Nation today, of which the consequences include the ongoing consequences
of an imposed Western democratic governmental structure that transformed
Navajo governance and leadership. Historically, the transformation of Navajo
governance, citizenship, and how we belong to each other within a nation
began with the American military defeat of the Diné in 1863, in which with
forced relocation to Hweéldi, headmen were stripped of their authority and
required to answer to Indian agents and military officers at Fort Sumner. At
the Bosque Redondo, American justice replaced Navajo sensibility regarding
justice with the establishment of a court of offenses to exact American justice
for Navajo offenders. One of the reasons for subjugating Navajos and remov-
ing them to a foreign land was to subject them to ethnic cleansing, where all

things Diné were to be erased and replaced with American institutions' values. Because the "experiment" of removal and the inculcation of American values of the Diné proved to be a disaster for several reasons, including the exorbitant cost of keeping prisoners at the reservation, the reservation was not becoming self-sufficient, and my ancestors never adapted to the reservation, a treaty between the Diné and the United States was drawn up. This treaty came about during a time when the United States was facing harsh criticism for the treatment of its Indigenous peoples by white settlers, with the Sand Creek Massacre receiving some of the harshest criticism.

In 1868, after negotiation between Navajo male leaders and U.S. representations, a treaty was drawn up that would release the Navajo people from the confines of the hated and alien reservation and send them back to their beloved homeland. Many of the provisions of the treaty that our male leaders agreed to continued U.S. claims to authority over the Navajo Nation and its peoples. It included provisions that indicate the position of limited power and authority that leaders had in the negotiations. For example, there was a provision that Navajos would allow a transcontinental railroad across their lands, and another that Navajo children would be schooled in American values. Furthermore, that the size of land decreed as Navajo land was severely diminished in size also spoke to the place from which Navajo men negotiated. For the Navajo people, however, the Treaty of 1868 is an important symbol of sovereignty and self-determination that is often invoked to announce the status of the Navajo Nation as a nation among nations.

Diné history is similar to those of other Indigenous peoples in the struggles our leaders and citizens face, and that it began with the imposition of foreign forms of government, judicial system, and leadership. It is, however, but one facet of what Navajo sovereignty and self-determination mean, as these essays demonstrate. The Navajo Nation, its leaders and citizens, might be constrained by the "domestic dependent" relationship with the United States, but it has not stopped Diné from being what it means to be Diné, and to reach into the past to the teachings of our ancestors who used their knowledge and experiences to survive the American war waged on them, and to perpetuate the teachings that have kept our people vibrant and alive. As many of these contributors note, and as my dear colleague Mohawk Audra Simpson declares, "We simply refuse to stop being Indigenous." We refuse to stop being Diné. Outside of the colonial gaze and the attempts to constantly monitor and surveil us as Diné, we faithfully practice who we are as Diné. Through the sharing of Diné teachings and the daily practice of *k'é*, Navajo principles of kin relationships, we keep alive the vibrancy of those thoughts and practices that saw our ancestors through some of the most horrific events in our history. We draw on the ceremonies and prayers that have within them First Teachings, thereby constantly re-creating a sense of community. It is those spaces of what some call "cultural sovereignty" and others "organic sovereignty," we affirm our nation as sovereign and our identities as distinctly Diné. These sovereign spaces also are places of freedom and liberation, because they are places where we are free to be who we are. They are spaces of respite and rest from the ongoing effects of colonialism.

Contributors note the multiple ways and layers of how we are Diné and how we practice sovereignty and self-determination. We work to transform governance by penning Navajo Fundamental Law and establishing the Peacemaking Court. We establish colleges and community schools that center on Diné philosophy and teachings. We establish a human rights commission to declare that we are a nation among nations. We draw on various media, art, and cultural events to remember and celebrate who we are as Diné. We write our own histories and narratives about being Diné and the value of our homeland. As the contributors note, as Diné we are a vibrant and flourishing nation and people who both celebrate and meet the challenges of a twenty-first-century modern tribal nation. There is still much to say, to think about, and to do to envision the kind of nation we want—one that meets the needs of our citizens. May these works of Diné leaders, scholars, and educators find fertile ground in our visions and imaginations.

NAVAJO SOVEREIGNTY

THE NAVAJO NATION

Navajo Nation Map

INTRODUCTION

S INCE TIME IMMEMORIAL, Navajo (Diné) people have determined their way of life. They lived life according to their needs. However, for the last 150 years, Navajo people have been confined into a "colonial box" where their rights, freedoms, power, authority, and autonomy are limited. This limitation frames Navajo sovereignty in the twenty-first century.

Prior to colonization, Navajo authority and autonomy was located in the extended family networks, clans, and "natural communities."[1] No one central leader controlled all Navajo families, clans, and "natural communities." In fact, if a decision was made in one "natural community," it did not have an impact, influence, or authority in all other "natural communities."[2] Individual family networks, clans, and "natural communities" exercised their power and authority on a daily basis without external intrusion. This way of life was impacted and altered by European and American invasions into Diné Bikéyah (Diné land) from the sixteenth century onward. For the most part, Navajo extended family networks maintained authority from the 1500s until the mid-1800s.

When Americans invaded the region in the nineteenth century, they started to subjugate Apache and Navajo peoples. Between 1864 and 1868, more than eight thousand Diné were imprisoned at Bosque Redondo in eastern New Mexico Territory. A treaty was negotiated with American officials in 1868, and the people were allowed to return home to a reservation. From 1869 to the late 1920s, Diné self-sufficiency thrived, although many people had a hard life. In the early 1930s, the federal government forced thousands of Diné to reduce their livestock (sheep, horses, cattle) herds to mitigate soil erosion on the reservation. Many people lost their self-sufficiency and sought wage labor in border towns and cities. Christian churches and boarding schools were established. Thousands of Diné children attended western schools for the first time. They changed Diné thought, language, and way of life.

The Bureau of Indian Affairs (BIA) created a Navajo "business" council in 1923 consisting of twelve delegates and twelve alternatives representing the five Navajo agency towns. Herbert J. Hagerman, special Department of the Interior commissioner to the Navajo reservation, presided over the council. The council's primary duty was to approve oil and other mineral leases. Along with a "business" council, the BIA implemented a chapter house system. Superintendent of Leupp Agency John G. Hunter created the chapter house system in the late 1920s; it was fed into preexisting, local sociopolitical structures.[3]

In 1936, the Department of the Interior secretary called for a constitutional assembly, and seventy-four individuals from all over the reservation came together to form a Navajo constitution. The secretary rejected the constitution, and instead issued a simplified set of bylaws called "Rules for the Tribal Council" that became the framework for Navajo government.[4] The Navajo council consisted of the seventy-four delegates called for the constitutional assembly. A federal official, the superintendent, and later the secretary "occupied a position beside the chairman in the conduct of council meetings."[5] Major amendments in the organization of the government or election procedures required secretarial approval. The basis for present-day Navajo government was constituted.

Attempts were made in the 1950s to develop a written constitution but failed because of the concern of secretarial oversight of the Navajo government. Nonetheless, the tribal council exercised a growing array of powers through resolutions, which were subject to secretarial veto. A tribal court system was established, reservation grazing regulations were adopted, a scholarship fund was created, the chapters were incorporated into the Navajo government, and the judicial branch was established.[6] In 1962, the resolutions were codified into a Navajo Tribal Code, outlining governmental powers and council procedures. In the 1990s, the Navajo Tribal Code was renamed the Navajo Nation Code.

From 1962 to 1989, the Tribal Code defined and expanded Navajo government and its authority. In 1989, then-chairman Peter MacDonald was placed on involuntary administrative leave pending a federal investigation into criminal charges. MacDonald and his supporters fought these actions, which led to a deadly confrontation in Window Rock, Arizona, on July 20, 1989, involving MacDonald's supporters, the tribal council, and the tribal police. Two people were killed and ten others injured in the altercation. In the fall of 1989, the tribal council enacted landmark changes to Navajo government. These changes created a Navajo government modeled on the American three-branch government system. Despite all of these changes, the Diné people have never sanctioned their current government.

Yet, with all the trauma, violence, and government changes, Diné people and their way of life continue. Diné people exercise sovereignty by various means, such as designating the Diné word *nááts'íílid* (rainbow) for sovereignty, the Navajo Nation Council codifying Diné bi Beenzhaz'áanii (Fundamental Laws), and individuals living by the philosophical principle of *Sa'ąh Naagháí Bik'eh Hózhǫ́ǫ́n* (SNBH).

Nááts'íílid symbolizes Navajo sovereignty. Nááts'íílid is seen on the Navajo Nation flag, where it arches over the nation and the sacred mountains. The colors of nááts'íílid are blue, yellow, and red. It is seen as protecting the land, environment, animals, plants, people, and way of life.

SNBH is a living paradigm. It is complex and simple, with many meanings and understandings for human beings. According to Navajo scholar Miranda Haskie, this principle is so powerful that when people "follow the path of SNBH, the natural teaching," we understand "the depth of our life." [7] She continues on, "We will believe in ourselves, have trust in ourselves, believe in what we are doing and we will understand and know where we are going in this life." [8] SNBH "represents the Diné traditional system of values and beliefs that provide teaching and learning of human existence in harmony with the natural world." [9]

SNBH is a pathway where Navajo people are taught and learn how to achieve a healthy well-being throughout life. [10] SNBH also encompasses a four-part planning and learning process central to the traditional Navajo way of knowing. [11] This process comprises *nitsáhákees* (thinking), *nahat'á* (planning), *iiná* (living), and *siihasin* (reflecting). [12] It is multidimensional and comprehensive. To understand SNBH is to understand the concept of wholeness, and achieving SNBH is completeness. [13]

SNBH provides individuals a way of acknowledging and overcoming the conflicts, difficulties, chaos, and contradictions in life. [14] SNBH recognizes that unsettling forces and change are normal; they are always present in life, and they were experienced repeatedly in the past. [15] These conflicts and changes are testimonies to the upheavals and displacements in Navajo history and illustrate how people are strong.

SNBH is also multidimensional ways and interconnected forces. Life is full of energies, and it's the responsibility of the community and of the person to know these energies and to use them wisely in their daily lives. Energies exist, and they represent positive and negative forces. These forces are in all living entities, and for a person and a community to achieve wellness, they must strive to ensure equilibrium and achieve symmetry. In other words, a person and community partake in moderation. Too much of any force is harmful to the individual and community. Each living entity is composed of halves of the whole, and achieving wellness is maintaining the equilibrium of both.

Diné bi Beenzhaz'áanii is interwoven with SNBH. In 2003, the Fundamental Laws were codified into Title One of the Navajo Nation Code. The Navajo Nation Council uses the Fundamental Laws to help govern, and the Navajo Supreme Court uses it to analyze legal cases. Along with the council, environmental grassroots groups such as Eastern Navajo Diné Against Uranium Mining (ENDAUM), Diné CARE (Diné Citizens Against Ruining Our Environment), Dooda Desert Rock, and Black Mesa Water Coalition evoke the natural law provision of the Fundamental Laws to help with their causes.[16] ENDAUM was successful in using the Fundamental Laws to justify a prohibition on uranium mining and milling on the Navajo Nation, although attempts are made every day to circumvent the prohibition by both corporations and Navajo government officials. Former Navajo Nation president Joe Shirley Jr. signed into law the Diné Natural Resources Protection Act of 2005, banning uranium mining and milling on Diné Bikéyah. This was a collaborative effort by activists, government officials, and state officials.

Diné bi Beenzhaz'áanii is rooted in cultural values, traditions, and ancestral knowledge. It is written in English, but the draft discussions on the legislation were in Diné. The Fundamental Laws are based on cultural knowledge respective of all elements on the earth and in the universe, and frame how the people live on the earth.

Chapter 1 declares the foundation of Diné law. It states, "Different thinking, planning, lifeways, languages, beliefs, and laws appear among us, but the fundamental laws placed by the Holy People remain unchanged. Hence, as we were created and with living soul, we remain Diné forever."[17]

Chapter 2 lays the groundwork for the various chapters of the Fundamental Laws. A list of rights and freedoms for each Diné person and the collective group is outlined. Some of the rights and freedoms include a government system consisting of *hozhóójí nahat'á* (executive branch), *naatáji nahat'á* (legislative branch), *hashkééjí nahat'á* (judicial branch), and *nayee'jí nahat'á* (national security branch). Diné bi Beenzhaz'áanii provides for the future development and growth of a thriving Navajo Nation regardless of the many different thinking, planning, lifeways, languages, beliefs, and laws that may appear within the nation.[18]

Chapter 3 covers traditional law. This chapter states that it is the right and freedom of the Diné to choose leaders of their choice, and for those leaders to carry out their duties and responsibilities in a moral and legal manner. It lists the duties of the executive, legislative, judicial, and security branch leadership. It calls for the people to respect and honor the elders and medicine people. The elders and medicine people can be called on to cleanse, protect, pray, and bless the leadership and the operation of the government. It also calls for the government and the people to respect the spiritual beliefs and practices of any person and to allow the input and contribution of any religion. Finally, it allows the people and government to incorporate practices, principles, and values of other peoples foreign to the principles and values of Diné bi Beenzhaz'áanii in the best interest and those necessary to provide the physical and mental well-being of each person.

Chapter 4 focuses on customary law. The main focus is to let the people know they have the right and freedom to a comprehensive Diné cultural education. They can learn *k'é* (relations), language, traditions, protocols, and cultural knowledge.

Chapter 5 is on natural law. Air, light, fire, water, earth, pollen—the six sacred and attendant mountains must be respected, honored, and protected. All creation on the earth and in the universe has a right and freedom to exist, and the people have a sacred obligation and duty to respect, preserve, and protect all. It states, "Mother Earth and Father Sky is part of us as Diné and the Diné is part of Mother Earth and Father Sky; the Diné must treat this sacred bond with love and respect without exerting dominance for we do not own our mother or father."[19] While love and respect are written down, the government and the people can benefit from natural resource extraction through a proper protocol of respect and offering. Natural resource extraction is a major source of revenue for the Navajo government's budget. Various Navajo grassroots groups contest this stringently and wholeheartedly. Many Native peoples have a similar ethical and moral approach to the usage of natural resources.

Chapter 6 centers on common law. This chapter focuses on the commonality of human beings and how life should be. For instance, it states, "The values and principles of Diné common law must be used to harness and utilize the unlimited interwoven Diné knowledge, with our absorbed knowledge from other peoples. This knowledge is our tool in exercising and exhibiting self-assurance and self-reliance and in enjoying the beauty of happiness and harmony."[20] In Diné common law, the need to compete in business for sustenance is acknowledged and encouraged. The Navajo Nation has several enterprises including the Navajo Nation Gaming Enterprise, which oversees four casinos at the moment.

The last part is a diagram of a Diné original law structure. It is designed to show the multidimensional and comprehensive motion. Traditional law, customary law, natural law, and common law are elements helping the people live in this world. The people are not above the laws but rather are guided by them. The laws are a pathway to happiness, prosperity, peace, and harmony. Diverging from these laws will cause challenges and difficulties to ensue.

SNBH and Diné bi Beenzhaz'áanii represent a traditional life framework, and Diné understandings of sovereignty are a part of this foundation. This foundation, however, is influenced by twenty-first-century realities and ways of life. The Navajo Nation is viewed as a domestic dependent nation by the federal government and western law. While the Navajo Nation and all Native nations in the United States are viewed in this fashion, they work diligently to exercise their power and authority conducive to their way of life and identity. Conversation, analysis, and dialogue are warranted to understanding and envisioning what sovereignty means to each specific Native nation and/or community. This anthology is only one Diné perspective; multiple views and thoughts are needed and warranted.

Several Native scholars such as Vine Deloria Jr., Taiaiake Alfred, Jeff Corntassel, David E. Wilkins, Tom Holm, Waziyatawin, Simon Ortiz, Joanne Barker, and Jennifer Denetdale have written on Native authority, autonomy, and sovereignty. Some of the scholars call on Native peoples to return to cultural epistemologies missing from many contemporary Native communities. For instance, in *The Nations Within: The Past and Future of American Indian Sovereignty*, Deloria distinguishes between nationhood and self-government:

> Nationhood implies a decision making that is free and uninhibited within the community, a community in fact that is almost completely insulated from external factors as it considers its possible options. Self-government, on the other hand, implies a recognition by the superior political power that some measure of local decision making is necessary but that this process must be monitored very

carefully so that its products are compatible with the goals and policies of the larger political power. Self-government implies that the people were previously incapable of making any decisions for themselves and are now ready to assume some, but not all, of the responsibilities of a municipality. Under self-government, however, the larger moral issues that affect a *people*'s relationship with other people are presumed to be included within the responsibilities of the larger nation.[21]

In *Peace, Power, Righteousness: An Indigenous Manifesto*, Alfred calls for reclaiming Indigenous space (intellectual, political, and geographic), developing an Indigenous consciousness, having a commitment to bettering Indigenous society, looking out for the dangers that might entice leaders, communicating the ideals to the community, and keeping in touch with historical teachings.[22] Alfred's call to develop an Indigenous consciousness is similar to Paulo Freire's call for *conscientização*. In *Pedagogy of the Oppressed*, Freire, a Brazilian educator, outlined a way the oppressed could be liberated:

In order for the oppressed to be able to wage the struggle for liberation, they must perceive the reality of oppression not as a closed world from which there is no exit, but as a limiting situation which they can transform. This perception is necessary but not a sufficient condition for liberation; it must become the motivating force for liberating action.[23]

Deloria, Alfred, and Freire provide insights into how Native nations can build their nations using cultural knowledge, even though it is fragmented in many Native communities. Carol Perry and Patricia Anne Davis, testifying at the Navajo Office of Government Reform public hearing in 2001, stressed the need to return to traditional Navajo governance:

The tribal governance standards of the past are not obsolete. They are appropriate and have stood the test of time. They were focused on maintaining the health and wellness of every member of the community. Safety, health, wellness, and protection were facilitated, not by dominance, confrontation, conflict, and coercion, but by ethics, communication, cooperation, and reverence for the creator and the laws of nature.[24]

Advocacy for traditional Navajo governance is part of the dialogue occurring among Diné people regarding sovereignty, power, and authority. The many challenges the Navajo Nation faces in the twenty-first century have increased the call for traditional governance as a way to rectify leadership corruption, lack of government efficiency, lack of confidence in the system, and an overall negative attitude toward contemporary Navajo government.

While some call for a restoration of traditional cultural epistemologies, others define tribal sovereignty in the twenty-first century by acknowledging traditional inherent forces with practical realities. For instance, in *American Indian Politics and the American Political System*, David E. Wilkins and Heidi Kiiwetinepinesiik Stark define sovereignty as such:

> Tribal sovereignty is the intangible and dynamic cultural force inherent in a given indigenous community, empowering the body toward the sustenance and enhancement of political, economic, and cultural integrity. It undergirds the way tribal governments relate to their own citizens, to non-Indian residents, to local governments, to the state governments, to the federal government, to the corporate world, and to the global community.[25]

In *The Third Space of Sovereignty: The Postcolonial Politics of U.S.-Indigenous Relations*, Kevin Bruyneel views sovereignty as the ability of a group of people to make their own decisions and control their own lives in relation to the space where they live and envision as their own.[26] In "Development, Governance, Culture: What Are They and What Do They Have to Do with Rebuilding Native Nations?" in *Rebuilding Native Nations: Strategies for Governance and Development*, Manley A. Begay Jr., Stephen Cornell, Miriam Jorgensen, and Joseph P. Kalt explain sovereignty as Indigenous control over the design of their own governing systems. They state that it may take some time, but once it is achieved, Native peoples are the ones who are most likely to create traditional or nontraditional systems that work, systems that are their own.[27] In *Indigenous Sovereignty in the 21st Century: Knowledge for the Indigenous Spring*, Michael Lerma believes that explaining Native sovereignty through federal Indian law and policy is a losing game that should be avoided if possible, but acknowledged and defended when necessary. He says, "Indigenous accounts of sovereignty are best understood in terms of ceremony, language, homelands, and sacred histories. Indigenous sovereignty, in reality, has nothing to do with Aboriginal Title."[28]

Not all Native scholars and intellectuals view sovereignty or the use of the word in a productive way. Vine Deloria Jr. also viewed *sovereignty* as a useful word to describe the process of growth and awareness that characterizes a group of people working toward and achieving maturity, but he also saw the limitation in a legal-political context where it can prevent solutions.[29] Joanne Barker sees sovereignty as historically contingent. She says, "What it has meant and what it currently means belong to the political subjects who have deployed and are deploying it to do the work of defining their relationship with one another, their political agendas, and their strategies for decolonization and social justice."[30] The specific social conditions must be considered, but also the incompleteness, inaccuracy, and troubled understanding of the term has to be acknowledged and analyzed.[31] In "Sovereignty," in *Sovereignty Matters*, Alfred rejects the term and the notion of Indigenous "sovereignty," and instead encourages people to restore cultural epistemologies to reflect their distinctive communities and a just relationship between the earth and the peoples.[32] In *X-Marks: Native Signatures of Assent*, Scott Richard Lyons argues that sovereignty does not exempt Native nations from a responsibility to be just.

A . . . pressing danger in my view is the use of Native nations and indigenous sovereignty for purposes that can be just as harmful and retrograde as anyone else's oppression. When gays and lesbians, workers, black people—or anyone— are harmed in the name of tribal sovereignty, then discourses other than nationalism are called for in the name of justice. . . . It is always the job of intellectuals to "look also at racism, political and economic oppression, sexism, supremacism, and the needles and wasteful exploitation of land and people," *no matter who perpetuates the* injustice.[33]

Other Native scholars want a comprehensive articulation of sovereignty. The discussion has to include place, body, home, visual, cultural, intellectual, and many areas of the Native way of life. For instance, in *Native Studies Keywords*, Michelle H. Raheja writes:

Filmmakers, artists, activists, and writers employ their work to imagine multiple forms of sovereignty and creative expression as well as to provide healthy critiques of legal discourses of sovereignty as they are articulated by both Native nations and settler-colonial states. If we are to imagine a future that takes seriously forms of sovereignty that pose radical, exciting, and therapeutic provocations and alternatives to settler-colonial jurisprudence and fixed representations of Native peoples, we must continue to encourage conversations that maintain spaces for articulations of sovereignty in the arts.[34]

Native peoples have endured many challenges to their way of life and identity over the past five hundred years, but they continue to function as distinct peoples. Each Native nation and community has a distinct and similar understanding and vision of what sovereignty, power, and authority means to the people. The understanding of sovereignty is reflected in the people's actions, perspectives, thoughts, and visions. What follows is only a small diverse glimpse of Navajo sovereignty.

This anthology is a contribution to the conversations, analyses, and dialogues taking place in Navajo chapter houses, in government offices, in schools, at flea markets, and all the different spaces around and in Diné Bikéyah. The book is divided into four sections, and these sections reflect various perspectives on Navajo sovereignty, power, and authority. The following questions frame the perspectives: (1) what is Navajo sovereignty, (2) how do various Navajo Nation institutions exercise sovereignty, (3) what challenges does Navajo sovereignty face in the coming generations, and (4) how do individual Diné envision sovereignty? While these questions frame the diverse perspectives, they do not limit what is shared and discussed in this volume. This book is for a diverse audience—not only other scholars, academics, and Navajo people themselves, but all Native people.

Native sovereignty is a complex subject to understand and reflect on because of the different histories and experiences of Native peoples. This book shows the diverse perspectives in one Native nation. Native peoples need to have more conversations, analyses, and articulations on the subject. The individuals in this anthology are only a small part of the conversation and by no means deliver the be-all and end-all perspective on Navajo sovereignty. This book will hopefully inspire and entice other Navajo and Native scholars and people to think, write, and analyze this complex, yet important, subject.

The first section of this book is about the law. Former Navajo Supreme Court Justice Raymond Austin and former assistant attorney general of the Navajo Nation Bidtah Becker are contributors. In "Diné Sovereignty, a Legal and Traditional Analysis," Raymond Austin examines the concepts of sovereign and sovereignty under American law, and discusses how these concepts are applied to Native nations in the United States. He further analyzes the concepts of sovereign and sovereignty using a Navajo traditional belief system, In "Sovereignty from the Individual Diné Experience," Bidtah Becker offers her personal insights into the Navajo Nation's internal workings to provide a distinct perspective on how Navajo sovereignty is viewed and exercised by the government. Her thoughts and writings frame how sovereignty might be understood and envisioned for the future of the Navajo Nation and its citizens.

The second section focuses on education. Manley Begay Jr. and Leola Tsinnajinnie contribute to this section. Begay examines educational sovereignty as a critical component of Native nation building. All Native nations in the United States are in the process of nation (re)building. Begay contextualizes the Navajo education system and what is needed to ensure the sovereignty of a Navajo child's education. Tsinnajinnie's chapter is a personal reflection on the concept of Navajo educational sovereignty. She shares her personal journey of education and how it ties into her work at the higher education level. Education is a very personal experience, and Tsinnajinnie beautifully shares and emphasizes the point of what it means for Navajo individual and educational sovereignty.

The third section is about research. Michael Lerma, along with Navajo healer Avery Denny, and Michelle Hale are contributors. Michael Lerma and Avery Denny's "Diné Principles of Good Governance" introduces the concept of good governance, then delves into the context of treaties and how foreign aid threatens Navajo good governance. They then develop a concept of good governance based on Sa'ąh Naaghái Bik'eh Hózhóǫn. In "Empowered Sovereignty for Navajo Chapters through Engagement in a Community-Planning Process," Michelle Hale investigates how the Navajo Local Governance Act of 1998 set the foundation for Navajo communities to empower the people. Navajo people have always planned, and she advocates for the people to maximize all opportunities with community planning.

The fourth section focuses on creativity and vision. Artist activist Colleen Gorman and artist, activist, and farmer Larry Emerson contribute to this section. Colleen Gorman's chapter brings insightful Indigenous knowledge to the discussion on Navajo sovereignty. Her piece demonstrates how Indigenous knowledge is linked to identity, language, and what it means to be a human being from a Navajo and Indigenous point of view. This discussion is warranted to understand what is important to an individual and group and how this importance can help revitalize, regenerate, and re-Indigenize Native peoples to the land, philosophy, and way of life. The book concludes with Larry Emerson's chapter. He rejects the Western concept of sovereignty and advocates the Diné methodology of *hózhóojí naat'á* (peacemaking) as a distinct, Native-centered way to engage the concept of sovereignty. He reflects and develops how to think about sovereignty from an inherent, original way of Diné thought. He feels a paradigm shift is possible, and a goal of Diné-centered concept of sovereignty leads to *hózhǫ́* (beautiful and happiness) and *k'é* (relations).

As previously mentioned, these chapters are only a small articulation of Navajo sovereignty; more individual perspectives will be needed.

NOTES

1. David E. Wilkins, *The Navajo Political Experience*, revised edition (Lanham, MD: Rowman and Littlefield, 2003).
2. Ibid., 69.
3. David E. Wilkins, *Diné Bibeehaz'áanii: A Handbook of Navajo Government* (Tsaile, AZ: Navajo Community College Press, 1987).
4. Ibid., 69.
5. Robert W. Young, "The Rise of the Navajo Tribe," in *Plural Society in the Southwest*, ed. Spicer E. and R. Thompson (Albuquerque: University of New Mexico Press, 1972).
6. Wilkins, *The Navajo Political Experience*, 89.
7. Miranda J. Haskie, "Preserving a Culture: Practicing the Navajo Principles of Hózhǫ́ dóó K'é" (PhD diss., Fielding Graduate Institute, 2002), 31.
8. Ibid., 31.
9. Ibid.
10. Ibid., 32.
11. Ibid.
12. Ibid.
13. John R. Farella, *The Main Stalk: A Synthesis in Navajo Philosophy* (Albuquerque: University of New Mexico Press, 1984), 153.
14. Deborah House, *Language Shift Among the Navajos: Identity Politics and Cultural Continuity* (Tucson: University of Arizona Press, 2002), 27.
15. Ibid., 27.
16. Dane E. Powell and Andrew Curley, "K'e, Hozhó, and Non-governmental Politics on the Navajo Nation: Ontologies of Difference Manifest in Environmental Activism," *World Anthropologies Network E-Journal* 4 (2009).

17. Navajo Nation, *Fundamental Laws of the Diné, Navajo Nation Code* (2002), No. CN-69–02, Window Rock, AZ: 2003.
18. Ibid.
19. Ibid.
20. Ibid.
21. Vine Deloria Jr. and Clifford M. Lytle, *The Nations Within: The Past and Future of American Indian Sovereignty* (Austin: University of Texas Press, 1998), 13–14.
22. Taiaiake Alfred, *Peace, Power, Righteousness: An Indigenous Manifesto* (Oxford: Oxford University Press, 1999), xx–xxiii.
23. Paulo Freire, *Pedagogy of the Oppressed, Thirtieth Anniversary Edition* (New York: Continuum, 2000), 49.
24. Carol Perry and Patricia Anne Davis, "Diné Sovereignty Is Spiritual Empowerment and Self-Identity," Public hearing, Window Rock, Arizona, August 16, 2001.
25. David E. Wilkins and Heidi Kiiwetinepinesiik Stark, *American Indian Politics and the American Political System Third Edition* (Lanham, MD: Rowman and Littlefield, 2011), 38–39.
26. Kevin Bruyneel, *The Third Space of Sovereignty: The Postcolonial Politics of U.S.-Indigenous Relations* (Minneapolis: University of Minnesota Press, 2007), 23.
27. Manley A. Begay Jr., Stephen Cornell, Miriam Jorgensen, and Joseph P. Kalt, "Development, Governance, Culture: What Are They and What Do They Have to Do with Rebuilding Native Nations?" in *Rebuilding Native Nations: Strategies for Governance and Development*, ed. Miriam Jorgensen (Tucson: University of Arizona Press, 2007), 52.
28. Michael Lerma, *Indigenous Sovereignty in the 21st Century: Knowledge for the Indigenous Spring* (Gainesville: Florida Academic Press, Inc., 2014), 46.
29. Vine Deloria Jr., "Self-Determination and the Concept of Sovereignty," in *Economic Development in American Indian Reservations*, ed. Roxanne Dunbar Ortiz (Albuquerque: University of New Mexico Press, 1979).
30. Joanne Barker, ed. *Sovereignty Matters: Locations of Contestation and Possibility in Indigenous Struggles for Self-Determination* (Lincoln: University of Nebraska Press, 2005), 26.
31. Ibid., 26.

32. Taiaiake Alfred, "Sovereignty," in *Sovereignty Matters: Locations of Contestation and Possibility in Indigenous Struggles for Self-Determination*, ed. Joanne Barker (Lincoln: University of Nebraska Press, 2005), 48.

33. Scott Richard Lyons, *X-Marks: Native Signatures of Assent* (Minneapolis: University of Minnesota Press, 2010), 163.

34. Michelle H. Raheja, "Visual Sovereignty," in *Native Studies Keywords*, ed. Stephanie Nohelani Teves, Andrea Smith, and Michelle H. Raheja (Tucson: University of Arizona Press, 2015), 31.

LAW

DINÉ SOVEREIGNTY, A LEGAL AND TRADITIONAL ANALYSIS

JUSTICE RAYMOND D. AUSTIN

INTRODUCTION

T IS THE SUMMER of 2014 and presidential politics are at full speed on the Navajo Nation. Seventeen candidates have declared for the office of Navajo Nation president.[1] Listen to KTNN, the Navajo Nation's radio station, and read the *Navajo Times*, the Navajo Nation's weekly newspaper, and you will notice a term the presidential candidates frequently use—*Navajo sovereignty*. At a recent presidential forum, two candidates said the following about Navajo sovereignty—Donald Benally: "I will never jeopardize the sovereignty of the Navajo Nation as your president"—Edison Begay: "We're never going to be sovereign just by saying we're sovereign."[2] Although we hear the words *sovereign* and *sovereignty* quite frequently throughout Navajo Country, the people who use them do not explain whether these concepts come from a distinctly traditional Navajo epistemology or not.

What do the concepts of sovereign and sovereignty mean? Are the words *sovereign* and *sovereignty*, as they refer to the legal and political status of the Navajo Nation, defined solely by American or Western legal and political understandings? Are the concepts of sovereign and sovereignty part of traditional Navajo beliefs, as understood and practiced by traditional Navajos? These and similar questions need to be debated because they go directly to the well-being and future of the Navajo people, Navajo Nation government, and

Navajo lands. The Navajo people should engage their leaders in dialogue and arrive at a consensus of what it means to be a sovereign Diné nation and to exercise Diné sovereignty. These discussions are necessary as we continue on the path to build and maintain an effective and efficient Navajo Nation government with strong, stable institutions.

This chapter is written particularly for the Navajo people, and its purpose is to inspire, and even provoke. That is, the Navajo people must discuss, intellectualize, and agree on a Diné sovereignty doctrine that is rooted in a distinctly Navajo epistemology. I first look at the concepts of sovereign and sovereignty under American law, then examine the application of those concepts to Indian nations in the United States. This application demonstrates that the American version of tribal sovereignty has had severe negative consequences and repercussions for the Navajo Nation and other American Indian nations in the United States. Can those negatives be neutralized through the implementation of a distinctly Diné sovereignty doctrine that is grounded in traditional Diné knowledge? I believe so. Different ideas need to come forth on this issue, and that is the major reason for this chapter. We need to begin discussions on developing our own Diné sovereignty doctrine by looking at the concepts of sovereign and sovereignty as they relate to the Navajo Nation using the Navajo traditional knowledge system.[3] More Diné knowledge holders—including ceremonial practitioners, traditionalists, and elders—scholars, leaders, and young people should realize the importance of this subject and contribute.

DEFINITIONS OF SOVEREIGN AND SOVEREIGNTY UNDER AMERICAN AND WESTERN LAW

According to the most widely used American law dictionary, a sovereign is a "state vested with independent and supreme authority."[4] As explained below, however, the modern Navajo Nation is not considered an independent state, as that term is used to generally define nation-states under international law.[5] A sovereign nation-state is defined as a "state that possesses an independent existence, being complete in itself, without being merely part of a larger whole to whose government it is subject."[6] The United States is a nation-state; the individual states of the United States are not nation-states. The modern American Indian nations are not independent nation-states because the United States ultimately controls their sovereignty. The pre–Columbian Navajo Nation (as were other Indian nations) would have met the definition of an independent sovereign state, although around the time of European discovery, considerable debate raged among European international law theorists on whether "uncivilized," non-Christian peoples had protectable rights (i.e., sovereign rights) to their lands, property, and political associations under natural law and the European Law of Nations.[7] Under the modern definition, a sovereign nation-state, like the United States, is a complete sovereign possessed of independent and supreme authority.

Sovereignty is the authority possessed and exercised by a sovereign state and is defined as follows: "Supreme dominion, authority or rule; the supreme political authority of an independent state."[8] The prevailing concept of nation-state is a Western construct. Modern American Indian nations in the United States do not fit into this Western construct of nation-state because they were colonized by the very European nations that developed that international law doctrine. This does not mean that American Indian nations do not have a right to self-government and self-determination, because they do. Although the words *sovereign* and *sovereignty* have been applied generally to American Indian nations in the United States, the more accepted terms currently used to describe their legal and political status are *domestic dependent nations* (semi-sovereigns) and *tribal sovereignty*.

AMERICAN INDIAN NATION SOVEREIGNTY UNDER AMERICAN LAW

The concepts of sovereign and sovereignty as they are applied to the legal and political status of American Indian nations in the United States primarily come from three cases decided by the United States Supreme Court in the early 1800s: *Johnson v. McIntosh*,[9] *Cherokee Nation v. Georgia*,[10] and *Worcester v. Georgia*.[11] These cases are called the Marshall Trilogy in federal Indian law, because Chief Justice John Marshall authored the opinions. U.S. courts use the Marshall Trilogy as the starting point for analyzing and determining the scope and nature of the sovereign status of Indian nations and Indian nation sovereignty under American law today. The Marshall Trilogy sets forth the foundational doctrines upon which most of United States federal Indian law and policy, both good and bad, were created, implemented, and exercised for nearly two hundred years now.

JOHNSON V. MCINTOSH

In 2005 it came to light that the first case, *Johnson v. McIntosh*, has a sordid history—collusion among the plaintiffs and defendants, fraudulent land purchases, and a feigned controversy that was decided by a land-speculating chief justice with a huge stake in the outcome.[12] Nonetheless, the case is still foundational law today and continues to be cited in court decisions. According to the U.S. Supreme Court, *Johnson v. McIntosh* is about the validity of land titles involving the same land. Which land title should United States courts recognize as valid—plaintiff Johnson's title, which came through direct purchase from Indian nations, or the title the United States granted to defendant McIntosh?[13] The title granted by the United States is the valid title, said the Supreme Court, because the European-derived doctrine of discovery had stripped Indian nations of their right to sell their lands to any party other than the United States.[14] The discovery doctrine under the Law of Nations essentially held that the first Christian European nation that discovers lands occupied by non-Christian, uncivilized peoples takes title to those lands upon discovery.[15] What about the Indian landowners—what rights do they have to their lands after discovery? The Supreme Court, in its interpretation and adoption of the discovery doctrine into American law, says the Indian nations are left with "a right of occupancy" of their lands, which can be extinguished through "purchase or conquest."[16] The discovery doctrine, as interpreted and adopted in *Johnson v. McIntosh*, gave the federal government practically unlimited power over Indian lands in the United States. Accordingly, in the ensuing years, the transfer of Indian lands, usually by treaties, became a one-way process, from Indians to white Americans.

On sovereignty, *Johnson v. McIntosh* said, the Indian nations' "rights to complete sovereignty, as independent nations, were necessarily diminished."[17] American Indian nations, including the Navajo Nation, were complete, independent sovereigns, as that term is known in international law, before European contact. Indian nation sovereignty, of course, is inherent, meaning the Indian nations have always had it; it is not granted by another sovereign such as the United States. Upon discovery by European nations, the discovery doctrine diminished the Indian nations' sovereign status. *Johnson v. McIntosh* said the Indian nations lost the sovereign power to sell their lands to private buyers.[18] *Johnson* did not say that Indian nations lost all sovereign powers and sovereign status through the discovery doctrine. Clearly, most of the sovereign powers of

Indian nations remained intact after discovery. The discovery doctrine is not an American Indian construct, so we will never know what the Indian nations would have argued if they had been parties to *Johnson v. McIntosh*.[19] The Indian nations simply were not there to protect their sovereign interests before the Supreme Court, and that fact alone says much about America's treatment of its Indigenous people.

CHEROKEE NATION V. GEORGIA

American Indian nations were complete, independent sovereigns during pre–Columbian times, but their sovereign status was diminished upon discovery. What is this diminished sovereign status, and what is it called? The answers lie in the second case of the Marshall Trilogy, *Cherokee Nation v. Georgia*. In late 1828 and in 1829, the state of Georgia enacted laws that added Cherokee lands to the state and extended Georgia's laws to those lands (effective June 1, 1830), thereby purportedly annulling Cherokee ownership and regulation of its lands.[20] In the mix was the national debate over removal of the southeastern Indian nations to lands west of the Mississippi River.[21] All niceties aside, *Cherokee Nation v. Georgia* is about the Supreme Court's denial of an Indian nation's attempt to invoke the court's power to prevent in the Deep South what we call "ethnic cleansing" today.

The Cherokees refused to recognize Georgia's laws and brought an original action[22] in the U.S. Supreme Court to enjoin Georgia from enforcing its laws. The court said:

> This bill is brought by the Cherokee nation, praying for an injunction to restrain the state of Georgia from the execution of certain laws of that state, which, as is alleged, go directly to annihilate the Cherokees as a political society, and to seize, for the use of Georgia, the lands of the nation which have been assured to them by the United States in solemn treaties repeatedly made and still in force.[23]

The court framed the issue as such: "Is the Cherokee nation a foreign state in the sense in which that term is used in the constitution?"[24] In other words, if the Cherokee Nation is a foreign nation, then the Supreme Court would have jurisdiction to decide the petition for injunction.

The Supreme Court first found that the Cherokee Nation was indeed a "state," because it had "a distinct political society, separated from others, capable of

managing its own affairs and governing itself," and the United States had recognized it as such by entering into several treaties with the Cherokee Nation.[25]
But was the Cherokee Nation a foreign state? The Court said no and dismissed
the petition, ruling that it did not have original jurisdiction. The Cherokee
Nation was not a foreign nation, but instead was a domestic dependent nation,
whose relation to the United States resembled that of a ward to his guardian.

> It may well be doubted whether those tribes which reside within the acknowl-
> edged boundaries of the United States can, with strict accuracy, be denominated
> foreign nations. They may, more correctly, perhaps, be denominated domestic
> dependent nations. They occupy a territory to which we assert a title independent
> of their will, which must take effect in point of possession when their right of
> possession ceases. Meanwhile they are in a state of pupilage. Their relation to
> the United States resembles that of a ward to his guardian.[26]

According to the Supreme Court, the discovery doctrine diminished the
Indian nations' complete, independent sovereign status to that of "domestic
dependent nations." The court said, as domestic dependent nations, the Indian
nations "look to our government for protection; rely on its kindness and its
power; appeal to it for relief of their wants; and address the president as their
great father."[27] In addition, the United States and foreign nations consider
Indian lands to be "so completely under the sovereignty and dominion of the
United States, that any attempt to acquire their lands, or to form a political
connexion [sic] with them, would be considered by all as an invasion of our
territory, and an act of hostility."[28]

Designation as domestic dependent nations turned out to be contradictory
for Indian nations. On the one hand, it protected Indian nation sovereignty;
on the other, it allowed federal courts to limit that sovereignty. For example,
in *Oliphant v. Suquamish Indian Tribe*,[29] Indian nations were stripped of the
sovereign power to prosecute non-Indians in their courts for crimes committed
on Indian lands. *Oliphant* said the Indian nations' exercise of criminal jurisdiction over non-Indians would be "inconsistent with their status" as domestic
dependent nations.[30]

Cherokee Nation v. Georgia holds that the relationship between Indian
nations and the United States is a guardian-ward relationship. When Navajo
Nation officials claim that the Nation has a trust relationship with the federal
government, they are talking about the guardian-ward relationship. Perhaps

Navajo officials do not know that the idea underlying the guardian-ward relationship is the pretense that Indian peoples are racially inferior to European peoples. Under the guardian-ward theory, the federal government, as trustee, has certain legal and moral obligations to Indian nations, the beneficiaries. Whether the trust relationship is legally enforceable is usually determined on a case-by-case basis.

Normally, if a federal statute expressly authorizes the federal government to undertake an obligation for the benefit of an Indian nation (e.g., management of the Indian nation's property) and the government fails to do so, a federal court will hold the federal government liable for damages for breach of fiduciary trust. As the U.S. Supreme Court held in *United States v. White Mountain Apache Tribe*,[31] a 1960 federal statute and comprehensive federal control of the property imposed a duty on the United States to maintain and preserve Fort Apache, which is located on the reservation, for the benefit of the Apache Nation. Contrast *White Mountain* with *United States v. Navajo Nation*,[32] wherein the Supreme Court held that the Indian Mineral Leasing Act of 1938, which required secretarial approval of Indian mineral leases, did not impose a trust duty on the United States, even though, as the Navajo Nation claimed, Secretary of the Interior Donald Hodel had caused the Navajo Nation to sign a lease with the Peabody Coal Company for below-market royalties for its coal.

WORCESTER V. GEORGIA

Chief Justice Marshall used the last case of the Marshall Trilogy, *Worcester v. Georgia*, to clarify the discovery doctrine, the doctrine of Indian nation self-government, and the doctrine of federal power over Indian affairs. Georgia officials arrested Samuel Worcester and several missionaries, all white persons, for violating state laws that required a license from the governor before residing on Cherokee lands and an oath to support and defend the state's constitution and laws.[33] All were convicted and sentenced to four years of hard labor in the state penitentiary. Worcester refused a pardon and brought his case before the U.S. Supreme Court, arguing that Georgia's laws violated "the constitution, laws and treaties of the United States."[34]

The Supreme Court first clarified its view of the discovery doctrine that it had incorporated into American law in *Johnson v. McIntosh* and subsequently used to characterize Indian nations as domestic dependent nations in *Cherokee Nation v. Georgia*. The court said the discovery doctrine did not transfer title to Indian land; it merely gave the first discovering nation, and any successor, the exclusive right to purchase lands that the Indian owners were willing to sell.[35] The court said:

> This principle [discovery doctrine] gave the nation making the discovery . . .
> the sole right of acquiring the soil and of making settlements on it. It was an
> exclusive principle which shut out the right of competition among those who
> had agreed to it; not one which could annul the previous rights of those who had
> not agreed to it. It regulated the right given by discovery among the European
> discoverers; but could not affect the rights of those already in possession, either
> as aboriginal occupants, or as occupants by virtue of discovery made before the
> memory of man. It gave the exclusive right to purchase, but did not found that
> right on a denial of the right of the possessor to sell.[36]

The United States, as the successor to Great Britain, assumed the "pre-emptive privilege" of purchasing the land from the Indians, when they were willing to sell.[37] *Worcester v. Georgia* explains how the discovery doctrine, as it was made part of American law in *Johnson v. McIntosh*, should be understood.

The discovery doctrine did not annul the preexisting sovereign status of American Indian nations and did not empower European sovereigns to interfere in Indian nation self-government. *Worcester v. Georgia* acknowledges that in pre-Columbian times, the Indian nations were complete, independent sovereigns and their sovereignty was as complete as the sovereignty of any European nation.

> America, separated from Europe by a wide ocean, was inhabited by a distinct
> people, divided into separate nations, independent of each other and the rest of
> the world, having institutions of their own, and governing themselves by their
> own laws. It is difficult to comprehend the proposition that the inhabitants of
> either quarter of the globe could have rightful original claims of dominion over
> the inhabitants of the other, or over the lands they occupied; or that the discovery
> of either by the other should give the discoverer rights in the country discovered,
> which annulled the pre-existing rights of its ancient possessors.[38]

After discovery, the Indian nations retained their original sovereign status as nations and all their sovereign powers, except for the surrender of their external sovereign power to treat or ally with nations other than the United States.

The Indian nations had always been considered as distinct, independent political communities, retaining their original natural rights, as the undisputed possessors of the soil, from time immemorial, with the single exception of that imposed by irresistible power, which excluded them from intercourse with any other European potentate than the first discoverer of the coast of the particular region claimed: and this was a restriction which those European potentates imposed on themselves, as well as on the Indians. The very term "nation," so generally applied to them, means "a people distinct from others." The constitution, by declaring treaties already made, as well as those to be made, to be the supreme law of the land, has adopted and sanctioned the previous treaties with the Indian nations, and consequently admits their rank among those powers who are capable of making treaties. The words "treaty" and "nation" are words of our own language, selected in our diplomatic and legislative proceedings, by ourselves, having each a definite and well understood meaning. We have applied them to Indians, as we have applied them to the other nations of the earth. They are applied to all in the same sense.[39]

Some Americans find it difficult to believe that Indian tribes of the United States are nations. As the Supreme Court said, since discovery, the European powers and the United States have dealt with the Indian tribes as nations and entered into over three hundred treaties with them; under international law, only nations can make treaties. In fact, the 1868 treaty between the Navajo Nation and the United States declares the Navajo Nation to be a "nation."[40] The Navajo Nation Code also declares that "the phrase 'Navajo Nation' [shall be used to describe] the lands and people of the Navajo Nation."[41]

Worcester v. Georgia acknowledges that American Indian nations are complete, independent sovereigns with all sovereign powers intact before and after European contact. When the United States declared its independence and succeeded to Great Britain's land claims, the Indian nations, in treaties, agreed to be under the protection of the United States and thereby lost their sovereign power to ally or make treaties with foreign nations. What does it mean to be under the protection of the United States? According to *Worcester v. Georgia*, it means a protectorate relationship where the Indian nations' right to self-government remains intact: "This relation was that of a nation claiming and receiving the protection of one more powerful: not that of individuals abandoning their national character, and submitting as subjects to the laws of a master."[42] The Supreme Court explained the protectorate relationship under international law this way:

The settled doctrine of the law of nations is, that a weaker power does not surrender its independence—its right to self government, by associating with a stron-
ger, and taking its protection. A weak state, in order to provide for its safety, may
place itself under the protection of one more powerful, without stripping itself of
the right of government, and ceasing to be a state. Examples of this kind are not
wanting in Europe. "Tributary and feudatory states," says Vattel, "do not thereby
cease to be sovereign and independent states, so long as self government and
sovereign and independent authority are left in the administration of the state."[43]

The discovery doctrine and the protectorate relationship that the Indian nations
have with the United States do not deprive the Indian nations of their inherent rights to self-government. According to the Supreme Court, it was Great
Britain's policy not "to interfere with the internal affairs of the Indians," and
although the Crown made alliances with them, it "never intruded into the interior
of their affairs, or interfered with their self government."[44] The United States
continued and furthered this policy through statutory enactments and treaties:

From the commencement of our government, congress has passed acts to regulate trade and intercourse with the Indians; which treat them as nations, respect
their rights, and manifest a firm purpose to afford that protection which treaties
stipulate. All these acts, and especially that of 1802, which is still in force, man-
ifestly consider the several Indian nations as distinct political communities, having territorial boundaries, within which their authority is exclusive, and having
a right to all the lands within those boundaries, which is not only acknowledged,
but guaranteed by the United States.[45]

The states of the United States do not have power over Indian nations
and cannot interfere with their right to self-government. *Worcester v. Georgia* reached the Supreme Court because Georgia had "seize[d] on the whole
Cherokee country, parcel[ed] it out among the neighbouring counties of the
state, extend[ed] her code over the whole country, abolish[ed] its institutions
and its laws, and annihilate[d] its political existence."[46] In effect, Georgia had
assumed power over Indian affairs. Was Georgia's conduct legal? No, said
the Supreme Court, because the U.S. Constitution grants Congress exclusive
power over Indian affairs: The Constitution "confers on congress the powers
of war and peace; of making treaties, and of regulating commerce with foreign
nations, and among the several states, and with the Indian tribes. These powers

comprehend all that is required for the regulation of our intercourse with the Indians."[47]

In fact, the states, including Georgia, had agreed that the territory of Indian nations were "separated from that of any state within whose chartered limits they might reside, by a boundary line, established by treaties: that, within their boundary, they possessed rights with which no state could interfere: and that the whole power of regulating the intercourse with them, was vested in the United States."[48] The laws Georgia enacted to annihilate the Cherokee Nation were held invalid. The court concluded as follows:

> The Cherokee nation, then, is a distinct community occupying its own territory, with boundaries accurately described, in which the laws of Georgia can have no force, and which the citizens of Georgia have no right to enter, but with the assent of the Cherokees themselves, or in conformity with treaties, and with the acts of congress. The whole intercourse between the United States and this nation, is, by our constitution and laws vested in the government of the United States.[49]

Worcester v. Georgia established several principles concerning Indian nation sovereignty that are still relevant today. These principles have been summarized as follows: "(1) the Indian tribes enjoy a sovereign right of self-government free from interference by the states; (2) their treaties must be honored as the supreme law of the land; (3) the doctrine of discovery and edicts from Europe do not divest Indian land or sovereignty; and (4) reservation borders are protective barriers against hostile states and land-hungry settlers."[50] The Supreme Court reversed the convictions of Samuel Worcester and the other missionaries and ordered their release. The *Worcester* decision, however, did not prevent the removal of the Cherokees and other southeastern Indians to the Indian Territory in the present state of Oklahoma.

TRADITIONAL NAVAJO VIEWS OF SOVEREIGN AND SOVEREIGNTY

Are there concepts of sovereign and sovereignty in traditional Navajo beliefs? This question, at first glance, seems pointless because the Marshall Trilogy recognizes that Indian nations are sovereign, although diminished, and can exercise tribal sovereignty. But it is the federal government, primarily the

U.S. Supreme Court, and not the Navajo Nation or Indian nations, that defines and determines the scope of those concepts. The federal government's brand of tribal sovereignty (known as federal Indian law and policy) controls and severely constrains Indian nations. Tribal sovereignty supposedly protects the Indian nations' exercise of governmental powers over activities on their lands, but in actuality it denies them the right to exercise regulatory and adjudicative powers over the conduct of outsiders on those same lands. The federal version of tribal sovereignty privileges non-Indian interests (primarily white interests) because the U.S. Supreme Court denies Indian nations complete control of tribal sovereignty. The Navajo Nation should be cautious of the federal government's brand of tribal sovereignty because it is a means of controlling Indian nations (and Indian peoples). We should not have to be reminded that the federal version of tribal sovereignty resulted in the termination of several Indian nations in the 1950s.

Congress, using plenary power, can extinguish the federal version of tribal sovereignty[51] and the U.S. Supreme Court now uses federal common law to limit tribal sovereignty.[52] American Indian scholars warn that "in a world where tribal political sovereignty is dependent upon federal acknowledgement, Indian nations will always be vulnerable to restrictions on their sovereignty, and perhaps even to the total annihilation of their sovereignty."[53] They rightly recommend "a reappraisal of the tribal sovereignty doctrine—one that is based in the concepts of sovereignty held by Indian nations and which responds to the challenges that confront Indian nations today. This account of inherent sovereignty should [allow] Indian people to exercise their own norms and values in structuring their collective futures."[54]

Navajo scholars also see a necessity for a Navajo sovereignty doctrine grounded in Diné knowledge and ways: "The Navajo people—from grassroots activists to writers—are not only disenchanted with the [Navajo] centralized government system but calling for and theorizing sovereignty from intellectual positions grounded in a distinctly Navajo epistemology."[55] The Navajo people seek government reform. Foremost in government reform should be to establish a Diné sovereignty doctrine that is rooted in the Diné lifeway (i.e., culture, language, spirituality, identity, and sense of place) and responds to contemporary and foreseeable challenges generated by Navajo societal changes and external non-Indian pressures. Doctrines of sovereign and sovereignty that are grounded in Navajo epistemology will inevitably be defined, controlled, and owned by the Navajo people, and serve as the foundation for the modern

Navajo Nation government and its laws and policies. Once the Diné sovereignty doctrine is in place, all Navajo Nation laws, regulations, policies, and plans should be amended, discarded, or newly enacted so they are in line with that doctrine.

That there is very little existing literature on the concepts of sovereign and sovereignty through a traditional Navajo lens (or even traditional American Indian views) should motivate us to locate principles in our oral traditions that will guide our discussions on how we understand those two concepts from a strictly Diné point of view. Traditional Navajos understand the world through a system of beliefs that emphasizes and expresses spirituality, universal relationships, clan relationships, and land ethics and a set of foundational, primordial doctrines that include *hózhǫ́* (harmony, balance, and peace), *hochxó* (disharmony), *k'é* (positive values), and *k'éí* (kinship system). What do the foundational doctrines and the system of beliefs say about the sovereign and sovereignty concepts?

Ask a Navajo person, "What is Navajo sovereignty?" and expect the response to be, "*Nááts'íílid nihinazt'íí*" (It's the sacred rainbow that surrounds us). And if you ask, "Where does the idea of the Navajo Nation as sovereign come from?" The response will probably be, "The Holy Beings."[56] The Great Seal of the Navajo Nation (adopted on January 18, 1952) and the Navajo Nation flag (adopted on May 21, 1968) use the rainbow to symbolize Navajo Nation sovereignty and its sovereign status.[57] Navajos probably associated the rainbow with Navajo Nation sovereignty and its sovereign status from the designs on the flag and seal. But why use the rainbow to represent sovereign and sovereignty on the flag and seal?

Navajos believe that the rainbow is sacred—it has its own unique traits, sacred name, prayers, songs, and stories as told in the Navajo Creation Scripture and Journey Narratives (Narratives).[58] The oral stories associate the rainbow with the Holy Beings and First Man. First Man was instructed on the powers of the rainbow in the First World as a means of protection, security, and travel. The Narratives teach that the Holy Beings also use the rainbow as a mode of travel between the spiritual realm and the human world, to shrink distances between points, and to bridge chasms.

The Narratives teach that the rainbow guards portals to special and sacred places. On some Navajo ceremonial sandpaintings, the rainbow guards the themes, figures, and design that animate prayer and healing, much like it does on the flag and seal. The rainbow is one of the major symbols on a Navajo traditional basket (used in Blessing Way Ceremonies and traditional weddings).

The three red, unclosed rings (opening at the east) on the basket surround and protect Navajo lands, the Diné lifeway, and the six sacred mountains (four are mentioned below—the other two are Huerfano Mountain and Gobernador Knob). The rings represent sunbeam and the rainbow. "The sacred rainbow that surrounds us" thus means the rainbow is guardian and protector of Navajo lands and resources, Navajo people and their society, and all that is Navajo—including government, laws, culture, language, and spiritual beliefs. The characteristics of the rainbow as expressed in the Diné system of beliefs, especially protector and guardian of all that is Navajo, reflect the Diné understandings of sovereign and sovereignty. The Narratives teach that the Creator and the Holy Beings created the Diné as a distinct people and gave the Diné a holy name, a distinct language, and spiritual ceremonies (or what non-Navajos call religion). The Holy Beings delineated lands with four sacred mountains and promised those lands to the Navajo people in perpetuity. The Narratives describe these as characteristics of Diné nationhood and complete, independent sovereign status. Any designation of the Navajo Nation as a "domestic dependent nation" is, thus, antithetical to the Creator's and Holy Beings' plan for the Navajo people. The Holy Beings placed within the confines of the sacred mountains a set of guiding foundational doctrines that serve as the wellspring for morals, values, customs, and traditions that the Diné use to exercise sovereignty as a distinct nation. Fundamental doctrines are primordial and intrinsic to the creation of the Diné as a distinct people.

The Diné language does not have a single word that translates to sovereignty, but that does not mean our ancestral, traditional Diné did not exercise sovereignty. The old-time Diné practiced what might be called "doing sovereignty" through traditional, internal self-governance and through international diplomacy and relations with non-Navajos. As a matter of self-government, the Diné chose their leaders by consensus and worked with them to govern in the best interests of the Navajo people using Fundamental Laws. Navajos used the k'é principle (i.e., values that promote peace, cooperation, and kinship) to make trade and peace agreements and military alliances with other Indian nations and colonial actors including Spain, Mexico, and the United States.

The closest single word to sovereignty is *naat'á*, which means government. The Narratives teach that the Holy Beings planted the six sacred mountains and blessed each with the characteristics of naat'á. The ancestors of the present Diné were instructed to use the characteristics for self-government and for dealing with non-Navajos in war and peace. Thus, the mountains are called

Dził Naat'á in ceremony, which broadly encompasses authority, power, laws, and leadership. Dził Naat'á is analogous to the Western concept of sovereignty because the sacred mountains are blessed with supreme authority and power. The Navajo belief that mountains hold ultimate authority and power on earth is vastly different from the Western practice that places ultimate authority and power in aristocracy.[59] The Navajo traditionalist's understandings of sovereign and sovereignty would indeed be difficult, if not impossible, for a non-Indian to comprehend.

The Navajo Nation began choosing leaders by popular vote following the creation of the present Navajo Nation government in 1923. Prior to 1923, the authority and power to choose leaders by consensus rested in the local people—a localized community usually bound by a common matrilineal clan. The leader (*naat'áanii*) used persuasive authority and power to serve and speak on behalf of the people. *Nahat'á* is "doing sovereignty," or the practical exercise of power, including planning, policy-making, problem-solving, and peacemaking (nonadversarial Diné dispute resolution). Nahat'á, in traditional governance, requires leaders to govern with wisdom, foresight, and persuasive authority. Primordial, foundational doctrines that the Holy Beings established, and are collectively called *beehaz'áanii bitsé siléí*, guided leaders while "doing sovereignty." Unlike a Western written constitution, humans cannot change the primordial, foundational doctrines.

Sovereignty and place (or land) are intertwined, and give real meaning to being sovereign. The traditional Navajo homeland (which is larger than the current Navajo homeland) is marked in each cardinal direction by a sacred mountain—Mount Blanca in the east, Mount Taylor in the south, the San Francisco Peaks in the west, and Mount Hesperus in the north. The Narratives teach that the Holy Beings planted a mountain in each cardinal direction and blessed each with tangible and intangible properties, including knowledge, governance, leadership, laws, and everything that the Diné would need to grow and prosper as a people or nation. The four sacred mountains define Navajo territorial sovereignty when considered under Navajo sense of place.

The four sacred mountains serve as pillars for a metaphysical, or cosmic, hogan that encloses Navajo lands, Navajo people, and the Diné lifeway. The Narratives and ceremonies declare that the sacred mountains and the cosmic hogan protect the Diné as an independent, distinct nation with complete internal and external powers. The federal brand of tribal sovereignty that diminishes the Navajo Nation to semi-sovereign with limited powers contravenes these traditional Navajo beliefs about the sacred mountains and the cosmic hogan. Territorial sovereignty, external sovereignty (interactions with other nations), and internal sovereignty (domestic interactions) are all derivatives of the four sacred mountains. Thus, a traditional leader would exercise internal sovereignty according to *Hózhóóji* (the Peace Way) and external sovereignty according to *Naayééji* (the War Way). Internal sovereignty allows exercise of powers on lands delineated by the sacred mountains (e.g., domestic matters), and external sovereignty allows exercise of powers beyond the sacred mountains and with other nations (e.g., treaty and alliance making with other nations and warfare).

Traditional Navajo expressions of sovereign and sovereignty were on display during the treaty negotiations at Fort Sumner, New Mexico, from May 28 to June 1, 1868, between the Navajo Nation and the United States. Barboncito, Navajo leader and negotiator for his people, negotiated from a position grounded in traditional beliefs on the first day of talks with General William T. Sherman, negotiator for the United States. When General Sherman asked, "We want to know . . . what you think of your reservation here (referring to the Bosque Redondo Reservation),"[60] Barboncito said:

> Our Grand-fathers had no idea of living in any other country except our own and I do not think it right for us to do so as we were never taught to. When the Navajos were first created[,] four mountains and four rivers were pointed out to us, inside of which we should live, that was to be our country and was given to us by the first woman of the Navajo tribe. It was told to us by our forefathers, that we were never to move east of the Rio Grande or west of the San Juan rivers and I think that our coming here has been the cause of so much death among us and our animals. That our God when he [*sic*] was created (the woman I spoke of) gave us this piece of land and created it specially for us[.][61]

Although accuracy of translation (from Navajo to Spanish to English) was a definite problem during the treaty negotiations, we can discern principles from Barboncito's words that reflect the traditional Diné's understandings of sovereign and sovereignty. Preeminent among these is the belief that humans did not grant sovereign status to the Diné. Accordingly, Diné sovereignty is also not granted by humans. Sovereign, sovereignty, land (or place), and the Diné go hand in hand, and they come from the Holy Beings. Barboncito's words reflect these beliefs: "When the Navajos were first created, four mountains and four rivers were pointed out to us, inside of which we should live, that was to be our country and was given to us by the first woman of the Navajo tribe."[62] The "first woman" is likely Changing Woman, the progenitor of the modern Diné during the episode called the "Re-creation of the Diné." Changing Woman set forth the foundational principles from which spring domestic laws and practices that are integral to doing internal sovereignty.[63] Barboncito mentions the four sacred mountains and land; these mountains and land manifest the Navajo Nation's sovereign status and contain all characteristics necessary for doing sovereignty.

Barboncito's words reference the cosmic hogan that encompasses the Holy Beings' gift of sovereign status to the Diné. The cosmic hogan enshrines the Diné as a distinct, independent sovereign nation with land boundaries accurately marked by the sacred mountains. The Narratives teach that all the tools for "doing sovereignty," including language, planning, frameworks, talking things out, foundational laws, lawmaking, government and governing, and leadership, were specifically implanted in the sacred mountains for use in the cosmic hogan. Barboncito also said, "Our Grand-fathers had no idea of living in any other country except our own and I do not think it right for us to do so as we were never taught to."[64] The traditional beliefs emphasize that the Holy Beings promised the Diné a nurturing environment conducive to growth and prosperity inside the cosmic hogan.

The sacrosanct covenant between the Holy Beings and the Diné, which ensures the permanence of the Diné on earth, is fully effective when they live on lands bounded by the four sacred mountains, follow the foundational, primordial laws, speak the Diné language, perform ceremonies, and perpetuate the Diné lifeway. Movement as a nation outside these boundaries can mean violation of the covenant and loss of the Holy Beings' protection. Barboncito implied a violation of the covenant, albeit forced, and its dire consequences when he said that our forefathers told us "never to move east of the Rio Grande or west of the San Juan rivers and I think our coming here (to Bosque Redondo Reservation) has been the cause of so much death among us and our animals. . . . [In our own country] we can raise a crop almost anywhere, our families and stock increase, here they decrease, . . . this land does not like us[,] neither does the water. . . . I think now it is true what my forefathers told me about crossing the line of my own country. It seems that whatever we do here causes death."[65]

The Navajo people can exercise self-government freely using Hózhóóji (the Peace Way) when they govern themselves using their own laws on their own land. Barboncito relayed this belief when he said, "I am speaking for the whole tribe, for their animals[,] from the horse to the dog, also the unborn,

all that you have heard is the truth and is the opinion of the whole tribe."[66]
These words illustrate the workings of traditional Navajo self-government (or
leadership), including the use of the foundational doctrines of k'é and k'éí,
and the principles of participatory democracy, talking things out, and consensual decision-making. Navajo oral accounts speak of a Navajo gathering
on May 27, 1868. At this gathering (participatory democracy), the points that
Barboncito later presented to the commission, as "the truth [and] opinion of the
whole tribe," were discussed (talking things out while guided by k'e and k'ei)
and agreed upon (consensual decision-making). Barboncito's words show that
"doing sovereignty" fosters universal relationships, which sustains the state of
hózhǫ́, and serves the best interests of not only the Diné, but all "beings"[67] that
compose creation. When Barboncito said, "I [speak] for the whole tribe, for
their animals[,] from the horse to the dog, also the unborn,"[68] he is explaining
to General Sherman that the proposed treaty will affect the Diné (present and
future generations) and the Diné lifeway, so he expects the general to negotiate
with humility, respect, and equality (or according to k'é).

Dealing with non-Navajos, or exercise of external sovereignty, is deemed
risky, so it must be done properly and according to the teachings of Naayééji.
Barboncito's strategy on handling General Sherman, a powerful enemy war
leader, illustrates the intricacies and workings of the Navajo metaphysical
world. Barboncito said to General Sherman:

> It appears to me that the General commands the whole thing as a god. I hope
> therefore he will do all he can for the Indian, this hope goes in at my feet and out
> at my mouth. I am speaking to you (General Sherman) now as if I was speak-
> ing to a spirit and I wish you to tell me when you are going to take us to our
> own country.[69]

Barboncito knows that General Sherman can either send the Diné home or to
the Indian Territory in Oklahoma, so he gains control of the general by "turn-
ing" him into a persuadable "god." A Navajo carrier of traditional knowledge
assumes and controls a "god's power" by becoming one with the "god," beginning from earth to feet to head—thus, Barboncito says, "this hope goes in at
my feet and out at my mouth."

Navajos have a fundamental principle that states, "Words are powerful";
thus, any desirable outcome is achievable. Barboncito skillfully uses this principle to achieve the result he wants for his people. In other words, General

Sherman as "spirit" has been manipulated through speech ("words are powerful") to act in a benevolent manner. Thus, Barboncito confidently says to General Sherman, "I wish you to tell me when you are going to take us to our own country." In the minds of the traditional Diné who witnessed the negotiations, it is already a done deal that the Navajo people are going home; it's just a matter of when that will happen. Barboncito probably used the "Hero Twins' (Monster Slayer and Born-for-Water) Journey to the Father," a War Way narrative, to persuade General Sherman as a "god." The Twins persuaded their father, the powerful "sun spirit," to give them unique weapons that they used to eliminate "monsters" that were destroying people and, thereby, made Navajo Country safe for the Diné.

Barboncito's words during the treaty negotiations in the summer of 1868 demonstrate the traditional Diné "doing sovereignty" the Diné way. "Doing sovereignty" follows either the Peace Way or the War Way and can delve into metaphysics because Navajo traditionalists believe in universal consciousness, universal kinship, and the interconnectedness of all creation. These same principles and procedures can apply in governance following establishment of our own Diné sovereignty doctrine.

In summary, I again stress that this chapter is for the Diné. We first have to understand that the principle of tribal sovereignty, as it has been applied to us, has been detrimental to our Diné lifeway and our sacred covenant with the Holy Beings. There is no guarantee that the Navajo Nation will exist in the future if we continue to depend on the federal government (and outsiders) to recognize and define our sovereignty and our sovereign status. The best protection for all Diné and the Diné lifeway is to formulate our own Diné sovereignty doctrine, a doctrine that is grounded in our own traditional knowledge and ways, and let it guide our nation forward.

NOTES

1. Cindy Yurth, "At Forum, Young Candidates Demand a Seat at the Table," *Navajo Times*, July 24, 2014.
2. Ibid.
3. Although the commentary on traditional Diné beliefs comes from my own understandings, I do not claim thorough knowledge on traditional narratives, doctrines, and spiritual beliefs.

4. Black's Law Dictionary, 7th ed., s.v. "sovereign."

5. The contemporary concept of the nation-state under international law comes from "European models of political and social organization whose dominant defining characteristics are exclusivity of territorial domain and hierarchical, centralized authority." S. James Anaya, *Indigenous Peoples in International Law*, 2nd ed. (New York: Oxford University Press, 2004), 22.

6. Black's Law Dictionary, s.v. "sovereign state."

7. Robert A. Williams Jr., *The American Indian in Western Legal Thought* (New York: Oxford University Press, 1990), 13–15, 44–50 (discussing Pope Innocent IV's commentary on Pope Innocent II's *Quod super his*—regarding the natural law rights of non-Christian peoples—and Alanus Anglicus's argument that non-Christian peoples had no rights to property or lordship); ibid., 87–108 (discussing the debates on the rights of American Indians in the Americas, including Franciscus de Victoria's lectures entitled "On the Indians Lately Discovered").

8. Black's Law Dictionary, s.v. "sovereignty."

9. *Johnson v. McIntosh*, 21 U.S. (8 Wheat.) 543 (1823).

10. *Cherokee Nation v. Georgia*, 30 U.S. (5 Pet.) 1 (1831).

11. *Worcester v. Georgia*, 31 U.S. (6 Pet.) 515 (1832).

12. Walter R. Echo-Hawk, a prominent Native American lawyer, summarized well the history of this case in his book:

> It is amazing that over 750 law review articles and several books have been written about *Johnson v. McIntosh* in recent times, yet it was not until 2005 that the first complete story of this case was told. In 1991, a law professor named Lindsay G. Robertson made a startling find: A trunk containing the complete corporate records of the plaintiff land companies in that case. The records reveal a truly sordid tale of collusion by many of the leading figures of the day, surrounding a fraudulent purchase of an enormous tract of Indian land by wealthy land speculators. They sought to validate their illegal purchase through a friendly lawsuit about a feigned controversy that was conceived and prosecuted by crafty lawyers—influence peddlers, really—and this case was decided by a chief justice of the Supreme Court who possessed an enormous stake in the outcome. The opinion thus produced contained far-reaching dicta that gravely compromised Indian land rights in the United States, even though no Indian tribes were parties to the case. This entire affair occurred within the context of speculation in land owned and occupied by Indian tribes. (footnote omitted)

The serious irregularities in this litigation brought to light by Robertson gravely impugn the legitimacy of the *Johnson* decision and should leave many to wonder whether the decision is entitled to receive continuing effect by the courts. Yet at this writing, *Johnson* does remain a landmark decision in the United States and several other settler states that restrict indigenous land rights. It provides the foundation for modern land ownership in those nations.

Walter R. Echo-Hawk, *In the Courts of the Conqueror: The 10 Worst Indian Law Cases Ever Decided* (Golden, CO: Fulcrum Publishing, 2012), 56.

13. Chief Justice Marshall framed the issue as whether Indian nations have "the power to . . . give, and of private individuals to receive a title which can be sustained in the Courts of this country." *Johnson*, 21 U.S. at 572.

14. 21 U.S. at 574.

15. 21 U.S. at 573–74. The court said, "This principle [discovery doctrine] was, that discovery gave title to the government by whose subjects, or by whose authority, it was made, against all other European governments, which title might be consummated by possession." The court then said that the Indian nations' "rights to complete sovereignty, as independent nations, were necessarily diminished, and their power to dispose of the soil at their own will, to whomever they pleased, was denied by the original fundamental principle, that discovery gave exclusive title to those who made it."

16. 21 U.S. at 587 ("The United States, then, have unequivocally acceded to that great and broad rule by which its civilized inhabitants now hold this country. They hold, and assert in themselves, the title by which it was acquired. They maintain, as all others have maintained, that discovery gave an exclusive right to extinguish the Indian title of occupancy, either by purchase or by conquest; and gave also a right to such a degree of sovereignty, as the circumstances of the people would allow them to exercise.").

17. 21 U.S. at 574.

18. Ibid.

19. As Echo-Hawk stated: "But what about the Indians? It was *their* property rights and sovereignty at stake, yet they were not a party to *Johnson*. As the oral argument began, only white people were in the courtroom. They would fashion the rules affecting Indians, just like they developed the law of slavery without the input, representation, or presence of the slaves. No one thought to ascertain the views of the Indian tribes in *Johnson*." Echo-Hawk, *In the Courts of the Conqueror*, 66–67.

20. David H. Getches, Charles F. Wilkinson, Robert A. Williams Jr., and Matthew L. M. Fletcher, *Federal Indian Law*, 6th ed. (Eagan, MN: West Publishing, 2011), 100.
21. Ibid., 96–98.
22. An original action in the Supreme Court invokes the court's original jurisdiction under Article III of the United States Constitution. The provisions applicable to this case state as follows: "The judicial power of the United States shall extend to all Cases . . . between a state . . . and foreign States"; and "in all cases in which a State shall be a Party, the supreme Court shall have original Jurisdiction." Art. III, Sec. 2.
23. *Cherokee Nation v. Georgia*, 30 U.S. at 15.
24. 30 U.S. at 16.
25. Ibid.
26. 30 U.S. at 17.
27. Ibid.
28. 30 U.S. at 17–18. This quotation is interpreted to mean that, as domestic dependent nations, Indian nations lost their right to enter into treaties with foreign nations.
29. *Oliphant v. Suquamish Indian Tribe*, 435 U.S. 191 (1978).
30. 435 U.S. at 208.
31. *United States v. White Mountain Apache Tribe*, 537 U.S. 465 (2003).
32. *United States v. Navajo Nation*, 537 U.S. 488 (2003).
33. *Worcester v. Georgia*, 31 U.S. at 537.
34. 31 U.S. at 536.
35. 31 U.S. at 543, 544–45.
36. 31 U.S. at 544.
37. 31 U.S. at 544–45.
38. 31 U.S. at 542–43.
39. 31 U.S. at 559–60.
40. Introductory whereas clause, Navajo Treaty of 1868.
41. 1 N.N.C. § 501 (2005 ed.)
42. *Worcester*, 31 U.S. at 555.
43. 31 U.S. at 561–62.
44. 31 U.S. at 547.
45. 31 U.S. at 556–57.
46. 31 U.S. at 542.
47. 31 U.S. at 559.

48. 31 U.S. at 560.

49. 31 U.S. at 561.

50. Echo-Hawk, *In the Courts of the Conqueror*, 118.

51. *Santa Clara Pueblo v. Martinez*, 436 U.S. 49, 56 (1978) ("Congress has plenary authority to limit, modify or eliminate the powers of local self-government which the tribes otherwise possess"); *United States v. Wheeler*, 435 U.S. 313, 323 (1978) ("The sovereignty that the Indian tribes retain is of a unique and limited character. It exists only at the sufferance of Congress and is subject to complete defeasance").

52. See, as examples, *Oliphant v. Suquamish Indian Tribe*, 435 U.S. 191 (1978) (Indian nations lack power to prosecute non-Indians for crimes committed on Indian lands); *Strate v. A-1 Contractors*, 520 U.S. 438 (1997) (Indian nations have no jurisdiction over non-Indians who cause vehicle accidents on state highways running through Indian lands); *Nevada v. Hicks*, 533 U.S. 353 (2001) (Tribal court has no jurisdiction over state officers who commit torts while executing a state search warrant on Indian lands).

53. Wallace Coffey and Rebecca Tsosie, "Rethinking the Tribal Sovereignty Doctrine: Cultural Sovereignty and the Collective Future of Indian Nations," *Stanford Law & Policy Review* 12 (2001): 194.

54. Ibid., 195–96.

55. Lloyd L. Lee, "Reclaiming Indigenous Intellectual, Political, and Geographic Space," *American Indian Quarterly* 32, no. 1 (Winter 2008): 97.

56. The supernatural beings that Navajos call the Holy People are credited with creating the Navajo people and setting forth foundational laws on which Navajo society rests.

57. Navajo Nation Council Resolutions No. CJ-9-52 (January 18, 1952) and No. CMY-75-68 (May 21, 1968). See also Dana E. Powell, "*The Rainbow Is Our Sovereignty*: Rethinking the Politics of Energy on the Navajo Nation," *Journal of Political Ecology* 22 (2015): 53.

58. The Narratives compose the oral history of the Navajo people beginning with creation. Raymond D. Austin, *Navajo Courts and Navajo Common Law, A Tradition of Tribal Self-Governance* (Minneapolis: University of Minnesota Press, 2009), xvii.

59. Carl Schmitt, *Political Theology*, trans. George Schwab (Cambridge, MA: MIT Press, 1985). "Sovereign is he who decides on the exception" (5). The exception "includes any kind of severe economic or political disturbance that requires application of extraordinary measures" (p. 5, fn 1).

60. Martin A. Link, *Treaty between the United States of America and the Navajo Tribe of Indians* (Las Vegas, NV: KC Publications: 1968), 1.

61. Link, *Treaty*, 2. Close to thirteen thousand Navajos were held as prisoners of war on the Bosque Redondo Reservation near Fort Sumner, New Mexico, from late 1863 to June 1, 1868. The Navajos signed the 1868 Navajo treaty and regained their freedom on June 1, 1868.

62. Link, *Treaty*, 2.

63. For a discussion of Changing Woman, the "Re-creation of the Diné," and Changing Woman's laws, see Austin, *Navajo Courts and Navajo Common Law*, 144–45, 157–58. There is also a female spiritual Being called "First Woman" who is paired with "First Man" in the Navajo Creation Scripture and Journey Narratives. Barboncito is likely talking about Changing Woman. For additional discussion of Changing Woman's laws, see *Riggs v. Estate of Attakai*, No. SC-CV-39-04 (Navajo Supreme Court, June 13, 2007).

64. Link, *Treaty*, 2.

65. Ibid., 2, 3.

66. Ibid., 4.

67. On the Navajo concept of "beings," see Austin, *Navajo Courts and Navajo Common Law*, 83–84.

68. Link, *Treaty*, 4.

69. Ibid.

SOVEREIGNTY FROM THE INDIVIDUAL DINÉ PERSPECTIVE

BIDTAH NELLIE BECKER

INTRODUCTION

P ROFESSOR LEE INVITED ME, and the other writers in this collection, to write essays about Diné sovereignty from our individual perspectives. As a lawyer for the Navajo Nation for just shy of thirteen years, I practiced something called tribal sovereignty. Since mid-May 2015, I have practiced that same concept of tribal sovereignty as the executive director of the Navajo Nation Division of Natural Resources in a nonlegal capacity. And while I could write about sovereignty from my individual professional experience as a Diné person, this essay is very much a reflection of my lifetime of personal experiences as a Diné woman with sovereignty and tribal sovereignty.

As a Diné person, I experience what sovereignty feels like—from when I was a young person who did not know the term *sovereignty*, to now as a parent and citizen of the Navajo Nation and also an employee of the nation. I studied sovereignty as an undergraduate international relations major, where I focused on Latin American studies, and it was as an undergraduate that I first theorized about sovereignty. My experience also includes living and working among the Ramah Indians of Nicaragua as a young adult. This essay is a reflection of my personal and professional experiences with sovereignty in the international sense, sovereignty as experienced by other Indigenous peoples, and a strong abstract and experiential focus on the sovereignty exercised by the

Navajo Nation as a body politic, and by the Diné people as a collected group of people and as individuals.

Professor Lee provided authors several questions to focus on, and I drafted this essay in direct response to those questions. At the same time, I attempted to bring out themes elicited from the questions into a cohesive conclusion. My conclusion is that sovereignty is a highly abstract concept and yet at the same time has a practical and tangible feel experienced by all human beings. The Navajo Nation exercises sovereignty in many forms both abstract and tangible. And while the Nation exercises sovereignty in many forms, depending on what the specific interest is that the Nation is advancing or protecting, the individual Navajo person exercises a form of sovereignty that I call *organic sovereignty*. From my individual perspective, this organic sovereignty has been, is, and will continue to be the great strength of the Navajo Nation.

TRIBAL SOVEREIGNTY

For purposes of this essay, and as a legal matter, the term *tribal sovereignty* refers to the sovereignty that an American Indian tribe enjoys as a body politic. In order to enjoy tribal sovereignty, the tribe must be recognized by the United States. If a tribe is not recognized, then the tribe cannot legally exercise the same political and legal control over its lands as tribes that are recognized. I discuss tribal sovereignty in more detail later.

ORGANIC SOVEREIGNTY

Organic sovereignty is a term that I landed on to describe the feeling that I have had ever since I can remember having cognition that I am a Diné person. Organic sovereignty describes those attributes of a group of people who choose to collect and identify themselves as a collective whole—even if the legal system does not recognize that group of people. The people organize first as an organic experience. For instance, the Ramah Indians of Nicaragua are considered a tribe by others and by themselves, but they do not have the same legal interaction with the state of Nicaragua as the federally recognized tribes of the United States of America. Yet there is no mistaking that the Ramah Indians are a group of people who are separately organized from the communities that surround them.

An organic sovereignty attribute may or may not continue over time. One example of organic sovereignty is language. One of the attributes that Diné people have organized around is the use of a common language. Today, many Diné, but not all, speak the Diné language. I contrast that with the language of the Ramah Indians. When I lived among them in 1993 and 1994, there was one Ramah who could fluently speak the language, and the common language was and continues to be a pidgin English unique to the Ramah. That organic sovereign exercise of utilizing a unique precontact language may have disappeared among the Ramah Indians, but the fact that the Ramah Indians are a collective group of people has not changed. Later, I describe in more detail the practice of organic sovereignty by the Diné people.

As referenced earlier, I utilized Professor Lee's questions for this essay, as I found his questions a useful framework. Also, I utilize the terms *Diné* and *Navajo* interchangeably, I think, because those terms are used individually on the Navajo Nation.

QUESTION 1: HOW IS NAVAJO SOVEREIGNTY UNDERSTOOD IN THE EYES OF WESTERN LAW?

As a strict legal matter, Navajo sovereignty would be understood in the same manner as the sovereignty of any Native American group of people that the United States recognizes as a tribe.[1] This type of sovereignty is referred to as tribal sovereignty. Precontact, tribes were the only sovereigns. Then the thirteen colonies formed along the Atlantic coast. They eventually became states and formed the United States of America. Today there are three sovereigns within the U.S. system: tribal, state, and federal.

The United States takes the legal position that it is the dominant sovereign and that tribes are domestic dependent sovereigns. This means that, according to federal law, tribes enjoy sovereign powers concerning its members, but not the full panoply of sovereign powers enjoyed by a sovereign nation recognized by the United Nations.

It is also important to note that sovereignty has an aspect of relativity, meaning that one is a sovereign to the extent that other sovereigns recognize it. Spain, Mexico, and the United States have all recognized the sovereignty of the Diné— but perhaps they did not always recognize the full legal sovereignty as would be defined appropriate by the Diné. Today, the fifty states of the United States and the other American Indian tribes also recognize the sovereignty of the Diné.

Sovereignty is also the concept that people have the authority to organize and govern themselves and practice self-determination. Currently the United States' policy is to support self-determination by tribal nations, as distinguished by the United States' historical policies toward native peoples, which included the distinct policies of termination and then later assimilation.

Policy is often very theoretical and often difficult to implement in a consistent manner. So while the law may define tribal sovereignty and policy may further inform that legal definition, the implementation may not always reflect that law and policy. In my professional life of working for the Navajo Nation and assisting in nation building, I have encountered differing attitudes and actions toward tribal sovereignty. For purposes of my daily work, I often imagine a tribal sovereignty continuum bookended on one end by the perspective that the Nation is 100 percent responsible for making and implementing its own decisions and the United States has no role in that decision-making, and on the other end by the perspective that the United States continues to "boss Indians around" such that the Nation is not responsible for making and implementing its own decisions. This latter perspective is affectionately referred to as "BIA," because the U.S. Bureau of Indian Affairs (BIA) has the most daily contact with tribes and continues to have great authority on tribal lands. Both Navajo officials and federal officials have beliefs or take action that fall anywhere on this continuum. Understanding where individuals fall on this continuum helps me navigate my day-to-day work, as I can better meet the individual expectations of individuals involved in some way in the Division's work of managing the Nation's vast natural resources and in nation building.

QUESTION 2: HOW DO VARIOUS INSTITUTIONS OF THE NAVAJO NATION EXERCISE SOVEREIGNTY?

I examine this question by asking how three institutions on the Navajo Nation exercise sovereignty. The three institutions are the Navajo Nation government, Tsé Hootsoi Diné Bi'Oltá, and the matrilineal familial institution.

NAVAJO NATION GOVERNMENT

The Nation is a three-branch government, which consists of (1) the legislative branch, which is the twenty-four-member Navajo Nation Council, several committees of the council, and several commissions; (2) the executive branch, which is headed by the president and vice president, and consists of twelve divisions and various other commissions or agencies; and (3) the judicial branch, which consists of the thirteen family/district courts and one appellate body called the Supreme Court. In addition, there are 110 chapters, which are local governments with responsibilities and authorities somewhat comparable to counties but uniquely Navajo.

The Navajo Nation exercises tribal sovereignty through a system of written rules embodied in various formats, including statutes and regulations, and unwritten rules or everyday practices that keep the wheels of government moving. In other words, the Navajo Nation exercises sovereignty in the same manner as all other governments—federal, state, county, and foreign. There may be differences in culture that the governments represent, and there may be limits on the sovereignty that the Nation exercises as compared to the sovereignty exercised by the United States, but the basic exercise of sovereignty is the same.

It is also important to note that for the most part the United States interacts with the national Navajo government, not the chapters or nongovernmental entities of the Nation. While at first this statement may seem controversial, this is similar in concept to the United Nations where only nation-states are members of the United Nations.[2]

MATRILINEAL CLAN SYSTEM

The matrilineal clan system is, from my perspective, the backbone of the Nation's tribal sovereignty, and may be the single greatest attribute of the organic sovereignty of the Diné people—past, present, and into the future. From time immemorial, Diné people have organized themselves and known themselves and other people who call themselves Diné through the matrilineal clan system. It is said that the clan system originated with four clans. The matrilineal clan system has grown from the original four to approximately ninety clans today. The growth is the result of an increase in Navajo peoples and the adoption of non-Navajo people, such as the Zia Pueblo people and Mexicans, into the clan system.

In this system, every Diné is asked to identify him- or herself by four clans. Generally, when introducing oneself, the person will introduce first his or her mother's clan, then his or her father's clan. Typically after that it is the mother's father's clan, and then the father's father's clan.

Many people believe we are still developing clans, and many believe that we are not. Some people believe clans can be adopted, while others believe they cannot. As a Navajo legal matter, the Navajo Supreme Court has ruled that a non-Navajo who marries a Navajo is subject to the Nation's civil and criminal laws.[3] This is significant because under the laws of the United States, tribes can criminally prosecute only members of federally recognized tribes. The Navajo Supreme Court is suggesting that a non-Navajo married to a Navajo is, in essence, a member of the tribe, whether or not that non-Navajo is a member of any federally recognized tribe, at least for criminal jurisdictional purposes. As a lawyer and tribal member, I believe this is a definitive assertion that clans are being added to the Navajo clan system today. I also believe that Diné people will fold this assertion of the Navajo Supreme Court into their everyday nonlegal life, because this assertion is a mere extension of the organic sovereignty of the matrilineal clan system.

I highlight the matrilineal clan system as an institution because it continues to be strongly practiced and revered, and just as the individual is the heart of organic sovereignty, the backbone that connects the heart with the body politic is the matrilineal clan system. As a Navajo woman and mother, I appreciate how differently the matrilineal clan system sees me as compared to how the mainstream American culture sees me. I do not want to sugarcoat the difficulties that exist for women within the Navajo Nation system. There are real challenges to Navajo women living in a poverty-ridden community where the majority of elected leaders are not women. These issues cannot be glossed over, but at the same time, I often feel that the strength and successes that I enjoy have come from the matrilineal clan system that recognizes the role of women as leaders of the family. More importantly, I do believe that the strength of my mother and my grandmother and the women who have come before me has reinforced the desire of individuals to self-identify as Diné and to carry on that strong desire to self-identify. The strong desire is more than simply becoming a citizen because one was born in a geographic area. It is a strong desire that recognizes the uniquely positive aspects of being Diné.

TSÉ HOOTSOI DINÉ BI'OLTÁ

Tsé Hootsoi Diné Bi'Oltá (TDB) is a Navajo-language immersion school for kindergarten through sixth grade located in Window Rock, the capital of the Navajo Nation. TDB is also an Arizona state public school. I have been an active parent at TDB, including having served as president of the Parent Advisory Council. Unlike the Navajo Nation, TDB is not exercising tribal sovereignty. Indeed, TDB cannot exercise tribal sovereignty because it is a creature of a state sovereign, not a tribal sovereign, as it is part of a school district created and regulated by Arizona state law.[4] In addition to not exercising tribal sovereignty, as a state entity it does not follow the laws of the Navajo Nation.

I have selected TDB because it is exercising a form of sovereignty that I call organic sovereignty. As described earlier, organic sovereignty is a common feature of a group of people who choose to organize themselves as a separate and distinct group of people. TDB is exercising the organic sovereignty of language—the language that is unique to the Navajo people. TDB is interesting because it is part of the Arizona state sovereign but it is exercising organic sovereignty that was practiced before the Western powers came onto the land. At the same time, this ancient organic sovereignty is rooted in modernity because TDB is also teaching the written language developed in the twentieth century. The written language came about post-contact but is very much organic sovereignty. What TDB is doing has been described as language preservation and at other times as language revitalization. For purposes of this essay, I will use the term *Navajo language preservation/revitalization*.

Importantly, before there was a TDB, the actions of individuals—not institutions—lead to the exercise of organic sovereignty by a state institution. My understanding is that TDB began as a program within an Arizona public school. The program began through the leadership of a handful of Navajo teachers and parents. After a few years of success, the Navajo parents worked with the school board, an elected body of five individuals who are currently all Navajo—and likely will be majority Navajo for a very long time—to create and authorize the creation of the immersion school. The Navajo individuals who were part of the creation of TDB, either in the role of a state-elected school-board official, an employee of a state public school, or as a citizen of the state of Arizona voting for the school board, utilized the system of the state of Arizona so that they could exercise Navajo organic sovereignty.

Of significant interest is that the organic sovereignty of language preservation/revitalization is being exercised through the institution of a state public school—a state that has a reputation for being hostile to utilizing any language other than English.

A critical lesson I have learned about sovereignty from my work with TDB is that the heart of sovereignty, especially organic sovereignty, is the individual. This became clear to me in 2014 when the school board was almost entirely replaced by individuals who led a recall election of the sitting school board; again, all these individuals were Navajo. After the new school board was seated, there were numerous rumors that the newly seated school board intended to shut down TDB as an immersion school. The TDB parents organized and attended a school-board meeting en masse to express their support for TDB. The newly elected board chair began the meeting by immediately stating that there was no intention on his part to end the immersion language school—to which there was immense applause. This was a strong tangible statement of organic sovereignty being exercised by the individual Navajo parents whose message was sent to an elected Navajo serving on a state of Arizona entity. I do want to point out that it was unclear if other members of the school board supported the chair's position, which is an interesting wrinkle in this discussion of organic sovereignty because if a different Navajo individual, one who does not support TDB was the chair, this situation may have played out entirely differently. It underscores the importance of the individual in the exercise of an aspect of the sovereignty of the state of Arizona and the organic sovereignty of the Diné. Both state sovereignty—not tribal—and Diné organic sovereignty are being played out at TDB, making it an infinitely fascinating case study.[5]

QUESTION 3. WHAT CHALLENGES DOES NAVAJO SOVEREIGNTY FACE IN THE COMING GENERATIONS?

For this question, I am defining Navajo sovereignty as tribal sovereignty of the body politic. Tribal sovereignty includes a set of laws that reflect a set of policies so that the Navajo Nation can be a self-governing entity. The challenges of the past will continue to be the challenges that Navajo sovereignty will face in the coming generations.

One challenge of the past and of today is that the Navajo Nation is made up of various types of land statuses. There is the Navajo reservation created through the Treaty of 1868 and continuously extended through various presidential executive orders. In Utah and Arizona, new reservation boundaries were drawn by Congress in 1933 and 1934, respectively, to incorporate those executive order lands within the Navajo reservation. A new boundary was not drawn in New Mexico; therefore, much of the Nation in New Mexico is colloquially referred to as "checkerboard," meaning that there are many different types of land status. In addition, there are the three satellite chapters that are also checkerboarded areas.[6] Finally, there are lands that are part of the Navajo Nation that were created pursuant to the congressional laws settling the land dispute between the Nation and the Hopi Tribe concerning the 1882 Executive

Order reservation. When the 1882 reservation was divided between the two tribes, many Navajo and Hopi were relocated. On the Navajo Nation, this lead to the creation of a new chapter, called Nahata Dziil, also known as "New Lands," which has a different land status for certain purposes than the land of the original reservation. These different land statuses make it difficult to govern because the Navajo Nation cannot always enact singular laws across the Navajo Nation for the purpose of having one set policy for the Nation. This is because, as a legal matter, the status of the land affects how the Nation's laws are enforced—if those laws can be enforced at all.

A specific example of this problem of different land statuses is the laws governing grazing. There are three different sets of laws: one for the reservation, one for the lands that were formerly part of the 1882 reservation, and one for the checkerboarded lands and Nahata Dziil Chapter. These three sets of laws reflect three different approaches on how to manage grazing. How a Navajo grazes on the New Lands is quite different than how a Navajo living on the formal reservation grazes. These different grazing practices affect the Navajo grazers and the natural resources that are utilized for the livestock in different ways.

Another challenge is poverty, which is both a challenge and a strength. It is a strength because it is a common rallying cry across the Navajo Nation that brings individual Diné together to focus on ameliorating the problem, including, at times, the three institutions discussed earlier in question 2. This is significant because these three institutions are to operate under a system of separation of powers. It is a challenge because tackling poverty is a monumental, draining task, but most tangibly, it is the greatest challenge the Navajo Nation faces because many Diné are choosing to leave the poor conditions of the Nation to build their lives elsewhere.[7] Some have described this phenomenon as a brain drain.[8] Whether or not it is a brain drain, it is a challenge to maintaining the culture and language of the Diné when people no longer live among one another.

At the root of tribal sovereignty, however, is organic sovereignty. Therefore it seems to me the greatest challenge to Navajo sovereignty is ourselves, the individual Diné. By ourselves, I mean the challenge to Navajo sovereignty are choices that individual Navajo people make. We can make choices that strengthen our organic sovereignty or that weaken our organic sovereignty. I focus on organic sovereignty, because it appears to me that organic sovereignty, more than tribal sovereignty in the Western sense, provides the pride that encourages individual Diné to continue to self-identify as Diné.

I say this because despite the fact that individuals are moving off the Navajo Nation, people are still enrolling themselves or their children or grandchildren to be citizens of the Navajo Nation. While there is certainly always a bit of coercion to identify as a member of any group, including as a Diné, for whom coercion is reinforced through the matrilineal clan system, it would seem to me that coercion weakens significantly when one leads a life far away from the Nation. Yet people living away from the Nation continue to choose to enroll their children or themselves in the citizenship of the Navajo Nation. I have interpreted this choice to mean that individual Diné are choosing to identify as Diné because of an individual desire to do so, and less so because of coercion. This is a positive statement of hope in the future of the Navajo Nation and Navajo sovereignty. So while we individuals may present the greatest challenges to ourselves as Diné people, we also present the greatest opportunity to find solutions to the challenges that face Navajo sovereignty.

QUESTION 4: HOW DO INDIVIDUAL DINÉ ENVISION SOVEREIGNTY, POWER, AUTHORITY, AND AUTONOMY FOR THE PEOPLE?

In my experience, each individual Diné reacts to this question differently. The individual person's reaction depends on how that person makes a living, where that person lives, what that person expects from the Navajo government, what that person expects from the federal government—the list of influencing factors goes on into the infinity of human identity. The most recent election debates concerning whether or not a Navajo presidential candidate should speak the Navajo language fluently demonstrated a divide among Diné on that issue and an example of how each Navajo uniquely reacts to any particular issue.

I provide one answer through the lawyer's lens that I wear. The Navajo body politic has sovereignty; it has power; it has authority; and it has autonomy. How much of any one of those four things it has depends on the issue in front of the body politic. When and how the body politic chooses to exercise any one of those four things differs depending on the issue in front of it. And the exercise of tribal sovereignty and the power and authority that comes with it is an ongoing experiment that the Navajo body politic hopes to utilize to improve the standard of living on the Nation so that the young Diné living off of the Nation will return home.

While it often seems to me that there are as many different visions of Diné sovereignty, power, authority, and autonomy as there are individual Diné, which is more than three hundred thousand visions if based on the number of enrolled citizens alone, the one common underlying theme that I repeatedly hear is that the Diné have not yet reached true sovereignty, power, authority, and autonomy for the people. Said another way, we are a developing Nation.

CONCLUSION

From my perspective, the Navajo Nation exercises tribal sovereignty and organic sovereignty. Organic sovereignty is a form of sovereignty unique and distinctive from the Western concept of sovereignty as defined by the term *tribal sovereignty* or as defined in the international system. At the heart of the Navajo Nation, tribal sovereignty is the individual Navajo person who is exercising organic sovereignty by continuing to self-identify as Diné, and thereby continues to be part of the collective group of people known as Diné. Tribal sovereignty and organic sovereignty complement one another. Indeed, tribal sovereignty and organic sovereignty can protect and promote the other. In its best light, sovereignty is a means for organic sovereignty to thrive. And in the end, the individual Diné has the power to make choices that will ensure a thriving Diné organic sovereignty, which is the heart of Navajo Nation tribal sovereignty.

NOTES

1. *Cherokee Nation v. Georgia*, 30 U.S. (5 Pet.) 1 (1831). In addition, for a good, brief, and readable explanation of the origins of federal Indian law and the concept of domestic dependent nations, see William C. Canby Jr., *American Indian Law in a Nutshell* (Eagan, MN: West Publishing, 2009). It is now in its fifth edition, but all of the editions contain this explanation.
2. See the United Nations' website to review the United Nations' charter. Two chapters of significant interest and relevance are Chapter II, which outlines the requirements to become a member states, and Chapter XI, which concerns "non-self-governing territories," which are "territories whose peoples have not yet attained a full measure of self-government." http://www.un.org.

3. This is to be contrasted with federal law, which states that a non-Indian is generally not subject to a tribe's criminal laws, even if the non-Indian is married to an enrolled member of that tribe and lives on that tribe's lands.

4. TDB is a school within the Window Rock School District. Of interesting notice, at the time of writing this essay, the Window Rock School District is legally challenging the Nation's tribal sovereignty. Specifically, the school district is challenging the application of the Navajo Nation's Navajo Preference in Employment Act at schools within the school district. TDB is not part of the legal action. The Piñon Unified School District, another Arizona school district, has also brought the same legal challenge.

5. One year later, I am happy to report that there is no more rumormongering about the school board eliminating TDB.

6. An interesting wrinkle with these satellite chapters is that in addition to parcels of land being set aside for the Navajo Nation or for individual Navajos, there are parcels of land within those chapters that are set aside for one of each of the three bands of Navajos for whom those chapters are named. The three bands are the Ramah Band, the Cañoncito Band, and the Alamo Band.

7. The on-reservation population decreased in 2010 from 2000, even though the birth rate has not declined.

8. Diné Policy Institute Brian Drain Study, http://www.dinecollege.edu/institutes/DPI/Docs/brain-drain-presentation.

EDUCATION

THE PATH OF NAVAJO SOVEREIGNTY IN TRADITIONAL EDUCATION

Harmony, Disruption, Distress, and Restoration of Harmony

MANLEY A. BEGAY JR.

INTRODUCTION

I N JUNE 2014, President Barack Obama, accompanied by First Lady Michelle Obama, made a historic visit to Indian Country, stopping at the Standing Rock Sioux Tribe in Cannonball, North Dakota.[1] Not only was it his first visit as president, but he was the first sitting president to visit Indian lands since Bill Clinton did so in 1999. After meeting with students at a local school, the president and First Lady emerged "stunned and emotional from a meeting with six students who spoke of lives affected by homelessness, alcoholism, poverty, and suicide."[2] President Obama said that he and the First Lady were "shaken because some of these kids were carrying burdens no young person should ever have to carry. And it was heartbreaking."[3]

Upon returning to Washington, DC, President Obama met with his staff and recounted his visit with the Native children. He stated that his administration needed "to aggressively build on efforts to overhaul the Indian educational system and focus on improving conditions for Native American youths." President Obama averred, "They knew I was serious because it's not very often where I tear up in the Oval Office. I deal with a lot of bad stuff in this job."[4]

Subsequently, at the White House's Sixth Annual Tribal Nations Conference, the Obama administration unveiled a set of reports, programs and other initiatives focusing on Native American children. The White House also presented a report stating Native American youths and their education system are in a "state of emergency," due in part to past "misguided federal policies," and that the educational, socioeconomic, health, and other issues facing young people on reservations are "nothing short of a national crisis."[5]

As I witness what appears to be yet another attempt by the federal government to revamp Indian education, I remain skeptical that this latest effort will finally address what is the core issue of education for Native peoples—the profound and wide-ranging consequences of colonization over hundreds of years. Past attempts by the federal government to overhaul Indian education have fallen short, and indeed failed because of a lack of funding, poor planning, short-term commitment, or because the federal government managed all or part of the process. It is imperative this latest initiative truly recognize the educational sovereignty of Native nations by allocating the requisite funds and placing Native peoples at the forefront and directly in charge of a complete overhaul of Indian education. Our people must be placed in positions of accountability and legitimacy whereby we own and exercise this aspect of our sovereignty. Until we accomplish this, the education of our children will continue to progress slowly—if at all.

In the light of the president's initiative to tackle the problems Native youths are facing, this chapter focuses on educational sovereignty, a critical component of Native nation rebuilding. The general public understanding of sovereignty is, as Wilma Mankiller, the late principal chief of the Cherokee Nation, stated: "The definition of sovereignty is to have control over your own lands, and resources, and assets, and to have control over your own vision for the future, and to be able to absolutely determine your own destiny."[6] Another way to explain sovereignty according to Peterson Zah, former Navajo chairman and president, is "by thinking about sovereignty as embedded in Diné way of life, culture, tradition, language, ceremonies, songs, and prayers. In other words, it is about who and what we are and how we want our children to live."[7] Indeed, one of our most valuable resources and assets is our youth and providing them an education that ensures a Native nation the ability to control its destiny and way of life.

Research has found that when Native peoples are in charge of their destiny, more successful development occurs than when outside governmental authorities are. Furthermore, the research reveals that Indigenous communities that have de facto decision-making control over their own assets and local governing apparatus have the greatest prospects of breaking the cycles of economic underdevelopment and social distress that have afflicted the vast majority of Indigenous communities over the twentieth and early twenty-first centuries. What I am referring to is *real self-determination* and not *self-administration*.[8] There is clear difference between actually governing and deciding how you are going to create your own future as opposed to managing and administering programs designed and managed by someone else.

Using the Navajo Nation as an example, I will discuss the integral role of an educational system as part of Native nation building by defining the components and their significance to educational sovereignty: What is traditional Navajo educational sovereignty? What were some of the traditional Navajo teaching practices of life, and what led to changes of these methods of teachings? How do traditional Navajos envision educational sovereignty, power, authority, and autonomy for the people? How is traditional Navajo educational sovereignty understood in the eyes of European interlopers? What challenges does Navajo educational sovereignty face in the coming generations?

Because Native languages are integral to sovereignty and education, I will use Diné foundational concepts of life to explain Navajo philosophy and values that underpin the meaning of educational sovereignty. Use of the Diné language allows for a more definitive and accurate understanding of how language and culture are wholly integrated together to understand Diné perspectives of the root of educational sovereignty. In other words, language and culture are inseparable. All in all, language, as Keith Basso observes, "emerges as a powerful vehicle of thought and a crucial instrument for accomplishing social interaction, as an indispensable means of knowing the world and for performing deeds within it."[9] In this writing, the Diné language serves as an entrance to the conceptual world of the Navajo by understanding the cultural assumptions and beliefs that are revealed in not only understanding the importance of Navajo heritage language but also in knowing what educational sovereignty means from a Diné perspective.

Sovereignty has been too often portrayed strictly in the European political and legal sense, which consequently severely diminishes and dismisses traditional Navajo (and other Indigenous) cultural views and conceptions of it. When this occurs, Navajo origins of sovereignty are neglected, oppressed, and disregarded. Because traditional Navajo beliefs of sovereignty are deeply rooted in the geneses of traditional Navajo ethos of life, the European interlopers to Navajo Country disrupted this philosophy of life.

HARMONY—EXERCISE OF TRADITIONAL NAVAJO EDUCATIONAL SOVEREIGNTY THROUGH NAVAJO TEACHINGS OF LIFE

Before the arrival of the Europeans, Navajo educational and child-rearing philosophical thought found that "child-rearing and indigenous education practices often go hand in hand. Within the context of the home and community, a child learns to develop her full potential as an individual and to harmonize that individuality with communal needs. This is done through a holistic system of education that teaches the child that all things in life are related."[10]

Central to the holistic system of education and teachings of the Navajo people are the Navajo Creation Scriptures and Journey Narratives, which includes *Shá bik'ehgo As'ah Oodááł*.[11] This life-teaching philosophy is better understood by parsing the words into its distinct parts:

> *Shá* refers to the sun, the path of the sun, and the sunlight as it passes during the day. *Bik'ehgo* means according to, therefore, *Shá bik'ehgo* signifies living according to the southerly pathway of the Sun. *As'ah* denotes far ahead into the future; to old age; essentially, making a life with health and strength of body, mind, and spirit, while avoiding problems that arise on the journey of life. *Oodááł* signifies the personal travel or journey to old age, walking to old age, or on the way to old age. *As'ah Oodááł*, in general terms, is having a healthy lifestyle and wellness at all times. This could be on a daily basis or a lifetime, short-term or long-term.[12]

Therefore the Navajo life-teaching mantra *Shá bik'ehgo As'ah Oodááł* loosely translates to "A Journey with Wellness and Healthy Lifestyle Guided by the Journey of the Sun."[13] This educational philosophy is taught to Navajo children from an early age in hopes of nurturing a child into adulthood with all the blessings of, among others, good thinking, planning, independence, strength, knowledge, health, happiness, and sense of hope. Embodied in this teaching philosophy was exposure to concepts embedded in the study of, among others, physics, economics, horticulture, math, genealogy, arts, law, environment, astronomy, and personal development that enabled one to live to an old age as a strong and sovereign human being.[14] In other words, this teaching philosophy rooted in the Navajo Creation Scriptures and Journey

Narratives serves as a complete sociological and anthropological scholarship of every feature of Navajo culture.

Being a sovereign human is based on building and maintaining strength of self and independence through proper traditional Navajo educational teachings. Therefore, primary to living as a sovereign Navajo person are the understanding and exercise of primordial concepts of *k'é* (kinship unity through positive values to include respect for all in the promotion of goodwill, peace, love, positive relationship, and solidarity) and *k'éí* (descent, clanship, kinship).[15] K'é, a key philosophical concept that underlies traditional Navajo culture, is an attribute of *Hózhójii*—the state of harmony, peace, beauty, wellness, and balance with all.[16] Further, to know Hózhójii, one must also know *Hochxójii*, the state of disharmony—another primordial concept of life, which is the antithesis of the Hózhójii. A purpose of Navajo life is to maintain balance and respect between the individual and the universe and to live in harmony and beauty with nature, the social milieu of family and community, and the Holy Ones[17] in hopes of achieving the state of *Sa'ąh Naagháí Bik'eh Hózhóǫn*.[18] As such, *Sa'ąh Naagháí Bik'eh* means:

> . . . the balance of our lives with the natural path of the sun. We strive to follow the established path of life, signified by the natural path of *Hózhóǫn Niidlį*, the sun, *Shábik'ehgo*, and this is the foundation of *iiná dóó á'ál'į'*, *Diné* life and culture. *Diné* values are established from the connection with the natural world, including comprehension of the cardinal directions, the circle of life, four seasons, and the creation stories. The goal is proper balance between *Sa'ąh Naagháí Ashkii* and *Bik'eh Hózhóǫn Atééd*. When we achieve the balance, *Sa'ąh Naagháí Bik'eh Hózhóǫn Niidlį*, and complete our life cycle, *Hats'íís dóó háni'haatih*, we have walked the right path and maintained our connection. Our human journeys, *Oodáál*, shall be helped by our human institutions, as we follow the natural path of the sun, *Shábik'ehgo*, in strength of body, mind, and spirit, *Bee yis'ah go oodáál*.[19]

Traditional Navajo lifeway teachings regarding life goals incorporate philosophical understanding and practice of *Hózhǫ́ogo Naashaadoo* ("Walking in beauty, peace, and harmony"), *Shił Hózhǫ́* ("Being happy and spiritually at peace"), *Hózhǫ́ogo shił haz'a* ("Having your domestic affairs in order"),[20] *Chánah* ("Being vigorous, healthy, and energetic, and/or having courage, vitality, and strength"),[21] and *T'ááhó ájít'éigo* ("Taking care of yourself physically, emotionally, socially, and spiritually," or "being self-reliant").[22] These practices are not easily acquired and require instilling cultural values and efficacy of personal responsibilities through a set of teachings rooted in the Navajo Creation Scriptures and Journey Narratives. Essentially, these primordial tenets are guided by the Journey of the Sun and are about "teaching and empowering individuals (from birth to adulthood) to be responsible for preserving and protecting their own and well-being of others."[23] For traditional Navajos, the definition of educational sovereignty is deeply embedded in Navajo ontology and epistemology.

In his chapter, Ray Austin states that a traditional Navajo denotation of sovereignty is *naat'á*, with its meaning deeply rooted in traditional Navajos belief "that the Holy Beings planted the six sacred mountains and blessed each with naat'á."[24] He goes on to say, "Thus, the mountains are called Dził Naat'á in ceremony, which broadly encompasses authority, power, laws, and leadership. Dził Naat'á is analogous to the Western concept of sovereignty because the sacred mountains are blessed with supreme authority and power."[25] With this foundational understanding of the traditional Navajo meaning of sovereignty, we are better able to begin to comprehend the precise meaning of educational sovereignty.

To the Navajos, the six sacred mountains represent the cosmic hogan—celestial dwelling place—within which resides the sovereignty of the Navajo Nation. Where, then, can we find traditional Navajo educational sovereignty? Navajos believe that sovereignty is deeply embedded in the cosmic hogan, and, therefore, Navajo educational sovereignty exists in the terrestrial hogan—earthly dwelling—as well.[26] Further, traditional Navajos believe that the primordial elements of life are earth, light, air, and water, which serve as the foundational geneses of traditional Navajo education of life.

As such, Navajo Creation Scriptures and Journey Narratives reveal that *Kǫ́* or *Hajiinéi Kǫ́* (Fire) undertakes a fundamental role in traditional Navajo teachings of life as verified by *Haashch'éélt'í* (Talking God), the First Teacher.[27] Navajo connotation of educational sovereignty then would be *Iiná ba naat'á*—deciphered as exercising sovereignty for the education of life.[28] In the terrestrial hogan, *Kǫ́* and *Honeeshgish* (Fire Stoker) reside in the center as teachers of life. The terrestrial hogan is the cornerstone of Navajo family life and teachings and was formed in the image of the sacred mountains.

The mountains in their sequential and foundational form and order serves as the life pillars, a philosophical structure in which an epitome of family is formed, lived, and prolonged on the path of *Sa'ạh Naagháí Bik'eh Iina* and *A'sah Na'adá*. *Iina Kǫ́* (Fire of Life) is always present with the *Honeeshgish* (Fire Stoker), as they are situated in its midst of a home, so that it has significance and connection to the constellation within the Universe; whereby the dome of the [terrestrial] Hogan represent the Universe and the constellations that were placed appropriately with *Náhookǫs Bikǫ́* serving as the "Light of Life" within the Universe. This is signified by placing the fireplace *Honik'eh* directly and between the entrance *Yah'ałníí'* or middle of the home. More importantly, it signifies the "Light of Life" amidst the constellations of appropriates stars relating and identifying with the fireplace of homes on Mother Earth. Furthermore, the dispositions of these set of stars bear their names *Átsé'etsózá, Átsé'etsoh, Dilyéhé, Hastiin Sik'ai'í*, and others in Diné myths and legends of the Holy Peoples' ventures in their time immemorial. This is why the grandparents tell and teach their children to respect nature in Mother Earth and Constellations in the Stars, to wake up early and be early risers in *"Yikááh Na'adá"* and to pray and offer to *Nihoogai or Hayoołkáál Diyiin Diné'é*, and *Haasch'ééh Diné'é* with white corn meal or *Naadą́'ałgaii*.[29] (Emphasis added)

Consequently, the cosmic and terrestrial hogan serves as an ontological and an epistemological creation and understanding of sovereignty in the education of individual Navajos and the Navajo Nation as a whole.

The established values and responsibilities firmly entrenched in the Journey of the Sun and the Universe have guided Navajo individuals since the beginning of time to ensure a long life full of happiness, harmony, peace, wellness, protection, contentment, and purpose. From birth, a Navajo child would be nurtured and educated with these teachings to become an adult who is able to live by and fulfill the following noted personal values and responsibilities:

Ádééhániih—Demonstrating concern for self and self-responsibility
Ádáhodílyin—Valuing the whole self (body, mind, spirit, and social relations) as well as one's place in the universe of all relationships
Ádaa áháyą́—Caring for self and one's place of dwelling and taking responsibilities
Ádaa hą́ą́hasin—Understanding limitation and the need to rest to replenish mind, body, spirit, and emotional needs.[30]

A confident, capable, autonomous, and self-determined Navajo individual with an appropriate traditional foundational education will be able to attain

A'daan Nitsi'dzi' kees—or the "ability to think for yourself"—a skill that requires higher-order thinking powers. A traditional Navajo education is based on an internal-external learning and teaching paradigm where the individual first develops a strong sense of internal identity and thereby gains a sense of self and purpose. With cognitive ability ingrained in clear reasoning and autonomous thinking, the individual can manage externally ideas and concepts with conscience of discernment. Having this self-confidence allows the individual to become knowledgeable about the world through trusting his or her abilities, knowledge, and skills toward attainment of a greater sense of accomplishment. Intellectual independence with a foundation of courage and strength of being brings forth creativity, unrestricted contemplation, and original thinking. This type of traditional Navajo education resulted in the development of a Navajo person who is an independent, self-motivated individual yet is also interdependent and recognizes that he or she is part of a larger whole. A Navajo individual of this sort is truly a sovereign human being.

This Navajo individual is then able to confidently define him- or herself as a five-fingered human being and *Diyin Nohookáá Diné'é*: Holy Earth-Surface-Person. Content and armed with the knowledge of life and self, the sovereign Navajo individual will realize that

> *Bíla'ashdla'ii* is an affirmation. We affirm our name, *nihízhi'*, *Diné*, which means the people, human, or beings with five fingers, *Bíla'ashdla'ii*. We also have a spiritual name, *Diyin Nohookáá Diné'é*, or Holy Earth-Surface-People. Through our name, we affirm the human in all tribes and nations, and respect for the individual, all our relatives, and all living beings, *ádil'ídlį*. Through respect, we affirm there is a proper place and value for all human beings.[31]

DISRUPTION—THE TURMOIL BY EUROPEAN INTERLOPERS ON TRADITIONAL NAVAJO EDUCATIONAL SOVEREIGNTY

The newcomers to the Western Hemisphere did not have a high regard for the traditional Indigenous educational and life philosophies, including those of the Navajo people. The most notable and prevailing view on the education of Native Americans by the U.S. government held true by many new to the Western Hemisphere was the infamous quotation by Captain Richard H. Pratt, "Kill the Indian, and save the man."[32] This cultural genocidal view did not suddenly appear; rather, it had been fermenting for centuries even before the first Navajo and European encounter.[33] The ultimate intent couched in numerous European governmental policies was to completely expunge the cultural practices of the Navajos as well as other Native peoples and have full access to the Indigenous souls and riches held on Indigenous lands.

Before the first European contact with the Navajo people, the die of cultural assimilation and genocide had already been cast. In 1493, the year after the "discovery" of the New World, Pope Alexander VI, issued his infamous Bull of Demarcation, in which Spanish explorers gave to Spain all the undiscovered country of the Southwest lying beyond an imaginary line one hundred miles west of the Azores and the Cape Verde Islands. Upon this and other decrees, Spain based her sovereign claims to the New World.[34,35] The Bull of Demarcation and later decrees gave the rights to colonize, exploit, and convert all non-Christian territory to Catholicism. These decrees treated all newly discovered nations and people as property of European nations and vilified all non-Christian governments the Catholic explorers found.[36]

As Don Francisco Vasquez de Coronado was exploring the southwestern part of the United States—specifically, what is now Arizona and New Mexico—he was under specific instructions mandated by the Bulls to colonize those who occupied the area and seize all riches found. While it is possible there was contact between the Spanish and Navajos during Coronado's first expedition (1540–42), there was no written account until the expeditions conducted in the 1580s by Francisco Sanchez Chamuscado, Fray Agustin Rodriquez, and Antonio de Espejo.[37] The 1581 to 1588 expeditions beyond Pueblo Country westward—in particular, the de Espejo expedition—mention contact with "warlike mountainous people" near the Little Colorado River.[38] The Spanish gave the Navajos two names—"Apache de Navajos" and "Querechos." The intent of these expeditions was to Christianize and civilize the Navajos and other Indigenous peoples, and appropriate their wealth.[39]

In 1541, Don Francisco Vasquez de Coronado reveals his cultural assimilation and genocidal intentions as he searched for mineral wealth, when he stated:

> I gave a detailed account of this expedition, which the viceroy of New Spain ordered me to undertake in Your Majesty's name to this country which was discovered by Friar Marcos de Niza, the provincial of the order of Holy Saint Francis. I described it all, and the sort of force I have, as Your Majesty had ordered

me to relate in my letters; and stated that while *I was engaged in the conquest and pacification of the natives of this province*, some Indians who were natives of other provinces beyond these had told me that in their country there were much larger villages and better houses than those of the natives of this country, and that they had lords who ruled them, who were served with dishes of gold, and other very magnificent things; and although, as I wrote Your Majesty, I did not believe it before I had set eyes on it, because it was the report of Indians and given for the most part by means of signs, yet as the report appeared to me to be very fine and that it was important that it should be investigated for Your Majesty's service, I determined to go and see it with the men I have here. I started from this province on the 23d of last April, for the place where the Indians wanted to guide me.[40] (Emphasis added)

These and subsequent Spanish expeditions led to the subjugation of most of the pueblos; however, the Navajos proved to be a formidable foe. Despite a Spanish invasion that led to Christian conversions, diseases, slavery, and suppression of the Navajo people, the Navajos withstood the assault through strength of cultural ways directly connected to the significance and practice of the Navajo Creation Scriptures and Journey Narratives. The Spanish were compelled to finally negotiate with the Navajo people. In fact,

there are no records of treaties prior to the 1620's. The earliest known peace treaty was arranged by a Spaniard named Fray Alonso de Benavides in his efforts to convert Dine to Christianity. This account dates back to the 1620's and there is apparently no record of the negotiation itself.[41]

Eventually, from 1706 to 1819, four treaties were negotiated between the parties[42] regarding peace, alliance, trade, and slavery.[43] When military victory was not possible, Spanish subjugations and manipulations ensued via these treaties. In the late eighteenth century, in an attempt to weaken and defeat the Navajos, the Spanish formed alliances with other tribes in the surrounding area.

Atrocities were committed on all sides. Constant raiding and slave-taking occurred. It is estimated that during the early 1800s more than 66 percent of all Navajo families had experienced the loss of members to slavery. Navajo children were taken from their families and sold at auctions in Santa Fe, Taos, and other places. Others were sent deep into Mexico to work in the silver mines. Most never returned. Many Navajo families retell stories of slaves taken or escaping during this time.[44]

The onslaught of the Spanish took its toll on the Navajo people into the early 1800s, adversely impacting the Navajo people by a reduction of its population, the spread of diseases, slave trade, and forced Christianization.

The Spanish colonial era faded into Mexico's independence from Spain in 1821; however, it did not decrease the number of battles and slave expeditions to Navajo Country by the Mexicans. The number of skirmishes and slave expeditions increased, prompting the negotiation of treaties between the Mexicans and Navajos from 1822 to 1844.[45] Under the banner of Mexican independence from Spain, former Spaniards—now Mexicans—lay claim to all land in the Southwest without agreement from the Navajos and other Native peoples from that area, which furthered colonization by the European intruders. The Mexican period between 1821 and 1846 continued a cultural disruption of life for the Navajos. The next wave of European intruders, the Americans, came under the banner of Manifest Destiny. The Americans proved to be the same as the Spanish and Mexicans in their intent because they also wanted access to Navajo land and the riches it held and to Christianize and "civilize" the Navajo people.

As early as the 1600s, American colonists expressed an aversion and disdain with how Native peoples were living and believed that reeducation was the best answer. Robert Gray, a supporter of the expansion of colonial Virginia, stated what was a familiar and prevalent view of Native people when he remarked, "It is not the nature of men, but the education of men, which makes them barbarous and uncivil, and therefore change the education of men, and you shall see that their nature will be greatly rectified and corrected."[46] Unfortunately, for the Indigenous people of this land, this lamentable sentiment became the mantra for American colonization for hundreds of years to come.

The American colonization policies of the Indigenous peoples of the United States in the seventeenth and eighteenth centuries were marked by two themes: to Christianize and civilize the American Indians.[47] To fulfill this distressing sentiment, the U.S. government passed numerous policies with the goal of complete assimilation of the Indigenous people.[48] This colonial mind-set that became U.S. federal Indian policy carried over into Navajo Country, beginning in the mid-nineteenth century, essentially when the United States declared war on Mexico in 1846. The result was "that the formerly Mexican territory was now a part of the United States of America and that the former Mexican citizens would be afforded the protection of the U.S. government."[49]

As the Spanish and Mexicans had done, the Americans unilaterally laid claim to Navajo land without Navajo consent.

The Navajo people had initially hoped that after the change in regime (Mexico to the United States), the United States would come to the aid of the Navajos and assist in recovering Navajos who were imprisoned or sold into slavery by the Mexicans. Instead, the Americans declared that they would protect the Mexicans from all "hostile" Indians. As a result of tremendous animosity between the Mexicans and Navajos, and, now the Americans, treaty making became rampant even though the treaties were consistently broken on both sides.

Between 1846 and 1868, treaties were signed between the Navajo Nation and the United States. Those previous to the 1868 treaty contained specific provisions for peaceful trading, the establishment of boundaries, beginning establishment of a reservation, protection by the United States, jurisdictional claim to Navajo land, hunting rights, armistice, returning or exchanging prisoners, and property.[50] Out of nine treaties, Congress ratified only two. The events leading up to the last treaty with the U.S. government, the Treaty of 1868, nearly devastated the Navajo people.

For more than 250 years of Spanish and Mexican onslaughts, the Navajo people endured, but not without a heavy loss of life and a relentless assault on culture and lifeways. Constant warfare, enslavement (estimates are as high one-third of the Navajo people were enslaved), treaty after treaty, diseases, and Christianization attempts took its toll. Finally, the Navajos had to contend with the Americans.

Hostilities between the Mexicans, Americans, and other Indian tribes against the Navajos were intense for two decades in the mid-1800s.

Navajos refer to the 1850s and early 1860s as a troubled period—*Nahonzoǫ odaa'*—during which they had to constantly move around in defense of their livestock and families. They had to keep ahead of their enemies at all times. No permanent structures could be built, and their hogans and cornfields often were discovered and burned. Sheep and horses were stolen. Families were massacred and children were taken to be sold. Enemies came from all directions: Utes, Comanches, Jicarilla Apaches, Zunis, New Mexicans, and Americans. Alliances were constantly shifting. Americans, French, Spanish, and in some cases

Mormons, reportedly furnished the Utes, Comanches, and Pawnees with guns, while the Navajos had to fight primarily with bows and arrows and spears.[51]

Notwithstanding the coming of the American Civil War, the United States declared an all-out war against the Navajos. This lasted nearly five years and culminated in a massive assault and subsequent pursuit, capture, forced march (the Long Walk), and four-year incarceration of Navajos in a makeshift concentration camp at Fort Sumner, New Mexico (known as *Hweeldi* by the Navajos), some three hundred miles from Navajo Country. Those events led to a substantial decrease in the Navajo population. Although the entire Navajo population was not imprisoned in the concentration camp at Fort Sumner, over eight thousand Navajos were, and it has been estimated that over three thousand succumbed to starvation, disease, poverty, misery, homesickness, frostbite, despair, killings, and kidnappings. What the Spanish and Mexicans could not do—pacify the Navajos—the Americans did, relentlessly. The American war on the Navajos ended with the signing of the Treaty of 1868, and the Second Long Walk began.[52]

Since the nineteenth century, traditional Navajo educational practices have been openly viewed as primitive and backward. In the ensuing hundred years, the Americans commenced cultural genocide—the provocation of the Navajos through education for assimilation and acculturation. This was an all-out effort by the U.S. government to eradicate all that was Navajo—lifeways, culture, language, and thought. It was a systematic eradication of Navajo lifeways by the Americans that took its toll on the Navajo people, resulting in massive trauma still being felt and experienced today.

DISTRESS—THE IMPACT OF THE EUROPEAN INTRUDERS ON TRADITIONAL NAVAJO EDUCATIONAL SOVEREIGNTY

It is remarkable testament to the strength and resiliency of the Navajo people's culture and lifeways that in the twenty-first century, they are still alive and flourishing. As of July 2011, the Navajo population exceeded three hundred thousand.[53] But even as the Nation grows more populous, there are inherent socioeconomic problems it must contend with.

The Navajo people are currently facing some serious educational, social, economic, and cultural challenges. The educational attainment rates are dismal at best,[54] the poverty rate is extremely high,[55] the unemployment rate is staggering,[56] and the language-retention rate is dropping.[57] These dire socioeconomic issues did not materialize suddenly; rather, they have been escalating for centuries. Essentially, many of these problems stem from the extreme historical trauma suffered by generations of Navajo people.

Dr. Maria Yellow Horse Brave Heart, PhD, first conceptualized the notion of historical trauma in the early 1980s in the course of developing an understanding as to why many Native Americans were not able to live "the American Dream."[58] She has written extensively on the topic, and in addition to the scholars and subject-matter experts cited in this essay, many others continue to contribute to the field.[59] Dr. Brave Heart defined "historical trauma" as "the collective emotional and psychological injury both over the life span and across generations . . . emanating from massive group trauma."[60] It is "the collective emotional and psychological injury both over the life span and across generations, resulting from a cataclysmic history of genocide."[61] The basis of this trauma is that Native Americans, for over five hundred years, have experienced and suffered physical, emotional, social, and spiritual genocide resulting from European and American colonialism. While many Indigenous peoples in the United States have outwardly adapted (e.g., many are healthy and economically self-sufficient), not all share that well-being.[62]

Dr. Brave Heart further notes that this wounding goes beyond the individual, but indeed affects the majority of a group of people. In her study "Living and Surviving in a Multiply Wounded Country," Martha Caberea found that "multiply wounded societies run the risk of becoming societies with intergenerational traumas. It is virtually a law that one treats others the way one treats oneself. Anywhere that large population groups are traumatized, the trauma is transferred to the next generation. Working with the multiple wound phenomenon means accepting that the wounds are collective as well as personal."[63]

For the Navajo people, "historical trauma" begins with the initial contact with the first European intruders—an ethnic genocide. As stated earlier, the Navajo Nation was decimated through disease, annihilation, forced assimilation, and U.S. expansion and military politics.[64] There was an immediate clash of philosophies between Native peoples, including the Navajo, and the first interlopers over land and differing ideologies: Europeans placed personal value in the ownership of land, whereas Native peoples considered land, plants, and animals to be sacred relatives, far beyond a concept of property.[65] Government policies, such as the Dawes Allotment Act of 1887, divided tribal community land among individual Indians in parcels, and the remaining unallotted lands were given to white settlers as "excess" lands. Armed conflict and the removal of American Indian nations from traditional lands became the norm.[66] Numerous American Indian nations faced "Long Walks," where many, if not the majority, died from disease, fatigue, and starvation. Thousands of Native people were forced to relocate to "reservations," which were operated like prison camps by Indian agents.[67]

Assimilation was not simply the confiscation of traditional American Indian lands, but the obliteration of American Indian languages, customs, traditions, and cultures. Established in 1824, the Office of Indian Affairs (later the Bureau of Indian Affairs) assumed the function of providing education for the Navajos as well as other American Indians. Boarding schools were thought to be the solution to the "Indian Problem," and Navajo and other Indian children were forced to leave their families and were relocated to schools without the opportunity to see their families for many years. They were forced to have their hair cut, given store-bought European-style clothing, and beaten for speaking their Native languages or following their Native religion.[68] "The boarding school graduates were then sent out either to make their way in a White world that did not want them, or to return to a reservation to which they were now foreign."[69]

Boarding schools resulted in devastating consequences for Navajo and other American Indian families and communities because "abusive behaviors—physical, sexual—were experienced."[70] These assimilative conditions under which Navajo and other Indian children were raised affected their future relationships. Navajo and other Native children left the schools spiritually and emotionally bereft, often with no foundation of healthy self-esteem and a sense of belonging to family or community. They had lost their Indigenous identity.

Traumatic stress is ongoing and, according to Brave Heart et al., includes historical trauma as well as microaggressions (e.g., subtle forms of racism). Similar to historical trauma, the effects of racism on Navajos, as well as other American Indian families, "have led to a deep sense of grief and loss."[71] This was and is the burdensome legacy of historical trauma the Navajos and other Native peoples have had to endure and contend with into the twenty-first century.

The causes of historical trauma and its continuing impact on Navajos and other American Indian people—children, parents, families, communities, and nations—are clear, and the effects are devastating. As Dr. Brave Heart has noted in her research and writings on this topic, "The effects of historical trauma include: unsettled emotional trauma, depression, high mortality rates, high rates of alcohol abuse, significant problems of child abuse and domestic violence."[72] That time does not always "heal all wounds" is emphasized by David Anderson Hooker and Amy Potter Czajkowski in their paper, "Transforming Historical Harms":

> It is clear that historically traumagenic circumstances that have not been healed, reconciled or made right can have continuing consequences at the individual, family, organizational, communal, regional, national and even international level for generations. This is seemingly true regardless of whether the original traumagenic policies or practices persist, because there are consequences to trauma that the mere passage of time does not heal.[73]
>
> When a trauma has not been healed, however, the traumagenic society reflects this continuing trauma through clear disparities in health, welfare, economic status, and mental, emotional, physical and spiritual distress.[74]

It has been well documented that the massive displacement of American Indian children has had long-lasting effects on the well-being of Navajo and other American Indian children, families, and nations. Other studies have corroborated these findings.[75] Taken as a whole group, American Indians demonstrate high rates of mental health problems and higher incidences of alcoholism (579 percent), accidents (212 percent), suicide (70 percent), and homicide (41 percent) compared to the general U.S. population. The problems experienced by American Indians are not specific to adults, but are also experienced by American Indian adolescents.[76]

Early American educational practices were rooted in a history of declining population, degradation and marginalization, enslavement, extermination, colonial ethnocentrism, epidemic diseases, ethnic cleansing, Christian conversions, racial prejudice, cultural genocide, land cessations, and displacement or forced removal of the Indigenous people. The educational experiments of the European invaders proved to be a total dismal failure.

RESTORING HARMONY—A RETURN TO TRADITIONAL NAVAJO EDUCATIONAL SOVEREIGNTY

Dating back to the arrival of the Spanish, every Indigenous transformation policy implemented by European interlopers on the Navajos has failed, except for one—self-rule.[77] The Indian Self-Determination and Education Assistance Act of 1975 (Public Law 93-638) encouraged the Navajo people that they would, finally, on their own, with appropriate assistance from the United States, begin to reclaim what was misplaced—traditional Navajo educational sovereignty. Under a renewed condition of freedom to educate Navajo children as the Creator and the Holy People intended, the Navajos, in earnest, began to reconstruct the educational systems on the Navajo Nation.

While Public Law 93-638 severely limited the ability of the Native nations to truly self-rule, the law did lead to the practice and implementation of Indigenous-run and managed educational, social, and economic programs. Interestingly, the Navajo Nation was ahead of the 1970s Indian political resurgence of educational self-determination by establishing the Rough Rock Demonstration School in 1966, the first Indian-controlled school in the United States.[78] Two years later, the first Indian college in the United States—Navajo Community College (now called Diné College)—was established on the Navajo Nation. Both of these educational institutions specifically emphasized the centerpiece of their purpose was "to enable Navajos to understand their heritage, language, history, and culture, and to transmit these values for the survival of Navajos as individuals and as a nation."[79] Establishment of these schools is the epitome of Indigenous nation (re)building and the restoration of harmony.

Since these schools were founded, there have been many successes as well as challenges on the Indigenous nation (re)building road. What is clear, however, is that when Native nations control their destinies, they are capable of accomplishing significant goals.[80] Since 1987, the research of the Harvard Project on American Indian Economic Development (which I co-direct) has focused extensively on the challenges of political and economic development and social well-being among Indigenous communities—not only American Indian communities in the United States, but also communities in Canada, Australia, Aotearoa (New Zealand), and Mexico.[81] The lessons here are striking, and several Indigenous nations—Mississippi Choctaw (U.S.), Navajo Nation (U.S.), Membertou First Nation (Canada), Citizen Potawatomie Nation (U.S.), and Winnebago Tribe of Nebraska (U.S.)[82]—from both the United States and non-U.S. context illustrate this point well.

These examples are illustrative of the positive impacts that local control over community resources, health care, education, and economic affairs generates in Indigenous communities. For example, U.S. government policies recognizing Indigenous communities' rights to such control appear to be centrally responsible for the fact that citizens of American Indian nations experienced increases in per capita income in the 1990s, which were approximately three times greater than the income increases witnessed on average across the remainder of the United States.[83] This economic development, in turn, has improved the ability of Indigenous community citizens to find economic opportunity within their communities as defined by them,[84] and thereby encouraged their return to communities. Further, where Native nations have freely exercised sovereignty, it also translates into improved health circumstances, such as decreased suicide rates.[85]

Amid what often seems like a sovereignty dance of two steps forward, three steps back, the Navajo Nation has taken a huge step forward in reasserting its political sovereignty over the education of its children. Through the Navajo Sovereignty in Education Act of 2005, the Navajo Nation took a bold step toward establishing more authority and jurisdiction over how its people are educated.[86] Aligned with traditional Navajo educational philosophy and beliefs, the vision statement of the Act avows "Diné Education is our strength to promote and foster lifelong learning," and the mission statement reads, "It is the educational mission of the Navajo Nation to promote and foster lifelong learning for the Navajo People, and to protect the cultural integrity and sovereignty of the Navajo Nation."[87] To ensure that the Act gained traction, the Navajo Nation Board of Education and Department of Diné Education were established and charged with overseeing the implementation of the legislation. Within the Act are sweeping directives and goals laid out for various entities, from U.S. federal and state governments to local government agencies. The Act further affects all educational institutions, from Head Start to higher education across the Navajo Nation. This legislation issued administrative and strategic guidelines in areas including, among others, administration, management, budgeting, curriculum, and funding. An important charge of the Act is the possibility of establishing a severely needed uniform and consistent educational system across the Navajo Nation, which would bring order and clarity to the current disparate, disjointed, multilayered, and indistinct educational systems. Clearly, the Act has an expansive mandate; however, if we want to create positive change for our children, we must ensure it is fully implemented.

Since the Navajo Sovereignty in Education Act was signed into law nearly ten years ago, questions remain about its impact. Is the legislation accomplishing what it set out to do? How has it impacted on the sovereignty status of the Navajo Nation? These and other questions have been asked, and answers remain elusive. What is constant is that this legislation provides us, the Navajo people, with a plan to increase control over how and what we teach our children. What seems to be lacking in the implementation of this Act is appropriate funding, collective support, and strategic thinking. As Navajo citizens, we must fully support this Act by reminding ourselves of what type of society we would like to see one hundred years from now, and beyond.

Although the path thus far has been an arduous one, I believe that the Act must come to fruition if the Navajo Nation and its coming generations are to become truly sovereign and capable of overcoming the nation (re)building challenges that it currently faces, and those that lie ahead.[88] The Act, if well implemented, can lead the Navajo Nation toward restoring its educational sovereignty with the ability to form well-developed Navajo individuals grounded in time-honored Navajo philosophies of life.

It is critical that we fully reverse centuries of deficits by collectively committing to the future of the Navajo Nation, our grandchildren, and those yet to be born. We must invest in education for independence, self-rule, and good governance. Those who inspire the minds of Navajo children with notions of sovereignty of action will determine the future for the Navajo Nation. As such, we must answer questions, such as: How do we want our children to evolve? What language(s) do we want them to speak? Where will they live? What kind of homes do we want them to live in? What kind of clothes do we want them to wear? What kind of music do we want them to listen to and sing? How do we want them to act? What kind of culture do we want them to have? What kind of jobs do we want them to have? The answers to these and other questions must be answered now; otherwise, our children will develop haphazardly.

The nation-(re)building tasks that lie ahead are great; however, I am confident that we as Navajo people will tackle these and others challenges and create a viable and admirable Navajo Nation with a sense of restored harmony and shared identity, where we all want to live. According to an African proverb, "The best way to fight an alien and oppressive culture is to embrace your own."[89] As such, traditional Diné educational sovereignty is a blueprint of how we, as Navajo people, can embrace our own culture for the current generation and the generations to come.

NOTES

1. On May 19, 2008, while on the presidential campaign trail as Senator Barack Obama, he visited the Crow Agency in Montana. See Jeff Zeleny, "Obama Adopted by Native Americans," *New York Times*, May 19, 2008.

2. Sari Horwitz and Katie Zezima, "How the Stories of Native American Youths Made Obama Cry in the Oval Office," *Washington Post*, December 3, 2014.

3. Ibid.

4. Vincent Schilling, "Obama Puts Native Youth Front and Center at 2014 White House Tribal Nations Conference," Indian Country Today Media Network, December 4, 2014, http://indiancountrytodaymedianetwork.com/2014/12/04/obama-puts-native-youth-front-and-center-2014-white-house-tribal-nations-conference.

5. Ibid.

6. Wilma Mankiller, *Governance, Leadership, and the Cherokee Nation*, "Leading Native Nations" interview series, Native Nations Institute for Leadership, Management, and Policy, University of Arizona, September 29, 2008, https://nnidatabase.org/db/video/wilma-mankiller-governance-leadership-and-cherokee-nation.

7. Manley A. Begay Jr., in discussion with Peterson Zah, former chairman and president of the Navajo Nation, January 6, 2015. Furthermore, throughout the article I use the term *Diné*, which is the traditional word to refer to the Navajo people. Navajo traditional medicine societies have also determined that our real name is Diyin Nohookáá Diné, which means Holy Earth Surface People. The designation of the term *Navajo Nation* was officially changed by the Navajo Nation Council in 1969 from *Navajo Indian Reservation*.

8. Miriam Jorgensen, ed., *Rebuilding Native Nations: Strategies for Governance and Development* (Tucson: University of Arizona Press, 2007), chapter 3.

9. Keith H. Basso, *Western Apache Language and Culture: Essays in Linguistic Anthropology* (Tucson: University of Arizona Press, 1992), xii.

   The 1960s and 1970s saw a proliferation of language-immersion and culture-based schools, and the Navajo Nation schools were the leaders in this movement. Since then, all of these trendsetting and successful schools on the Navajo Nation no longer practice the needed language-immersion curriculum to strengthen Navajo language and culture loss that are occurring at a rapid pace. As such, and, unfortunately, only one school is truly based on language immersion, and that school is Tséhootsooí Diné Bi'Olta Immersion School in Fort Defiance, (Navajo Nation) Arizona. For the Navajo Nation to further curb the loss of its language and culture, more language-immersion schools, such as Tséhootsooí Diné Bi'Oltá Immersion School, are needed.

10. Lorie M. Graham, "The Past Never Vanishes: A Contextual Critique of the Existing Indian Family Doctrine," *American Indian Law Review* 23 (1998): 7.

11. "Sha' bik'ehgo As'ah Oodááł: Living with Wellness and Health Guided by the Journey of the Sun," Navajo Health and Wellness Curriculum for Health Promotion, Division of Public Health, Chinle Comprehensive Health Facility, Chinle, Arizona (2006). This curriculum was developed by Navajo cultural teachers, philosophers, and healing practitioners. The contributors were Annie Kahn, Avery Denny, Benjamin Barney, Victor Clyde, Gerald King, Johnson Dennison, Mae Bekis, Ruth Roessel, Ursula Knoki-Wilson, William Clay, Frank Morgan, Jennie Joe, Jill Moses, Michelle Kierstead, Carol Leonard, Leon Ben, and Marie Nelson.

12. Ibid.

13. Teachings are also embedded in the four directions of the path of the sun, and are depicted as *Hayoołkááł* (Dawn), *Nahoodetłiizh* (Daylight), *Nohootsoi* (Evening Light), and *Chahałheeł* (Darkness).

14. Traditional Navajos believe that a goal in life is to reach at least 102 years of age.

15. Raymond D. Austin, *Navajo Courts and Navajo Common Law: A Tradition of Tribal Self Governance* (Minneapolis: University of Minnesota Press, 2009), 83–95.

16. Michelle Kahn-John, "Concept Analysis of Diné Hózhó: A Diné Wellness Philosophy," *Advances in Nursing Science* 33, no. 2 (April–June 2010), 113–25.

17. Ronald Schenck, "Navajo Healing," *Psychological Perspectives: A Quarterly Journal of Jungian Thought* 19, no. 2 (1988): 223–40.

18. *Bitsé siléí/Biníí'siléí*, Cornerstones of Navajo Culture. As such, it is said: "*Sa'ąh Naagháí Bik'eh Hózhǫ́ǫ́n Niidlį* means the holistic or holy path of male and female beings. Navajo philosophy tells us that everything we are and do as Diné people is a reflection of our Diné origin. A reflection in which we are considered sacred people from the bottom of our feet to the top of our heads, and that we are all bounded by the laws of nature. In this respect, we are all very sacred, yet very susceptible to things that are considered natural order of life; that we have to atone to what we violate, hurt, or destroy that is considered sacred in places, animals, birds, reptiles, amphibians, and even insects. The universe, Mother Earth, and nature was created and set in ways accordingly to the four sacred directions in time and balance; balance and time that revolves each day as revolution by the sun, moon, and stars. The balance therein dictates the seasonal changes in *Daan* (Spring), *Shį* (Summer), *Aak'eed* (Fall), and *Hai* (Winter)." http://www.navajocourts.org/Harmonization/Bitsesilei.htm.

19. Ibid.
20. Navajo Health and Wellness Curriculum for Health Promotion, "Sha' bik'ehgo As'ah Oodááł."
21. These authors confirm the definition of the word *chanah*.

    Mary C. Sobralske, "Perception of Health, Navajo Indians," *Topics of Clinical Nursing* (October 1985); Leon Wall and William Morgan, *Navajo English Dictionary*, rev. ed. (New York: Hippocrene Books, 1994); and Robert W. Young and William Morgan, *The Navajo Language: A Grammar and Colloquial Dictionary*, rev. ed. (Albuquerque: University of New Mexico Press 1987).
22. Further, *T'ááhó ájít'éigo* is depicted as follows: "Throughout these various stages in growth and development for a child, teachings in the form of discipline is recognized and strongly and emphasized in the native term *Na'nitin bee adiihwii'nííł* and *T'ááhó ájít'éigo*. In English, it would best be termed as *self-determination*. The basis of such teachings are like the pillars of life, and the teaching of such discipline starts at the conception stages of a child and commences throughout his/her life. A reason why this is important information is that when a person is respectively taught in this manner, the person should not have any difficulty living a life into [adulthood]. Generally speaking, the facts of life are emphatically taught and stressed especially at the puberty stage. [For example,] a young woman will be taught the basic fundamentals of life in womanhood, motherhood, and parenthood; involve in being a mother/parent, being a mother of the house, performer of duties around the home as cooking, weaving, personal hygiene for the family and a teacher as well" (Judicial Branch of the Navajo Nation n.d.).
23. Ibid.
24. Raymond D. Austin, this volume, 32.
25. Ibid., 32–33.
26. The terrestrial or earthly hogans of the Navajo (male, female, and sweat lodge) is designed and constructed according to the spiritual dimensions of the cosmic hogan. "The original Diné home known as the *Hooghan* was constructed at the emergence by the *Diiyin Diné'e* with plans and urgings of the Coyote and *Haasch'éélti'í*. The construction was originally planned and based on the Sacred Mountains, respectively; *Sisnaajini*/Mt. Blanca, *Tsoodził*/Mt. Taylor, *Dook'oosłííd*/San Francisco Peak, *Dibétsaa*/La Plata Mountains, *Dził Ná'oodiłi*/Huerfano Peak, and *Cho'ółí*/Gobernador Mountain. The fifth and sixth mountains were placed toward the east to serve as the doorway and excess to the Sunrise each day" (Judicial Branch of the Navajo Nation n.d.).

27. Manley A. Begay Jr., in discussion with Johnson Dennsion, Navajo educator and traditional healer.

28. Ibid.

29. *Aspects and Perspectives of Diné Traditional Teaching*, Navajo Courts, http://www.navajocourts.org/AspectsDineTeaching/hooghan.pdf

30. "Sha' bik'ehgo As'ah Oodááł: Living with Wellness and Health Guided by the Journey of the Sun," Navajo Health and Wellness Curriculum for Health Promotion, Division of Public Health, Chinle Comprehensive Health Facility, Chinle, Arizona (2006). This curriculum was developed by Navajo cultural teachers, philosophers, and healing practitioners.

31. *Bitsé siléí/Biníí'siléí*, Cornerstones of Navajo Culture, http://www.navajo courts.org/Harmonization/Bitsesilei.htm

32. David Wallace Adams, *Education for Extinction: American Indians and the Boarding School Experience, 1875–1928* (Lawrence: University Press of Kansas, 1995), 51–55. See also "Official Report of the Nineteenth Annual Conference of Charities and Correction" (1892), 46–59, reprinted in Richard H. Pratt, "The Advantages of Mingling Indians with Whites," in *Americanizing the American Indians: Writings by the "Friends of the Indian" 1880–1900* (Cambridge, MA: Harvard University Press, 1973), 260–71.

33. For further discussion of European thought on the "savage" and how it originated in Europe, see Robert A. Williams Jr., *Savage Anxieties: The Invention of the Western Civilization* (New York: Palgrave Macmillan, 2012).

34. H. Vander Linden, "Alexander VI and the Demarcation of the Maritime and Colonial Domains of Spain and Portugal, 1493–1494," *American Historical Review* 22, no. 1 (1916): 3.

35. For further discussion, see the *American Historical Review*, "Coverage: 1895–2008" (vols. 1–113).

36. For further discussion, see "Moving Wall: 5 years, JSTOR Subjects(s): American Studies, History," *JSTOR Collection(s): Arts & Sciences I Collection, For-Profit Academic Arts & Sciences I Collection* (Oxford University Press on behalf of the American Historical Association).

37. Robert A. Roessel Jr., *Dinétah: Navajo History*, ed. T. L. McCarthy, Navajo Curriculum Center and Title IV-B Material Development Project, Rough Rock Demonstration School, Rough, Rock, Arizona, 1983, vol. 1, p. 43.

38. Ibid. See also Harriet Koenig and Seymour H. Koenig, "Acculturation in the Navajo Eden: New Mexico, 1550–1750," *Archaeology, Language,*

and Religion of the Peoples of the Southwest (New York: YBK Publishers, 2005), 108–11.

39. In fact, in ibid., 108, Koenig aptly states, "For adventurers and entrepreneurs, the prospect of untold mineral wealth accessible from the Rio Grande Valley persisted. For colonizers, there was the lure of land for agriculture and cattle grazing. For administrators, it was land-grants for political power and influence. For Franciscans, it was the prospect of another kind of wealth and power: additional souls to be saved and new missions built. For all, prospect of a sizable yet subservient, if not, submissive, Indian population established the scale of these several competing but overlapping agendas, and enlivened the dreams of would-be colonizers."

40. "Coronado's Report to the King of Spain Sent from Tiguex," October 20, 1541. Letters from Francisco Vazquez de Coronado to His Majesty, in which he gives an account of the discovery of the province of Tiguex, *New Perspectives of the Southwest, Archives of the West to 1806*, episode 1, PBS, http://www.pbs.org/weta/thewest/resources/archives/one/corona9.htm.

41. Michael Lerma, "Remembering Naat'áannii: Exploring the Efficacy of Traditional and Contemporary Diné Governance" (PhD diss., University of Arizona, 2010), citing David M. Brugge and J. Lee Correll, "The Story of the Navajo Treaties, Navajo Historical Publications," documentary series, no. 1 (Window Rock, AZ: Research Section, 1971).

42. Lerma, "Remembering Naat'áannii." Citing David E. Wilkins, *The Navajo Political Experience*, rev. ed. (Lanham, MD: Rowman and Littefield, 2003), 21–22.

43. Ibid.

44. Nancy C. Maryboy and David Begay, "A History of Utah's American Indians, Chapter Seven," in *Utah History to Go*, http://historytogo.utah.gov/people/ethnic_cultures/the_history_of_utahs_american_indians/chapter7.html.

45. Lerma, "Remembering Naat'áannii, 21–22.

46. Amos Yong and Barbara Brown Zikmund, *Remembering Jamestown: Hard Questions about Christian Missions* (Eugene, OR: Wipf and Stock Publishers, 2010), 75.

47. The Declaration of Independence reads: "He has excited domestic insurrections amongst us, and has endeavored to bring on the inhabitants of our frontiers, *the merciless Indian savages*, whose known rule of warfare, is undistinguished destruction of all ages, sexes and conditions" (emphasis added, http://www.constitution.org/us_doi.pdf). For additional information, see Adrian Jawort,

"The Declaration of Independence—Except for 'Indian Savages,'" *Indian Country Today Media Network*, May 1, 2014, http://indiancountrytodaymedia network.com/2014/05/13/declaration-independence-except-indian-savages.

48. Margaret Connell Szasz, *Indian Education in the American Colonies, 1607–1783* (Albuquerque: University of New Mexico Press, 1988).

    Some of the early colonial policies include 1609 Charter of Virginia Company of London; 1617 King James Order for Special Collections in Churches; 1629 Charter of the Massachusetts Bay Company; 1648 Parliament approved final bill ushering in the Society of for the Propagation of the Gospel in New England (New England Company); 1650 Harvard Charter; 1769 Dartmouth College Charter.

49. Lerma, "Remembering Naat'áannii." Citing Myra Ellen Jenkins and Albert H. Schroeder, New Mexico Cultural Properties Review Committee, and New Mexico State Planning Office, *A Brief History of New Mexico*, 1st ed. (Albuquerque: University of New Mexico Press, 1974).

50. Lerma, "Remembering Naat'áannii," 90–97.

51. Nancy C. Maryboy and David Begay, "A History of Utah's American Indians, Chapter Seven," in *Utah History to Go*, http://historytogo.utah.gov/people/ethnic_cultures/the_history_of_utahs_american_indians/chapter7.html.

52. Treaty between the United States of America and the Navajo Tribe of Indians, concluded June 1, 1868, ratified July 25, 1868, and proclaimed August 12, 1868. Article VI states: "In order to insure the civilization of the Indians entering into this treaty, the necessity of education is admitted, especially of such of them as may be settled on said agricultural parts of this reservation, and they therefore pledge themselves to compel their children, male and female, between the ages of six and sixteen years, to attend school; and it is hereby made the duty of the agent for said Indians to see that this stipulation is strictly complied with; and the United States agrees that, for every thirty children between said ages who can be induced or compelled to attend school, a house shall be provided, and a teacher competent to teach the elementary branches of an English education shall be furnished, who will reside among said Indians, and faithfully discharge his or her duties as a teacher. The provisions of this article to continue for not less than ten years." To this day, this provision has not ever been fulfilled by the United States government.

53. Bill Donovan, "Census: Navajo Enrollment Tops 300,000," *Navajo Times*, July 7, 2011. Note: the Navajo Nation requires a blood quantum of one-quarter for a person to be eligible for enrollment as a citizen/member.

54. Marcia Gentry and C. Matthew Fugate, "Gifted Native American Students: Underperforming, Under-Identified, and Overlooked," *Psychology in the Schools* (2012): 3–4. Gentry and Fugate found, "Currently, U.S. citizens are concerned about a high unemployment rate that exceeds 9%, while the unemployment rate on the Navajo nation is 42%, with 40% of families living in poverty" (Navajo Nation Division of Economic Development, n.d.). In short, many Diné children face a "triple threat" to their academic achievement because they deal with poverty, marginalization of their culture, and the challenges of living in a remote, rural area without the technology and basic resources taken for granted in many schools and communities. According to a report by the Navajo Nation Department of Diné Education (DoDE) made to the U.S. Department of Education (USDOE, 2011a), only 17 percent of tribally controlled schools made annual yearly progress under No Child Left Behind during the 2007–2008 school year. Although the report shows slight gains in reading achievement, from 27 percent proficient in 2004–2005 to 35 percent proficient in 2009–2010, "the performance record in mathematics is more erratic, and leaves one doubting that the educational system has improved in any substantial way since 2004–2005" (2–3). Table 1 contains the Native American mathematics achievement statistics for eighth-grade students in Arizona, New Mexico, and Utah, the three states in which the majority of Diné students attend school, compared with national averages according to the NAEP data (Mead et al., 2010). The DoDE Office of Educational Research and Statistics reported 2000 census data showing that of the 167,528 Diné in the Navajo Nation, only 55.9 percent held a high-school diploma, and only 7.3 percent held a bachelor's degree or higher. Furthermore, statistics reveal that despite a growth in population of approximately 45,000 people between 2000 and 2009 (Navajo Nation Division of Economic Development, n.d.), enrollment in grades 1 through 12 has steadily declined—from 55,648 in 2000 to 38,990 in 2009 (Navajo Nation DoDE, 2011b). Reasons for this decline were not given but can be partially attributed to children who do not attend school or who drop out of school.

55. The Demographic Analysis of the Navajo Nation Using 2010 Census and 2010 American Community Survey Estimates, Arizona Rural Policy Institute, Center for Business Outreach, W. A. Franke College of Business, Northern Arizona University, p. 34, states: "Poverty rates on the Navajo Nation Reservation (38%) are more than twice as high as poverty rates in the State of Arizona (15%). Almost half (44%) of all children under 18 years of age are

considered to be living in poverty, while one-third (34%) of tribal members between 18 and 64 also live in poverty. Almost one-third (29%) of persons living in families on the Navajo Nation live in poverty, twice the rate of families living in poverty in the State of Arizona (13%), for example. More than one-third of all persons over age 65 (39%) also live in poverty, five times higher that the State of Arizona (8%) for this age group. Poverty rates are consistent for Navajo Nation tribal members residing in all three states." http://www .indianaffairs.state.az.us/Documents/Links/DemoProfiles/Navajo%20 Nation.pdfhttp://www.indianaffairs.state.az.us/Documents/Links/Demo Profiles/Navajo%20Nation.pdf.

56. "By different estimates, the unemployment rate hovers between 47% to more than 60%." Frederick H. White, acting executive director of the Division of Natural Resources, Navajo Nation, July 20, 2011, in response to advance notice of pro-posed rulemaking notice, 76 *Federal Register* 30881 (May 27, 2011) by the U.S. Department of the Interior, Office of Natural Resource Revenue, http://www.onrr.gov/Laws_R_D/PubComm/PDFDocs/AA00/ AA00%20Navajo%20Nation%20Comments.PDF; Alysa Landry, "Navajo Nation Economic Growth Creating Jobs and True Independence," Indian Country Today Media Network, August, 28, 2013, http://indiancountry todaymedia network.com/2013/08/28/navajo-nation-economic-growth -leading-red-tape-freedom-151046; prepared statement by Vice President Rex Lee Jim, New Mexico State Senate, Health and Human Services Committee Meeting, Santa Fe, New Mexico, June 25, 2012; 2008 Needs and Assessment Report, First Things First, Navajo Nation Regional Partnership Council, 13–14, http://www.azftf.gov/RPCCouncilPublicationsCenter/ Navajo_Nation_Need_and_Assets_Report_2008.pdf.

57. According to the U.S. Census Bureau, "68% of residents of the Navajo Nation Reservation and Off-Reservation Trust Land, Ariz.-N.M.-Utah, age 5 and older who spoke a language other than English at home." See Julie Siebens and Tiffany Julian, *2011 American Community Survey Briefs*, Table S0601, Native North American Languages Spoken at Home in the United States and Puerto Rico: 2006–2010, U.S. Department of Commerce, U.S. Census Bureau, Economics and Statistics Administration, December 2011.

Prebble Ramswell stated, "As late as 1930, 71% of Navajos spoke no English, as compared with only 17% of all American Indians at the time (Census Bureau, 1937). The number who speak Navajo in the home remains substantial—148,530 in 1990, or 45% of all American Indian language speakers" (Census Bureau, 1993).

"At present, many Navajos of all ages speak the language, and more than half of their population speaks Navajo at home. Many parents still teach their children Navajo as their first language, and the Navajo continue to use their native language for everyday communication. US Census data show that between 1980 and 1990 the percentage of Navajos ages 5–17 who spoke only English rose from 12% to 28%, and by the year 2000, the figure reached 43% (University of Arizona, 2008). In 1848, the number of Navajo Indians was approximately 12,000. By 1900, the number had grown to 20,000, and by 1950 the number had reached 69,000, despite a growing trend of learning English. The numbers continued to grow: in 1990, the US Census listed 148,000 speakers of Navajo and 178,000 by 2000. In 2010, that number had decreased slightly, indicating a possible stabilization, with 170,000 speakers.

"The problem with such numbers is that the population of Navajos is also increasing. As such, though the number of speakers has increased, the percentage of Navajo speakers remains at about 50%. Further, there is cause for concern. Today, fewer than five percent of Navajo children under age 5 are speakers of the language (Speas, 2012). Whether the growing trend will cease and the numbers stabilize or decrease remains to be seen, but one fact remains: the Navajo have without a doubt, defied the odds and succeeded in sustaining their language while most other American Indian tribes in the United States have not." See Prebble Q. Ramswell, "Ayali: Is It Time to Say Good-bye to American Indian Languages?" *Indigenous Policy Journal* 23, no. 1 (Summer 2012): 9.

58. Dr. Maria Yellow Horse Brave Heart, "Welcome to Takini's Historical Trauma," http://historicaltrauma.com/

59. Additional sources on this topic include: D. Brown, *Bury My Heart at Wounded Knee* (New York, Holt, Rinehart and Winston, 1970); Vine Deloria and Daniel R. Wildcat, *Power and Place: Indian Education in America* (Golden, CO: Fulcrum Publishing, 1991); P. Freire, *Pedagogy of the Oppressed* (New York: Seabury Press, 1968); Lorie M. Graham, "The Past Never Vanishes: A Contextual Critique of the Existing Indian Family Doctrine," *American Indian Law Review* 23 (1998): 1–54; David Anderson Hooker and Amy Potter Czajkowski, "Transforming Historical Harms," Presented by Coming to the Table, A Project of Eastern Mennonite University's Center for Justice and Peacebuilding (2013), http://comingtothetable.org/wp-content/uploads/2013/10/01-Transforming_Historical_Harms.pdf; and Winona LaDuke, "An Indigenous View of North America," *Lineup* 2, no. 1 (1995): 28.

60. Dr. Maria Yellow Horse Brave Heart et al., "Historical Trauma: Boarding School Trauma," http://historicaltrauma.com/htboardingschools.pdf.

61. Brave Heart, "Welcome to Takini's Historical Trauma."

62. Ibid.

63. Martha Caberea, "Living and Surviving in a Multiply Wounded Country," (1995), http://www.medico.de/download/report26/ps_cabrera_en.pdf. http://www.medico.de/download/report26/ps_cabrera_en.pdf.

64. Dr. Maria Yellow Horse Brave Heart and Lemyra M. DeBruyn, "The American Holocaust: Healing Historical Grief," American Indian and Alaska Native Mental Health Research, Centers for American Indian and Alaska Native Health Colorado School of Public Health/University of Colorado Anschutz Medical Campus (1998), www.ucdenver.edu/caianh.

65. Ibid.

66. Ibid., 62.

67. Transcending Historical Trauma, Wisdom of the Elders website, http://discoveringourstory.wisdomoftheelders.org/resources/transcending-historical-trauma.

68. Vine Deloria related that American Indians and Native Alaskans were unable to legally practice their religions until 1978. See Vine Deloria, *Custer Died for Your Sins: An Indian Manifesto* (Norman: University of Oklahoma Press, 1988).

69. Peter Farb, *Man's Rise to Civilization: The Cultural Ascent of the Indians of North America* (New York: Penguin, 1978, 1991), 257–59.

70. Brave Heart and DeBruyn, "The American Holocaust: Healing Historical Grief," quoting M. Beiser, "Editorial: A Hazard to Mental Health: Indian Boarding Schools," *American Journal of Psychiatry* 31, no. 3 (1974): 305–6; Maria Yellow Horse Brave Heart, "The Return to the Sacred Path: Healing from Historical Trauma and Historical Unresolved Grief among the Lakota" (PhD diss., Smith College, 1995); E. Dlugokinski and L. Kramer, "A System of Neglect: Indian Boarding School," *American Journal of Psychiatry* (1974): 131, 670–73; M. H. Irwin and S. Roll, "The Psychological Impact of Sexual Abuse of Native American Boarding School Children," *Journal of the American Academy of Psychoanalysis* 23, no. 3 (1995): 461–73; J. Noriega, "American Indian Education in the United States: Indoctrination for Subordination to Colonialism," in *The State of Native America: Genocide, Colonization, and Resistance*, ed. M. A. Jaimes (Boston: South End Press, 1992), 371–402; H. Tanner, "A History of All the Dealings of the United States

Government with the Sioux," unpublished manuscript (1992). Prepared for the Black Hills Land Claim by order of the U.S. Supreme Court, on file at the D'Arcy McNickle Center for the History of the American Indian, Newberry Library, Chicago.

71. Laurelle L. Myhra, "'It Runs in the Family': Intergenerational Transmission of Historical Trauma Among Urban American Indians and Alaska Natives in Culturally Specific Sobriety Maintenance Programs," American Indian and Alaska Native Mental Health Research, Centers for American Indian and Alaska Native Health, Colorado School of Public Health/University of Colorado Anschutz Medical Campus, p. 19, www.ucdenver.edu/caianh.

72. Brave Heart, "Welcome to Takini's Historical Trauma."

73. Hooker and Czajkowski, "Transforming Historical Harms," 17.

74. Ibid., 52–53.

75. See, for example, Joseph Westermeyer, "The Ravage of Indian Families in Crisis, in American Indian Families," supra note 100, at 47; 1974 hearings, statement of Dr. Joseph Westermeyer; statement of Dr. Robert Bergman, Indian Health Service. See generally Christopher Bagley, International and Transracial Adoptions (New York: Avebury, 1993); Catherine M. Brooks, "The Indian Child Welfare Act in Nebraska: Fifteen Years: A Foundation for the Future," 27 Creighton L. Rev. 661, 668 (1994) (citing a study by Dr. Carol Locust of the University of Arizona College of Medicine on the adverse effects of being adopted into off-reservation, non-Indian homes); refer to David Fanshel, Far from the Reservation: The Transracial Adoption of American Indian Children (Lanham, MD: Scarecrow Press, 1972) (noting that the removal of Indian children from their families and communities may be the "ultimate indignity to endure," but is nevertheless a desirable option).

76. Brave Heart and DeBruyn, "The American Holocaust: Healing Historical Grief," citing Albright LaFromboise and Harris (2010); LaFromboise, Medoff, Lee, and Harris (2007); Stewart-Sabin and Chaffin (2003); Stiffman, Silmere, and Brown (2007); and Yoder et. al (2006).

77. The ebb and flow of European Indigenous policy in the United States as it impacted on the Navajo is as follows: Spanish Colonial Period (1492–1821), Mexican Colonial Period (1821–46), American Colonial Period (1846–present). The American Colonial Period, as it impacted all Native American is as follows: International Treaties (1776), Law and Military Expansion (1830), Military Invasion (1865), Termination through Allotment (1885), Indian

Reorganization Act (1934), Termination through De-Recognition (1953), Self-Determination (1970), Nation Building (2000).

78. Robert Roessel states that "Rough Rock in 1966 was the first school in which the local all-Navajo school board determined the curriculum, the amount of time spent on each subject, the requirements for teachers, the textbooks to be used, and so forth." See Robert A. Roessel, "Navajo Education, 1948–1978: Its Progress and Its Problems," Navajo Curriculum Center, Rough Rock Demonstration School, *Navajo History*, vol. 3, part A, Rough Rock, Arizona, Navajo Nation, Arizona, 1979, 49–58. See also Robert A. Roessel Jr., "Navajo Education in Action: The Rough Rock Demonstration School," Navajo Curriculum Center, Rough Rock Demonstration School, Chinle, Arizona, 1977. Further, Hildegard Thompson reveals, "Before the mid-1970's—Rough Rock, Rock Point, and Borrego Pass—were under the complete management of local Navajo school boards. A contract was made with each local board whereby federal funds for school operation were turned over to the board. Thus, these three schools will operate in a fashion similar to local public school, with the local school boards setting policy within defined guidelines, as well as managing school funds and employing staff in accordance with legal requirements." In Hildegard Thompson, *The Navajos' Long Walk for Education—Diné Nizaagóó Bíhoo'aah Yíkanaaskai: A History of Navajo Education—Diné Óhooł'aahii Baa Hané Tsaile* (Navajo Nation, AZ: Navajo Community College Press, 1975), 172.

79. Roessel, "Navajo Education, 1948–1978."

80. For examples of Indigenous success in economic development, education, social, culture, law, etc., refer to "Honoring Nations Tribal Governance Success Stories, Honoring Contributions in the Governance of American Indian Nations," the Harvard Project on American Indian Economic Development, John F. Kennedy School of Government, Harvard University, http://www.hks.harvard.edu/programs/hpaied. See also Eric Henson et al., *The State of the Native Nations Conditions under U.S. Policies of Self-Determination, The Harvard Project on American Indian Economic Development* (New York: Oxford University Press, 2007); Miriam Jorgensen, ed., *Rebuilding Native Nations: Strategies for Governance and Development* (Tucson: University of Arizona Press, 2007).

81. Stephen E. Cornell and J. P. Kalt, "Where's the Glue? Institutional and Cultural Foundations of American Indian Economic Development," *Journal of Socio-Economics* 29 (2000); Stephen E. Cornell and J. P. Kalt, "Reloading

the Dice: Improving the Chances for Economic Development on American Indian Reservations," in *What Can Tribes Do? Strategies and Institutions in American Indian Economic Development*, ed. J. P. Kalt and S. Cornell (Amer Indian Studies Center, University of California, 1992), 1–59; Stephen E. Cornell and J. P. Kalt, "The Redefinition of Property Rights in American Indian Reservations: A Comparative Analysis of Native American Economic Development," in *American Indian Policy: Self-Governance and Economic Development*, ed. L. H. Legters and F. J. Lyden (Santa Barbara, CA: Greenwood Press, 1994); and Joseph P. Kalt and J. B. Taylor, *American Indians on Reservations: A Databook of Socioeconomic Change Between the 1990 and 2000 Censuses* (Cambridge, MA: Harvard Project on American Indian Economic Development, 2005), http://www.ncaiprc.org/pdf/AmericanIndians onReservationsADatabookofSocioeconomicChange.pdf.

82. For more information, see Peter J. Ferrara, *The Choctaw Revolution: Lessons for Federal Indian Policy* (Washington, DC: Americans for Federal Tax Reform Foundation, 1998); Kalt and Taylor, *American Indians on Reservations: A Databook of Socioeconomic Change*; Harvard Project on American Indian Economic Development, "Choctaw Health Center, Mississippi Choctaw," Tribal Governance Success Stories: Honoring Nations 1999; Harvard Project on American Indian Economic Development, "Choctaw Community Injury Prevention Program, Mississippi Choctaw," and "Family Violence & Victim's Services, Mississippi Choctaw," Tribal Governance Success Stories: Honoring Nations 2003. See Ruggles M. Stahn, Dorothy Gohdes, and Sarah E. Valway, "Diabetes and Its Complications Among Selected Tribes in North Dakota, South Dakota, and Nebraska," *Diabetes Care* 16, no. 1 (January 1993). See also Jorgensen, *Rebuilding Native Nations*, chapter 7, p. 179; chapter 9, p. 235; and chapter 2, p. 39; Harvard Project on American Indian Economic Development, "Economic Development Corporation: Ho-Chunk Inc. Ho-Chunk, Inc. Winnebago Tribe of Nebraska," Tribal Governance Success Stories: Honoring Nations 2000, http://www.ihs.gov/winnebago/ and http://www.hochunkinc.com/index.html.

83. Notably, these rates of increase in Indian reservation incomes were not confined to only those reservations where Indigenous governments undertook much-publicized gaming casinos; the rate of income growth on reservations both with and without such gaming operations was also approximately three times the growth in income seen on average across the rest of the United States. See Kalt and Taylor, *American Indians on Reservations*.

84. For a discussion about development, governance, and culture, see Manley A. Begay Jr., Stephen Cornell, Miriam Jorgensen, and Joseph P. Kalt, "Development, Governance, Culture: What Are They and What Do They Have to Do with Rebuilding Native Nations?" In Jorgensen, ed., *Rebuilding Native Nations*, chapter 11 and chapter 2.

85. Michael J. Chandler and Christopher E. Lalonde, "Cultural Continuity as a Hedge Against Suicide in Canada's First Nations," *Journal of Transcultural Psychiatry* 35, no. 2 (1998): 193–211; and Michael J. Chandler and Christopher E. Lalonde, "Cultural Continuity as a Moderator of Suicide Risk among Canada's First Nations," in *The Mental Health of Canadian Aboriginal Peoples: Transformations, Identity, and Community*, ed. L. Kirmayer and G. Valaskakis (Vancouver: University of British Columbia Press, forthcoming). Draft version available electronically at http://web.uvic.ca/~lalonde/manuscripts/2004Transformations.pdf.

Note: According to the Native Nations Institute (2004), "In the first of these papers, the authors consider the effect of 'cultural stability' on suicide rates of First Nations youth, using data from 1987 to 1992. Adolescent suicide is an enormous problem in some First Nations but unknown in others. The authors develop measures of 'cultural stability' that take account of First Nations communities' differential efforts to preserve and rehabilitate their cultures. The measures include factors such as the active pursuit of land claims, the takeover of social service management, and investments in cultural activities, most of which also can be seen as measures of assertions of self-government. The paper systematically compares suicide rates in communities that are acting more to preserve and rehabilitate their cultures with rates in communities that are acting less. The results indicate that suicide rates are lower in indigenous groups who are acting to take control of their own futures. In other words, the authors establish a strong link between First Nations' success at practical self-government and certain health outcomes among their youth. In the second paper, the authors update their research with youth suicide data from 1993-2000 and add several more measures of cultural continuity. Again, these can be interpreted as measures of the extent to which First Nations are exercising self-governance. The findings hold over the longer, 14-year period, which leads the authors to consider policy implications. While they make no specific recommendations, they nonetheless stress the importance of indigenously designed, as opposed to centrally imposed, policy designs."

86. The Navajo Nation has the following types of educational institutions: Arizona, New Mexico, and Utah public schools; Navajo-sanctioned college preparatory schools; Navajo Nation–run colleges and universities; Navajo Medicine Man apprentice schools; Head Start schools; Bureau of Indian Education schools (also, grant contract schools); and parochial schools.

87. Resolution of the Navajo Nation Council, 20th Navajo Nation Council Third Year, 2005, an Act Relating to Education, Enacting the Navajo Sovereignty in Education Act of 2005 (CJY-37-05); Amending Titles Ten and Two of the Navajo Nation Code.

88. Testimony by Timothy Benally, Acting Superintendent of Schools, before the U.S. Senate Committee on Indian Affairs, *Navajo Nation Department of Diné Education: Hearing on Indian Education Ensuring the Bureau of Indian Education Has the Tools Necessary to Improve*, 113th Congress, May 21, 2014. Benally stated, "A profile on education and schools on the Navajo Nation shows that 17 school districts are operating schools on the Navajo Nation with a total of 244 schools. The Navajo Nation is situated within three states: Arizona, New Mexico, and Utah. There are a combined total of 38,109 Navajo students in all schools on the Navajo Nation. Based on the most recently available data, 23,056 Navajo students attended public schools on the Navajo Nation, which comprises 60.5% of all students. 48,172 Navajo students also attended public schools located off of the Navajo Nation. The Bureau of Indian Education operates 31 schools; 25 Navajo schools and seven Navajo residential halls receive federal grants pursuant to P.L. 100-297 (Better known as Grant Schools); and one and P.L. 93-638 contract school. In School Year 2012-2013, a total of 8,079 students attended Bureau of Indian Education-operated schools and 6,974 students attended P.L. 100-297 grant and P.L. 93-638 contract schools. BIE- operated schools and grant/contract schools collectively educated 39.5% of all Navajo students, with 21.2% attending BIE-operated schools and 18.3% attending grant/contract schools."

89. African proverb.

I AM YOUR NALI

LEOLA TSINNAJINNIE

N MANY RESPECTS, I had a very privileged upbringing. My parents were both college-educated elementary teachers who taught on the Navajo reservation. I rode to school with them each morning in our trusty 1980s family station wagon. I had my own room in a mobile home that included two bathrooms, a fireplace, and basic comfort utilities. The trailer was first parked at the renowned self-determination site at Pine Hill School campus (Manuelito 2005). This is where my parents began their teaching careers until they decided to move to my Nali's home community of Na' Neelzhiin. Essentially, my only concerns were the social challenges that came with being the sole English-only speaking student in my class each year. From childhood, I enjoyed school, and I eventually made the decision to become an academic after graduating from college and realizing the world was not centered on the nine-month calendar. In 2007, in the midst of my doctoral studies, my mother suddenly passed away, collapsing on the evening of her very last day at Torreon Day School. She had devoted nineteen years of service, and had just made the decision with my father to continue their commitment to the school, despite questions of retirement stability. Administrative ownership was leaving the governmental hands of the Bureau of Indian Education (BIE) for the next school year. My father honored the decision he made with my mother, and even now continues to teach sixth grade at our community-driven school, Na Neelzhiin Ji' Olta'. I share my narrative in order to highlight the educational accomplishments of my parents, grandparents, and ancestors. Without their sacrifices and the structures they laid into place, I would not have the opportunity to make a contribution to an anthology on Navajo sovereignty. In hindsight, I see that the steps I walked were written on my behalf over 150 years ago.

According to the Office of the Navajo Nation Scholarship and Financial Assistance (ONNSFA), the purpose of the Chief Manuelito Scholarship is to provide high-achieving Navajo students with funding for postsecondary expenses (2016). This scholarship is emblematic of my individual path and vision toward Navajo educational sovereignty. Navajo educational sovereignty is political, social, spiritual, and clanship based for the purpose of sustainability and nation building. In this chapter, I will address these themes by way of my experiences with ONNSFA, teaching, research, and my family history. American Indian education scholars have previously provided thoughtful discussion on the self-determination schooling practices of Navajo communities (Lee 2015; Lomawaima and McCarty 2006; McCarty 2002; Manuelito 2005; Rosier and Holm 1980). As a Diné individual, I will offer my vision of sovereignty, power, authority, and autonomy for our people through the lens of how our ancestors have navigated my path.

OFFICE OF NAVAJO NATION SCHOLARSHIP AND FINANCIAL ASSISTANCE

While attending awards ceremonies at my small, Catholic, off-reservation high school, I made it my goal to earn the Chief Manuelito Scholarship as at least one Navajo senior did each spring. There was a pride in knowing that those older brothers and sisters were being recognized for their scholastic achievements and were being supported by our Nation in their transition into higher education. When my opportunity came, I scarcely met the requirements, but I qualified. I did not receive a scholarship from my destined university, so it was "the Manuelito" that essentially paid for my tuition and allowed my parents the means to help me in other ways. Although I qualified for in-state tuition due specifically to residing within reservation boundaries, I did not understand sovereignty as an eighteen-year-old, but I understood that being Indigenous/Diné meant belonging to a system of relationships. I saw that the system of relationships was ultimately responsible for my entrance into college. I had not heard or studied Manuelito's stories, but I revered him and our leaders for their warriorship in establishing the roots of my education. After finding my way into American Indian studies at the University of Arizona and the University of New Mexico, I realized the power within peoplehood, nationhood, women, treaties, and the fight for self-determined education (Holm, Pearson, and Chavis 2003; Denetdale 2006; Lee 2008; Niethammer 2004). What I also knew, according to family history, was that my ancestors had escaped the Long Walk for their ability to find meaningful relationships with Zia Pueblo. Those relationships with Pueblo peoples have stemmed into a personal and professional base of happiness. Native nation-to-nation collegiality became an emphasis in my pedagogy and research methodology. My focus was less local.

By the time I was in the latter stages of completing my doctorate, I became more aware of the scholarship assistance offered by my chapter, Torreon/Star Lake. I was living an hour and a half away in Albuquerque, but I could have been in Tucson for the lack of physical connection I was making to my home community. Nonetheless, I applied for the scholarship, and as an applicant, I needed to address the community at a chapter meeting. I showed up at 10 a.m. sharp and sat there with my sister and dad, watching as people sat in their parked vehicles while no one was inside the building. We later learned that it takes a while before enough people show up to create a quorum, and that the process of addressing the community would not be an in-and-out affair. It required hours of waiting for the meeting to start and the agenda item to get onto the floor. Until this item, the meeting essentially took place in Navajo, with the exception of a few outsider presentations. These hours gave me sufficient time to question my entire identity. Ultimately, this portion of the chapter meeting was clearly a crowd favorite. Hearing from community students elicited so much positive energy in the room. My address, spoken mostly in English, was heard and approved with all the others. I remain so grateful for this lesson in what it truly means to make a promise to make a contribution to your community, or give back. My promise was to give back by becoming a professor. As scholars who live and operate outside our four sacred mountains, we make sense of our Diné selves in a variety of ways. For myself, I seek to provide that sense of familiarity in the front of and within a college classroom. I seek to honor the lived experiences of my students and provide the tools necessary to allow their learning to be filled with empowerment over understanding Native-centered sociopolitical concepts. Learning how to earn approval from my Navajo elders and *naat'áanii*, in this way, was as meaningful to my final stages of schooling as my graduate-level defenses.

TEACHING

Teaching is sovereignty. My first Native college instructor gave me the actualized picture of someone who taught in higher education from an Indigenous perspective. Despite the fact that the class was within the constructs of a university English 101 course, within our intellectual space, we were a sovereign entity. As I moved into upper-division and graduate-level courses, the spiritual element entered those same spaces. In these experiences, Native teachers maintained the highest level of scholastic expectations within a context of *cultural sovereignty* (Coffey and Tsosie 2001). Prayers are offered, food is shared, relationships are recognized, and Indigenous resilience is the ultimate decolonization *project*, as termed by Smith (1999).

These college teacher-mentor elders shaped the realization that I could strive to share those same gifts with the next generation. As a doctoral student, I took every opportunity I could find to begin to shape my own teaching spaces. I drove to Gallup or Santa Fe each week to reach them. A majority of the college students I have worked with are Navajo or Pueblo. My courses meet curricular criteria as prescribed by course-catalog descriptions and departments, but concepts are largely absorbed through discussion and storytelling. This is where sovereign spheres have the potential to come to life and to stay with students on their educational journeys. How do the lessons we learn and read about in Native studies courses make sense in our everyday lives, as well as in planning for our futures? As Navajo and Native people, especially, this is the core of how we live our sovereignty while earning credentials recognized and authorized by Western society.

In education, Western society has forced a framework that privileges United States' history, colonization, Christianity, and conquest (Jacobs 2006; Lomawaima and McCarty 2006; Pewardy 2005). In more recent generations, force comes disguised in the form of hegemony (Mihesuah 2006). Navajo/ Native people must directly confront these Eurocentric traditions through decolonization and anti-racism (Battiste 2013; Brayboy 2005; Fletcher 2008; Wilson and Yellow Bird 2005). To strengthen, recognize, or begin to affirm the centralization of the students' core values, I begin most of my courses by asking each student to visually express their personal theoretical frameworks. This creation becomes their reference for cultural sovereignty. The pieces also serve as an avenue for me to respect and understand where each student is holistically coming from, no matter their background. Furthermore, students present their pieces to each other and find value in both their commonalities and differences. We refer to this activity throughout the term, and remain connected to each other upon completion of the class by having shared this space. Navajo students tend to identify places, grandparents, parents, children, clanship, educational goals, language, prayer, and history as representing their deepest core values. The ultimate goal is to recognize individual sovereignty in order to create a shield from oppressive remnants of the past or forces of the present that threaten our sense of who we are as *the People*.

RESEARCH

Honoring individual and group empowerment through research is another avenue for which Navajo educational sovereignty can be embodied. A great movement I had the opportunity to touch upon was the successful Higher Learning Commission (HLC) reaccreditation process completed in 2013–2014 at the Southwestern Indian Polytechnic Institute (SIPI), the tribal college operated by the BIE located in Albuquerque, New Mexico. I was a faculty member who had the fortune of implementing the Introduction to Native American studies course into the curriculum, and continuing the longtime Contemporary Indian Issues course. Within the context of reaccreditation, a major goal was to emphasize student growth in cultural legacy, one of four general education competencies, which was based in the understanding of Native and non-Native histories. Serving at a small college with such integral responsibility to multiple Native nations, I was a member of several key faculty-driven committees. As such, I promoted the direction of cultural legacy toward nation building and community engagement, and suggested the school utilize its self-determination-oriented value statements as the basis for articulating what this meant. Prior to my arrival, and after, the mobility of the faculty, leaders, and students has led to numerous grant awards, including the outstanding success of the Wakaneja Sacred Little Ones Project (Lansing 2014). Another award was the nation-building grant from the American Indian Higher Learning Commission (AIHEC) in 2014, to which I served as a team member.

In my area of the grant, students engaged in two courses designed to steer their nation-building goals within an Indigenous education and decolonization framework (Brayboy 2005; Brayboy 2012; Cajete 2000; Jorgensen 2007;

Wilson and Yellow Bird 2005). A phenomenological study was completed to document the experiences of the participants. The study sought to answer the question: "How do Indigenous students plan their academic, career, and cultural goals in relationship to nation building in practice?" Students developed strong family, community, and education-oriented conceptions of nation building. Students equated nation building with family, education, unity, collaboration for the greater good, core values, Native language preservation, Indigenous tradition, diversity, and practicing self-determination. Students emerged from the courses being able to articulate clear connections between nation building and the pathways they want to take as educated community members. Every student expressed their intent to explicitly continue exploring nation building in higher levels of college coursework or apply it in their careers, driven by the goal of contributing to their respective communities. The project experience allowed for tribal college students to see themselves, through the stories of guest speakers and project oriented lessons, as community-driven nation builders. Three of the seven student participants were Navajo. One of the three is from my community chapter. I often felt at home teaching at the BIE institution whose dated campus buildings largely resembled my elementary school and whose students were related to me through friendships, networks, and clanship. While the structural struggles inherent in the federal legacy has been well documented, the resilience of Native people and our cultural sovereignty remains strong at SIPI (Khachadoorian 2010).

FAMILY HISTORY, CLANSHIP, AND COMMUNITY

The federal legacy of American Indian education, defined as Eurocentric education designed for Natives by non-Natives, also remains deeply embedded into my family history and the future of Navajo peoples (Lomawaima and McCarty 2006). My paternal grandmother, Iola Tsinnajinnie (Táchii'nii), attended Albuquerque Indian School (AIS) and graduated in 1932. She was a boarding school student who attended AIS at a time when starvation and brutality was not a mainstay of her experience. She had positive stories to share, yet the mission of survival, as a Native woman, was still to play the game of Westernized schooling. As a mother to our family and community, she carefully paved educational pathways and served as leader, principal, and teacher at Torreon Day School from 1944 to 1969. Her picture is displayed on our chapter wall along with others who have made strong positive impacts. Her observation on the emerging language shift from Navajo to English was that the educational practices of teaching English worked a little too well. My father was included in this shift, yet he can understand and write Navajo.

My maternal and first clan is Filipino. My mother was born and raised in Hawaii, but became a beloved member of Torreon community. For this, I am ever grateful for being shaped into someone who did not feel like I had to choose one side over another. She did the weaving for us. My Filipino identity is not the reason for being unable to speak Diné bizaad. Having studied our educational history, I realize that my English-only speaking ability is linked most directly with survival skills of the twentieth century under the heavy pressures of the era of termination and relocation (Wilkins 1999; Wilkins 2003). Thus, I have had to learn to think proactively about how I assert my sovereignty as a Diné woman. I may not speak Navajo, but I do believe language is at the core of our existence as a distinct people Indigenous to our land. Giving back to my nation through education and honoring my family legacy, especially in our community, is my practice of Navajo educational sovereignty.

By 2012, I was in the position to address my chapter community again. On this occasion, I was delivering the commencement address at our local border town high school whose student population was predominantly Navajo but whose administrative leadership was dominantly non-Navajo. I could finally demonstrate that I had completed the degree I had been talking about at each scholarship approval meeting in Torreon. It was important to me that I begin my speech in Navajo, although the plan was to share an inclusive message for all the graduates. My Aunt Mary Tsinnajinnie Cohoe worked with me on this opening greeting, and I practiced for weeks. When the time came, I carefully spoke each word in our language. After the ceremony, a Navajo lady rushed to the stage and said I made her so proud that she wanted to give me the necklace she was wearing. She said very lovingly that, to her, I was full Navajo. After all the years leading up to this, I became emotional. Later I learned she was an aunt, and the necklace was handed down to her from many generations. It was stolen from my suburban home two weeks later. When I saw her again and shared the news, she told me that now this meant the necklace would exist spiritually to always protect me.

While I still become anxious in settings where I must learn how to navigate, I am always secure in knowing the necklace is there. Whether in an educational forum, a ceremonial setting, or a chapter event, I know that my kinship, my family history, and my community identity will always be my sovereignty.

VISION

As stated earlier, Navajo educational sovereignty is political, social, spiritual, and clanship-based for the purpose of sustainability and nation building. In sharing my experiences, I offered one Diné perspective. In my vision, I extend that perspective into how this articulation of Navajo educational sovereignty serves as a means to recognizing and practicing inherent power as both collective individuals and as a people. Navajo educational sovereignty may be further strengthened through (1) language, (2) tribal colleges, (3) Native American studies programs, and (4) the power of young leaders.

LANGUAGE

As community members, scholars, activists, students, elders, athletes, workers, servicemen, servicewomen, mothers, fathers, sisters, brothers, and all our collective identities, we must commit ourselves to engaging or supporting the critical livelihood of our Diné bizaad. Whether we engage in research, lobbying, teaching, or silent prayer, we must remain rooted in what connects us to each other and our land.

TRIBAL COLLEGES

In 1968, our Nation established the first tribally controlled college in the United States: Diné College (Diné College 2016). We are now witnessing the rise of Navajo Technical University, which offers a Master of Arts degree in Diné Culture, Language, and Leadership (Navajo Technical University 2016). Our tribal colleges represent the epitome of Navajo educational sovereignty, as they are the result and practice of hundreds of years of political and social self-determination in the face of colonial onslaught (Wilkins 1999). These colleges offer the intersection of Western knowledge and traditional core values at some of the highest levels of schooling. Thus, we must also support the kinship in the national (United States) and global context of Indigenous education.

NATIVE AMERICAN STUDIES PROGRAMS

Within this kinship and context, Navajo educational sovereignty is reinforced through alliances with Native American studies and Indigenous studies programs. Located within high schools, tribal colleges, universities, and across the globe, these programs offer the power of networking, critical discourse, and the propensity to mobilize on Indigenous issues from politically promoting the articles of the United Nations Declaration on the Rights of Indigenous Peoples (UNDRIP) to ensuring our families have access to healthy water. Lloyd L. Lee has previously argued the viability of utilizing UNDRIP as a tool for the Navajo Nation (Lee 2014). The connections are inherent.

THE POWER OF YOUNG LEADERS

Finally, the relationship between our elders and our elders-in-training, as discussed by Emerson (2014), is where the power of Navajo educational sovereignty has the greatest potential. Sovereignty is sacrifice (Moore 2013). As long as we are willing to sacrifice individually for the sake of our peoplehood, sovereignty is alive. I see elders and elders-in-training willing to make sacrifices to preserve and enhance the beauty of Diné and all Indigenous life. When appropriate, we can sit at the same table and respect the value of what each of us brings. When college graduates are met with the embrace of eager open-eared chapter leaders, and community elders are cared for daily by their humble, willing, grown children, our power as a nation is infinite.

A FINAL NOTE

As the Harvard Project has argued, the Navajo nation-building approach is to plan for long-term sustainability (Cornell and Kalt 2007; Jorgensen 2007). I realize that rebuilding Native nations is to recognize that we have flourished as nations prior to Euro-American invasion. My tendency toward utilizing the term *nation building* in my discussion is to highlight the ongoing growth of ourselves as a people prior to this invasion, in the midst of colonization in its most brutal forms, and as we continue to decolonize while building forward. Our survival is a part of our growth.

Navajo educational sovereignty is joining together in collective minds, hearts, and hands to plan for healthy vibrant communities. In some capacities, it is to open meetings with an elder prayer and turn over the sacred space to the children so they may operationalize their knowledge. It is also vice versa. It is mutual loving respect and a common goal. Our survival has grown into a capacity in which we may share sacred spaces that allow for seamless recognition of formal titles while privileging kinship. Formal titles need not be hidden because they honor the sacrifices and the survival of our ancestors' spirits. The titles are community owned. Clanship is the means through which we own them.

I am your Nali.

RESEARCH

DINÉ PRINCIPLES OF GOOD GOVERNANCE

AVERY DENNY AND MICHAEL LERMA

INTRODUCTION

R ECENTLY THE COAUTHORS discussed good governance with members of the Navajo Nation Council legislative staff. All individuals were legitimately concerned about the current and future issues of the Navajo Nation Council. At the heart of these recent conversations are principles of good governance. There are hundreds of Native nations that could potentially be having this exact conversation now and in the very near future.[1] This chapter will present several two-dimensional illustrations (figures) on the principles of good governance. First, we discuss the role of inductive and deductive reasoning so that implicit assumptions are overtly stated and clear to the reader. We believe that discussions of good governance are hindered by unclear assumptions made visible during more concrete discussion of "foreign aid." Foreign aid, perhaps, should be viewed as a *Nayéé*, or "monster," to be possibly eliminated or allowed to live in some form that makes peoples' lives better. Then, we offer a concept of good Diné governance based on the assumption that the concept will require further fine-tuning. We believe more traditional knowledge holders should provide more guidance on this front at a later time.

From a normative perspective, good governance should possess four necessary conditions: (1) replicability, (2) reliability, (3) validity, and (4) setting.[2]

The traditional Navajo or Diné model of decision-making is next presented as it applies to inductive decision-making and policy-making. This process takes the form of developing a concept of good governance based on *Sa'ah Naagháí Bik'eh Hózhǫ́ǫ́n*. We more concretely apply Sa'ah Naagháí Bik'eh Hózhǫ́ǫ́n via the management of *Hózhǫ́* and Nayéé. Readers can also think about these applications in terms of foreign aid. We believe that by offering an admittedly subjective model that is consistent with Navajo philosophy, we begin the conversation about the subjective decision-making inherent in advocating for other preexisting European philosophy governance models. Critics have warned us that calling our model subjective only weakens our argument. We reject this idea because we are not selling an idea. Our elders say that the knowledge is there for us to better our lives, but there is no reason to impose or force the knowledge on others.

WHAT IS GOOD GOVERNANCE?

The term *good* governance is highly subjective. While we offer a concept of good Navajo governance in a subsequent section, for now we wish to critique the current ideas about contemporary good governance. We argue that subjectivity is key to conceptual stretching.[3] Conceptual stretching occurs when ideas, such as governance, are defined using terms foreign to another culture. In this case, *Naat'áahji*, or Navajo Leadership Way, was once a method of good Navajo governance.[4] This is an important assumption as we accept Naat'áahji is a legitimate form of good Navajo governance. After 1868, *Naat'áanii* (Traditional Navajo Leaders) seemed to have intentionally stopped practicing some portions of their leadership ceremonies.[5] Many, maybe 51 percent of the population, possibly rejected post-1868 leadership because it seemed to have lost its efficacy. This Naat'áahji leadership vacuum was based on emerging factions over the "correct" leadership, economic collapse, and old age taking the signers of the Treaty of 1868.[6] We now argue that many historians and community members have stretched the idea of pre-1920s Navajo society as "leaderless" or having "no government." This era of supposed no government also suffers a stretch of its own.

This stretch could have occurred on at least two levels: Chapter governance and the origins of the Navajo Nation Council are often correctly attributed to federal intervention. This does not make them solely U.S. projects. The formation of the 110 chapters of the Navajo Nation government was a federal institution building project carried out on behalf of Navajo peoples.[7] Beyond the scope of this research are questions about whether the chapter system relied on *k'é* or clan-based networks of pre-contact Diné political economy. If so, we have one example of a stretch by allowing some Navajo words to be replaced with the phrase *chapter house*. We suspect the root of k'é remains in place today in the chapter house system. Another potential stretch involves the formation of the Navajo Nation Council.[8] Originating in 1922, the "Business Council" was steadily stretched into its current form today.[9] So which is the "good" government? Again, this is a loaded question leading to subjective answers. There may be a way to back away from loaded questions by exploring some basics of Western-derived logic behind Naat'áahji philosophies of leadership.

When we assume that a term, such as *good*, is objective, we begin the stretch. The very notion of political philosophy must be addressed for a brief moment. Consider the distinction between inductive and deductive logic. Inductive logic involves using a specific example to make a generalization about a phenomenon.[10] Essentially, the previous paragraph took an inductive leap by discussing an anecdotal story that some may reject as subjective. The story, in our minds, still reflects a larger and more general problem in Indian country. We are implying that our observations are representative of a larger fact. In this way, we are taking a leap of faith with what we observe. As a result, there is a varying degree of subjective decision-making within our (and all) inductive leaps. The difference here is that we admit to this fact while others hide it. This notion of inductive reasoning is also applicable to governing a people. Somewhere along the way, a group of people took an inductive leap of faith and assumed that a particular existing philosophy would ensure a good result. The history of how Navajo people came to inherit their current government can be reviewed elsewhere.[11] What all of these accounts of Navajo governance share in common is their documentation of various inductive leaps made by Diné policy-makers beginning with the first encounter with Spaniards. These inductive leaps have remained obscured, unexplored, or intentionally hidden until now.

In contrast with inductive logic is deductive logic. In deductive logic—on a very basic level—if the premises are true, then the conclusion must also be true. One inductive conclusion drawn from interactions we have had with people interested in Navajo politics is that they all seem to have full confidence in their conclusions. In other words, many individuals are positive that their inductive arguments are actually deductive. An example of this problem recently emerged in the 2014 Navajo Nation presidential election. At the risk of appearing to take sides, this example is only being raised to present problems with drawing conclusions in a very biased manner. We choose not to take a position on the issue because it is moot. Candidate Chris Deschene was heavily criticized over a debate on his Navajo-language fluency. Some, including representatives of the Navajo Nation, wanted to test his fluency.[12] When Deschene refused to take the test, many that had already decided they were against his candidacy used this event to draw conclusions about his inability to speak Navajo. Opponents of Deschene might reason that (premise) if he will not take the test, then (conclusion) he must not be fluent. This idea is represented as an inductive form of reasoning. Deschene's refusal to take the test (a single event), is generalized into a broader conclusion about his fluency. Obviously, or perhaps not, this is flawed reasoning.

A problem emerges when other single events conflict with the broader generalization of fluency. There is video of Deschene speaking Navajo.[13] Some elders say he is fluent. At the first presidential debate, Deschene stated that he is learning Navajo.[14] Had Deschene's opponents correctly understood their positions as inductive, they would be forced to acknowledge the evidence that Deschene is fluent. In reality, many individuals for and against Deschene have chosen to engage in a shouting match with an apparent belief that their "inductive reasoning" can only lead to their own conclusions on his fluency. Those in favor of Deschene might say, "Because he spoke Navajo on video (premise of a single case event), we may generalize that he is fluent." Meanwhile, individuals opposed to Deschene might state, "Because he said he was learning Navajo at a debate (premise of a single case event), we may generalize that he is not fluent." In this example, the word *fluent* is being stretched.

More generally, we believe many political debates are not deductive in at least one sense. The conclusions drawn (based on premises) may not necessarily be true. We don't mean that individuals are lying. But we do mean that the premises are debatable in the sense that they are subjectively framed as correct. As with Deschene, it is not clear if he is actually fluent, and it is also not clear what fluency means. Perhaps some of the more "traditional" opinion holders do have some deductive logic on their side. Hence, a brief detour into Navajo philosophy will expound on this assumption.

Governance is a word applied to many methods of leading people. Hence, the word has been stretched to fit Native nations past and present. As previously stated, a series of inductive leaps exists somewhere in the history of Navajo and colonial actor interaction.[15] The result is the adoption of Western philosophy–based governance institutions. But, from the Navajo point of view, there are just a few simple deductions to draw. People want access to the sacred elements: *Kǫ', Tó, Niłchi, Tádídíín dóó Nahadzaan*. In English, they are called fire, water, air, and pollen/earth. These four elements give humans life, and they can all take life away depending on if humans have too much or too little of all four. If the premises are true, then so must the conclusion also be true. How humans obtain these elements is an inductive logic decision.

In this sense, our discussion should probably not assume that a preexisting Western model will solve the problems of the Navajo Nation. Rather, our discussion should surround the appropriate subjective decisions regarding distribution or coordination of resources. A more Diné way of looking at resources is through the lens of the four sacred elements. When this discussion does not occur, many policy-makers simply inject current-day problems with a ready-made distribution scheme from some place other than Diné Bikéyah, or the Navajo homeland as demarcated by the four sacred mountains. One example might be Navajo presidential candidates' language fluency. Very little, if any, discussion has been focused on a traditional Diné fluency test or even if one might exist. The subjective and inductive leaps about how a particular system of government will resolve the Navajo Nation's current issues miss the point. These subjective decisions do more to confuse the people than they do to resolve the peoples' problems. We believe this space of ambiguity is most dangerous. Within the space of ambiguity is leeway for a handful of individuals to take advantage of the Navajo constituency. We argue that contemporary Navajo policy-makers are counting on the Navajo constituency to remain unclear on the matters raised here so far. This confusion allows "business as usual" to continue, and deserves further elaboration.

"FOREIGN AID MONSTERS" AND THE NAVAJO NATION: STRINGS ATTACHED!

One of the most egregious examples of conceptual stretching currently ongoing in the popular narrative of Native nation and U.S. interaction is the very existence of Indigenous and Navajo sovereignty. Simultaneously, international interaction brings up serious issues about good governance for some constituents. Few have addressed Indigenous and colonial actor interaction in terms of current-day international relations.[16] To date, there is no treatment of Navajo and U.S. interaction within an international relations frame. Yet, framing the issue as international relations opens the door for using well-crafted strategies of interaction. In other words, we can describe the relationships between Navajo Nation leaders, its citizens, and the United States and its citizens. But can we explain them?

It is now necessary to deviate a bit from the discussion on current-day interaction. Diné philosophy discusses the origin of Nayéé Neezghání and Tó Bájísh Chíní. In short, twin boys were born in order to eliminate various "monsters" that were taking the lives of the humans or the five-fingered earth-surface people (aka *bilá ashdla'*). In these oral accounts, all living beings are considered people. Some accounts detail a chipmunk assisting the Hero Twins in their efforts to rid the world of the monsters, or Nayéé. All of these accounts have survived through ceremonial songs, prayers, and narratives generally known as *naaghái*.

Diné knowledge holders and medicine people understand and retell the lessons contained in the tribulations of the Hero Twins. Our current task is to relate these lessons to twenty-first-century international interaction. Typically, although there is always some variation, Monster Slayer, also known as *Nayéé Neezghání*, is credited with learning and understanding protection ceremonial knowledge. His knowledge is dangerous, and many consider it "scary" today. Monster Slayer would often encounter specific monsters, such as a monster that could stare at you until you lost your life. Other "peoples," which Western epistemologies might understand as animals, offered advice and assisted in distracting these monsters. Born for Water, or *Tó Bájísh Chíní*, was also very important in the process of eliminating human plagues. He was needed to provide a process for post-protection healing. He healed the people with his songs and prayers in order to restore balance and harmony. This is also typically known as hózhǫ. One of the larger lessons in these accounts involves the necessity not only to compartmentalize protection and healing processes, but to demonstrate how both are needed. But not all the monsters were eliminated.

Some of the monsters begged for their lives. Can we frame foreign aid as a monster? Monster Slayer took pity on between four and seven monsters. Depending on whom you ask, you may hear about the following seven monsters:

Greed/Poverty
Hunger
Lice
Sleep
Jealousy
Old Age
Death

Each of these monsters said they could motivate the five-fingered earth-surface people to take care of themselves, take care of their clan-based obligations, and ultimately live long lives. The rest of the monsters were placed deep into the ground. Mother Earth, or Shimá Nahaadzáán, would "seal" the monsters so that they lay dormant forever. We believe the idea was to remove one of the four sacred elements. Either fire, water, air, or pollen/earth was removed from the monsters, and this deprivation caused them to go dormant. The people were warned to never bring the monsters to the surface again, or they would wake up and take lives.

Our position is that, indirectly, foreign aid is a monster. Aid has appeared to foster greed, hunger, and jealousy. This imbalance has created a scenario in which elite Navajo leaders have allowed their own greed to create hunger and jealousy to take more control than they should have. Leaders have failed to protect their citizens from these monsters due to attractive foreign aid. Citizens have become impotent in the face of greed, hunger, and jealousy.

RELATIONSHIPS IN FOREIGN AID ANALYSIS: MANAGING GREED, HUNGER, AND JEALOUSY

In order to systematically understand the relationship between monsters and contemporary foreign aid, we need to lay out some key components of contemporary aid.

Native Nations:
Leaders of the Navajo Nation (LNN)
Constituents of the Navajo Nation (CNN)
Colonial Actor Nations

Colonial Actor Leaders (CAL)
Colonial Actor Constituents (CAC)

Selectorate theory is an emerging approach to strategic state-to-state inter-action.[17] Selectorate theory is especially relevant when there are clear power disparities. We may understand this as greed. Selectorate theory showcases some striking explanatory power when applied to the Navajo Nation. To make sense of this approach, we must define the Navajo Nation's selectorate. Navajo citizens eligible to vote are the selectorate. In the United States, if you can vote, you are also a member of the U.S. selectorate. Put simply, nonessential and replaceable members of the population make up a nation's selectorate.

The winning coalition is a minority of the selectorate. Navajo voters that voted for Russell Begaye are members of the winning coalition. President Begaye needed loyalty from a subset of the voters in order to be elected. Just how many votes Begaye needed to win the presidency should have dictated the strategy by which candidates planned their victories. Larger selectorates require different strategies than smaller selectorates.

Nations with a large winning coalition are better off if they maintain loyalty through public goods provisions. A public good cannot be exclusively distrib-uted to those that voted for Begaye. Clean air, good roads, and clean water are examples of public goods. Figure 5.1 illustrates the relationships between selectorate and winning coalition within a large winning coalition nation.

On the other extreme are military junta or dictatorship nations that require a small winning coalition. Loyalty is maintained through the provision of private goods. With private goods, leaders may exclusively distribute to each individ-ual winning coalition member. Contracts to build pollution-control devices to maintain clean air and water, and contracts to build and maintain roads are private goods. Exclusive natural resource access is also a private good. Private-goods provisions are lucrative to maintain loyalty. We see private-goods dis-tributions as greedy, leading to jealousy and hunger. Figure 5.2 depicts how a small winning coalition nation works. Hence, it is critical to accurately esti-mate the size of the Navajo Nation selectorate and winning coalition. Smaller winning coalition nations are more susceptible to foreign (U.S.) influence through foreign aid. Hence, foreign aid compromises the ability for recipient nations to maintain a good governance apparatus.

An old saying of the Navajo Nation is "Foreign aid comes with strings attached." Many in the Navajo Nation government have complained that money

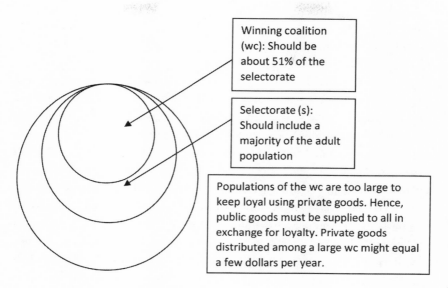

Winning coalition (wc): Should be about 51% of the selectorate

Selectorate (s): Should include a majority of the adult population

Populations of the wc are too large to keep loyal using private goods. Hence, public goods must be supplied to all in exchange for loyalty. Private goods distributed among a large wc might equal a few dollars per year.

FIGURE 5.1. Selectorate theory showcasing a large selectorate and winning coalition. Loyalty of the selectorate must be maintained using public goods. It is inefficient to keep large winning coalition selectorate loyal via private goods. Based on Bueno de Mesquita 2009.

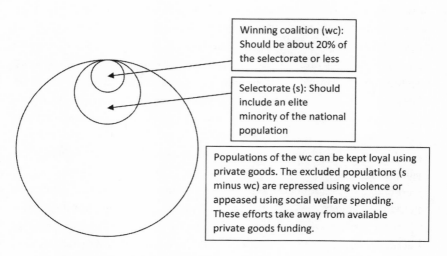

Winning coalition (wc): Should be about 20% of the selectorate or less

Selectorate (s): Should include an elite minority of the national population

Populations of the wc can be kept loyal using private goods. The excluded populations (s minus wc) are repressed using violence or appeased using social welfare spending. These efforts take away from available private goods funding.

FIGURE 5.2. Selectorate theory showcasing a small selectorate and winning coalition. Loyalty of the selectorate must be maintained using private goods. Based on Bueno de Mesquita 2009.

from Window Rock, the capital of the Navajo Nation, comes with so many regulations about spending that the money is not useful when it makes it to the local level. Interestingly, those that end up with the money may be accused of greed. Those that are left out may be accused of jealousy. Both of these scenarios lead to poverty. The same can also be said of federal money pouring into the Navajo Nation. When Window Rock receives money from the U.S. government, the United States wants something in return. The history of Navajo and colonial actor interaction details the benefits of war, trade, and peace.[18] The relationship continues today via resource extraction and foreign aid exchange.

The contemporary interaction between the United States and the Navajo Nation is one of international trade. Two nations have interacting political economies today. Yet, when trade policy is too heavily influenced by the one side, the chances of building good governance institutions are minimized. This outside influence will only further promote current income disparities on the Navajo Nation. Foreign aid relations have created more greed, jealousy, and hunger. The U.S. government is contributing (under treaty obligations) foreign aid to the Navajo Nation. Perhaps not coincidentally, the Navajo Nation is selling resources to U.S. corporations for under fair market value.[19] U.S. corporations end up selling Navajo natural resources for a profit to U.S. citizens.[20] This is not an accident. Selectorate theory details the explanation for why this process started back in 1848 and continues to this day.

Selectorate theory might make more sense when applied to the interaction between the Navajo Nation and the United States. There are four key groups to identify. Two groups tie into each nation. The Navajo Nation has leaders and constituents. The United States also has leaders and constituents. Each of these tie into each other as members of the selectorate, winning coalition, and leadership. Each of these must distribute public and private goods. One assumption is that each set of leaders wishes to personally, or as a party, remain in power (greed, jealousy, and hunger) for as long as possible. Each of the leaders must distribute public and private goods to their respective winning coalitions.

Foreign aid, as a function of policy concessions, works hand in hand with international trade. The more foreign aid impacts trade policy for a recipient nation, the less likely the recipient nation can retain the ability to sustain good governance practices that serve their own domestic and international interests. The United States is a large winning coalition nation. U.S. leaders retain loyalty during election cycles based on securing Navajo resources. These resources are distributed as public goods to U.S. citizens. The United States relies on a distribution scheme that allows for U.S. corporations to also serve the selectorate. U.S. corporations serve their leaders and the U.S. selectorate by providing jobs, cheap energy, water, and the like.

The second part of the equation is the Navajo Nation relationship to the interaction. Navajo leaders must participate in selling their natural resources to the United States, via corporations, for under fair market value. This is a clear threat to Navajo good governance practices. Foreign aid comes with strings attached. U.S. interests "abroad" are better represented if the foreign aid is distributed only to puppet democracies or moderate to small winning coalition nations as represented in figure 5.1. This includes the Navajo Nation as a moderate to small winning coalition nation. When the Navajo Nation has a small winning coalition, the United States is capable of purchasing policy concessions from Navajo Nation leaders with less money using private goods. The evidence suggests that the Navajo Nation is, indeed, a small winning coalition nation.[21] Currently, Navajo leaders do not need the loyalty of the Navajo constituency to remain as leaders. So long as Navajo leaders have a small winning coalition, they may buy the loyalty of winning coalition members with private goods.

U.S. leaders win because they obtain cheap natural resources from the Navajo Nation. Navajo citizens must bear the cost of Navajo leaders giving a policy concession to the United States, leaving citizens hungry. Foreign aid, then, buys a policy that should serve Navajo citizens and sells it to the United States in exchange for foreign aid. Selectorate theory, then, is certainly not an example of good governance for Navajo citizens. The foreign aid with strings attached model here is a snapshot of what is likely going on between the United States and all Native nations.[22] This issue should be on our minds as we explore good governance. What, then, constitutes an objective measure of good governance for the Navajo Nation or any Native nation?

PRINCIPLES OF GOOD DINÉ GOVERNANCE

Thus far we have discussed threats to good governance but have not discussed good governance itself. Over the past four years, the authors and staff members at Diné Policy Institute (DPI) have been discussing the concept of good governance. The word *concept* is not to be taken superficially. In relation to

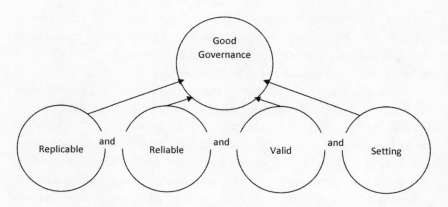

FIGURE 5.3. Two-level view of good governance model.

the conceptual stretch issues raised earlier, we have worked to ensure there is a definitive model in place for "good governance." Based on the concept-building approach, we now provide a two-level view of good governance.[23] Concepts connect a basic theoretical level label to secondary mid-level necessary conditions. Necessary conditions must be observed in the environment to verify the conditions are present. There is a case study (data/observation) level that is intentionally omitted here for the moment. We encourage future research along case study lines. We will also tie our research to current case study research. Figure 5.3 is a representation of good governance.

The label here is "good governance," but we can call it anything. We openly admit that good governance is a very abstract and theoretical construct. Hopefully, concept building will make it less abstract. Just as water is also called H_2O, the necessary conditions (hydrogen and oxygen) must be present or it is not really water.[24] We can call good governance anything we want—dictatorship, democracy, etc.—but one thing that is present in all good governance models is that they last a long time. Even dictatorships are good . . . for the dictators and the winning coalition! Hence, all good governance models have the following necessary conditions: (1) they are all replicable, (2) they are reliable, (3) they are valid, and (4) they have a setting. Note that these necessary conditions are reflected in the two-level view in figure 5.3. Data/observations, or cases, for each necessary condition can be explored independent of this research. The argument here is that you cannot have good governance if you are missing one of the four necessary conditions. This model is general enough that it should incorporate any form of government currently in existence today—thus making the need for an example unnecessary. This is both a strength and weakness because, in its present form, figure 5.4 explains everything and, thus, explains nothing. Yet, we need to start here because this is largely the basis for mainstream political theory today.

An aside would be to review how many political theorists have always discussed their models of governance as ones meant to monopolize resources and distribute them to society's upper echelons. Marx and Engels are obvious exceptions, but there are others.[25] John Locke, for example, may espouse a system of governance that reliably allows for a few to mix their hands with natural resources. Once the mixing has occurred, the individual "owns" the resultant property.[26] As an individual acquires more property, the person becomes "happier." The individual, then, should allow for governance that guides the pursuit of life with liberty to acquire all that one can so long as the acquisition does not spoil.[27] This model was strongly influential on the U.S. Constitution. Insofar as political philosophy goes, many in the United States consider the ability to pursue life, liberty, and happiness as synonymous with governing institutions that replicate such opportunities. A handful of white men (some of them slave owners) were able to utilize the same model to enrich themselves.[28] The U.S. constitutional model, in relation to Locke's philosophy, is quite replicable and reliable. The evidence for its replicability involves how the current U.S. model has lasted since 1787.[29] Various U.S. institutions have replicated the constitutional model, with some drastic changes, into the present time.[30] Perhaps the biggest question here, then, is whether the U.S. constitutional model is a valid reflection of Locke's theory.

This debate aside, the U.S. constitutional model in place today does replicate the hierarchy of leadership along race and class lines per the Aboriginal Title model.[31] This model of hierarchy has been successfully imported from Europe throughout the Americas since 1492 and has led to interesting economic development patterns today.[32] Like any model of good governance, the inductive decisions cannot be assumed without further elaboration. Can we simply assume that the aforementioned foreign models of governance, complete with their systematic monopolization of resources in the hands of an elite few, will further the interests of Navajo citizens? We believe this is the exact issue at play in contemporary Navajo governance problems.

CONCEPT OF DINÉ GOOD GOVERNANCE

Our examination of contemporary governance and nation-to-nation inter-action hopefully brings the most salient issues into focus. So far, few have addressed any inductive decisions about coordinating resource access. Instead, individuals appear tied to a confusing sampling of assorted governing institu-tions with minimal questioning. Some remain tied to a biblical model and are surprised when the model produces a Locke-style top-down set of institutions that enrich only a few.[33] Others may rely on a Bureau of Indian Affairs (BIA)–style bureaucracy and remain surprised when policies from the top rarely, if ever, impact the lives of Navajo citizens in a positive way or in a timely fash-ion. We invite others to individually peruse their own analysis of the origin of their potential models for good governance. We expect that individuals will find, repeatedly, that every model imported into the Navajo Nation will do precisely what it was designed to do. Discovering what these models were meant to do in their original setting is the responsibility of the advocate to clearly understand and present to the people. We take this responsibility seri-ously, and so advocate for a traditional Navajo (Diné) perspective on good governance here.

Figure 5.4 is a two-dimensional representation of Sa'ąh Naagháí Bik'eh Hózhǫ́ǫ́n. This is the model we now propose as a way to address contempo-rary issues on Diné Bikéyah, or the Navajo homeland.[34] This model can be located and applied to various other questions including language,[35] educa-tion,[36] astronomy,[37] and governance.[38]

Figure 5.4 is not very different from figure 5.3 except at the case-study (or data and observation) level. Additionally, the model is normatively advocating for the Sa'ąh Naagháí Bik'eh Hózhǫ́ǫ́n good governance model. Figure 5.4 attempts to link Navajo philosophy with contemporary Navajo practice. This concept-building approach can be applied to any political theory, but here it is only applied to Navajo political theory. Much of the evidence represented at the case-study level is contained in the oral accounts of Navajo philosophy.[39] We leave the details of case-study accounts to other scholars in order to focus more on mid-level links to theoretical (basic) level. It is recounted here briefly and should be further investigated by other scholars since additional refine-ment will only improve the model.

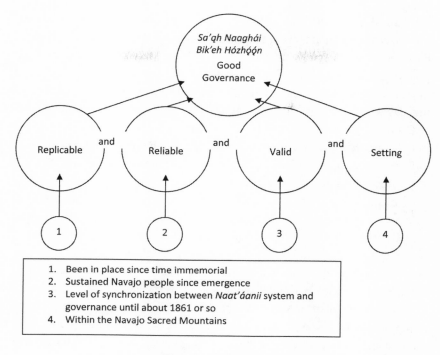

FIGURE 5.4. Three-level view of good governance
model reflecting Sa'ąh Naaghái Bik'eh Hózhǫ́ǫn.

Case-study-level accounts can be linked to a set of necessary conditions
for Sa'ąh Naaghái Bik'eh Hózhǫ́ǫn good governance. For example, figure 5.4,
observation 1 indicates that Sa'ąh Naaghái Bik'eh Hózhǫ́ǫn good governance
has been in place since time immemorial. If we assume that Sa'ąh Naaghái
Bik'eh Hózhǫ́ǫn good governance is a model of political theory, we might
also conclude the model was used by Navajo people to traverse at least four
(some say five) worlds into today.[40] We can reimagine "the journey narratives"
through a political theory lens.

An example of a problem in Navajo oral accounts involves a crisis of leadership. Diné knowledge-holders might call this the Navajo Emergence, or
Hajiineí. It is said that animals tried leading but failed because of their inherent
shortcomings. As a result, via the use of Sa'ąh Naaghái Bik'eh Hózhǫ́ǫn, *Dził
Naat'aah* (Mountain Philosophy) was implemented. *Diyin Dine'e* (Holy Ones)

recognized a problem and gave the Navajo people four sacred mountains. These sacred mountains were to be used by the people to govern.[41] Some of the directives included living within the four sacred mountains. We now interpret Mountain Philosophy as appropriate for use as a model for domestic and international relations today.[42] Many elders and knowledge holders believe, to this day, that Navajo people lived good lives up until the time of interaction with Spain, when evidence of treaty making emerged around 1706.[43] Much more evidence exists supporting how Sa'ąh Naagháí Bik'eh Hózhǫ́ǫ́n good governance has been in place and replicated since time immemorial.[44] There is also evidence that the model was quite reliable.

Evidence supporting the existence of Sa'ąh Naagháí Bik'eh Hózhǫ́ǫ́n good governance is also interrelated to evidence that the model has reliably allowed Navajo people to weather serious crises. This is represented in figure 5.4, observation 2. Readers may refer to the Dził Naat'aah model as an example. Still, another example is the separation of the sexes crisis weathered by using Sa'ąh Naagháí Bik'eh Hózhǫ́ǫ́n good governance. Oral accounts detail how women and men stopped collaborating. Women and men lived apart, and things started to fail. It is said that crops did not grow and rain did not provide water. Sexual misbehavior among the separate genders led to the birth of Nayéé. Diyin Dine'e, after careful thought and concern, gave the people songs and prayers to bless and protect themselves via the Warrior Twins. The Warrior Twins ended up eliminating most of the monsters except for six that begged for their lives.[45] The six monsters persuaded the Warrior Twins that they could assist humans if they were allowed to live. These six monsters are poverty, jealousy, hunger, thirst, lice, and sleep.[46] It is said these monsters are here today. Still, Sa'ąh Naagháí Bik'eh Hózhǫ́ǫ́n good governance reliably allowed for the recovery of the people on these two occasions, as well as many more in a manner that validly reflected the philosophy itself.

In an effort to validly reflect Sa'ąh Naagháí Bik'eh Hózhǫ́ǫ́n good governance, DPI discussed the monsters in a contemporary context. DPI set out to reflect a management system for facilitating Diné citizen the ability to attain a good and long life. In other words, Sa'ąh Naagháí Bik'eh Hózhǫ́ǫ́n could be a contemporary method of distributing public goods to citizens in order to offset the negative impact of Nayéé. Figure 5.5 is a revision of what first appeared as a restructuring question.[47] (The original figure is located in the appendix as figure 5.7. It is a deviation from the concept-building method.)

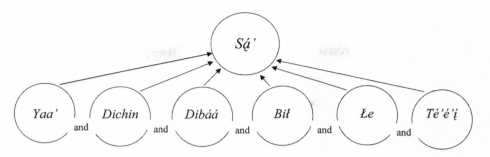

FIGURE 5.5. Current model for managing the six monsters with
us today. This model is more consistent with concept-building
methods, although the original figure (5.7) is also good.

Each of the six Naayéé' are contemporary-day social problems that must be
addressed via policy language. We opted to leave out monsters that we decided
could not be treated today. Contemporary distribution of public goods could
solve many of these ills, leaving room for individuals to achieve their own
goals. All monsters are social ills harming people today. *Yaa'*, or lice, involves
cleanliness. *Dichin* is hunger, *Dibáá* is thirst, *Bił* is sleep, *Łe* is jealousy, and
Té'é'į is poverty. The key is to maintain a proper distance from each of these
monsters in order to attain *Sá*, which is glossed over in English as long life,
wisdom, and knowledge, among other things.[48] In the same way that people
must maintain a proper distance from and toward the four sacred elements, one
must also keep a proper distance from and toward the six monsters.[49] Thinking
of these monsters along a concept-continuum line may further clarify these
complex issues.

Figure 5.6 is a representation of one of the six monsters, Té'é'į, or poverty,
originally represented in figure 5.5. The concept continuum represents some
complex ideas. First are protection songs, prayers, and stories. In terms of
poverty, one must learn to protect oneself and one's family from poverty. In
the past, adults were expected to make a home by marrying, establishing a
hogan, having children, and providing for their family both within the hogan
and through the clan relationship to extended family. This past expectation can
easily be imagined today as many individuals try to provide for their families
and extended relations. Some are successful and avoid poverty while others
struggle. It is possible that contemporary Diné continue to utilize a process of

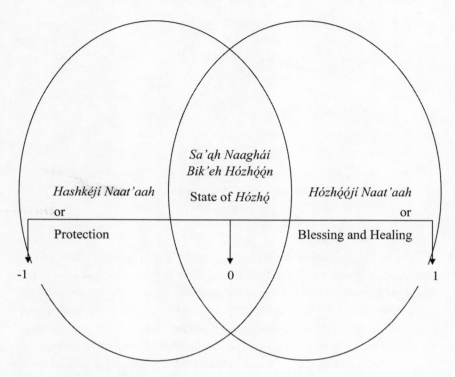

0 = A proper level of wealth

1 = Too much wealth in the hands of too few people

-1 = Too much poverty in the hands of too many people

FIGURE 5.6. Concept continuum of a given monster such as Té'é'í,
or poverty, and how it relates to Sa'ąh Naagháí Bik'eh Hózhǫ́ǫ́n.

healing and protection to ensure their families remain in balance—meaning
they are not too wealthy and not too impoverished. Protection ways can be
harsh at times. Still, protection is not enough. People also must bless and heal
themselves and their family in order to ensure that poverty does not get out of
hand. It is said that humans cannot properly handle poverty, or any other monster, with only blessing and healing way. Simultaneously, it is not enough to
simply protect one's self and one's family. Poverty cannot be simply contained
in a cage or jail. It moves and it is free. Remember that poverty begged for its

life and was allowed to live so that humans would be motivated to keep their fiscal life in proper order. This ideal seems as true today as it was long ago. The songs and prayers given to Navajo people for healing and protection are to be utilized in order to maintain Sa'ąh Naagháí Bik'eh Hózhǫ́ǫn.

In other words, even if there is no problem, the balance must be maintained by using songs and prayers, just as Monster Slayer and Born for Water once maintained balance. If an imbalance does occur, known as *anáhóót'i'*, or the emergence of a problem, the songs and prayers become even more important. This anáhóót'i' may be considered in degrees of urgency. You'll note in figure 5.6 that one could theoretically measure the distance from zero or *Hózhǫ́*. Although not exact, perhaps there is a cutoff point at which a situation is no longer Hózhǫ́ and becomes a matter of *Hóxchǫ́*, also known as drift away from Hózhǫ́. This is certainly an area that needs further study. For now, we only need to know that any distance, toward −1 or toward 1, requires maintenance. When maintenance of Hózhǫ́ is neglected or impacted by a larger issue (an unexpected event), the level of urgency increases. We know that when a situation drifts closer to a −1 or a 1 on the scale of maintenance, it becomes imperative to increase the level of urgency regarding attention to the problem. Figure 5.6, again, involves poverty. The more people we find impoverished on the Navajo Nation, the higher level of urgency it deserves by policy-makers. Ideally, these monsters must be maintained at or near zero for as long as possible. This model assumes that monsters move about, and it is the earth-surface people's responsibility to react accordingly.

These ideas are further reflected using the number line in figure 5.6. This information is interesting and, at times, difficult to fully comprehend. The proper method is to keep monsters at or near the zero designation. We assume these ideals move in time, perhaps by the second. Every now and then a miracle related to poverty may occur. We suspect that this is possible when both *Hashkéjí* and *Hózhǫ́ǫjí* completely overlap one another. This is the perfect balance and the ideal state of Sa'ąh Naagháí Bik'eh Hózhǫ́ǫn. This perfect state is fleeting, and may only last for a split second. These moments of perfection—miracles—may only occur briefly, but should be cherished since poverty will continue to move on its own and disrupt balance.

As poverty is diminished and poverty moves into the positive (blessing) range, there can be more unintended problems. This idea may be counterintuitive for some readers. The reason that this is a problem is because Navajo philosophy assumes that if too few people become extremely wealthy the like-lihood that others will be impoverished will increase. So this is the idea that there is too much of a blessing. Perhaps it can also be understood as "too much of a good thing." The people may get jealous or the imbalance may create poverty for those left out. When too many people are impoverished, more protections must be in place. When negative and positive are in balance, things are good. One final note involves the monsters themselves: Navajo phi-losophy holds that it is humans who must adjust to monsters. As stated ear-lier, one cannot expect the monsters to sit still and remain encaged. In many ways, the monster discussion truly does reflect issues on the Navajo Nation today. Too many remain impoverished. Too few remain wealthy. It is possible to redraw figure 5.6 for each monster. We believe, however, it is now self-explanatory how figure 5.6 would describe and explain how Sa'ąh Naagháí Bik'eh Hózhǫǫn can be used as a model of governance to properly manage all other monsters.

We already know that the current governing model used by the Navajo Nation has failed its people. The 2014 campaign season exposed many issues. Many candidates are career politicians, giving rise to the criticism that they are "old guard" and afraid of meaningful change. The debate rages on about the traditional perspective on female leaders. Those in favor of female leaders point to their female deity leaders. Those opposed to female leaders are criti-cized for adopting patriarchic practices from the United States. Many candi-dates emerged with new ideas that threatened the status quo. Some of these candidates alienated their constituents by, perhaps, being too honest about not knowing all of the answers or not making promises they did not believe they could keep. Few citations are offered here so as not to imply any allegiance or criticism of particular candidates. People remain impacted by all six monsters today. A majority of Diné citizens remain needlessly impacted by at least one of the monsters. Even current and future leaders suffer from the ills of wealth, jealousy, hunger, and sleep. How do we strike a balance?

Poverty is an issue of not having enough access to the four sacred ele-ments. With a lack of access, some people find themselves in a poor condition. The simple answer is to increase access to opportunities for securing the four sacred elements. This is not the same as simply providing food. When an indi-vidual has water, they can quench their thirst. When an individual has fire, they can cook and stay warm. When the person has clean air, they can breathe. With access to pollen they can plant their corn, squash, beans, and tobacco. It truly is a matter of dislodging the current status quo in order for the citizens to have true access to their sacred elements. This is the potential role good governance can play. Sa'ąh Naagháí Bik'eh Hózhǫ́ǫ́n might call for *Naat'áanii* to step up and provide institutional pathways to the sacred elements as public goods. Access need not be privatized and handed out to members of the winning coalition. Clearly, the status-quo governing style has operated in favor of privatizing access to the four sacred elements. Water, for example, is often sold to urban centers. The incentive for tribal leaders to privatize access is great.[50] We leave a diagnosis of current Navajo leadership to the reader and suggest they utilize figure 5.7 as a guide. Are Navajo leaders out of balance?

It is important to note how the current Navajo Nation government and its officials have all lodged themselves in place as a function of private goods access points via the U.S. government. Reconfiguring current institutions to allow access to the four sacred elements as a public good would threaten the private access that grocers, resource-extraction corporations, and fast-food restaurants currently have on the Navajo people today. This explains why powerful individuals on the Navajo Nation today have no interest in changing the status quo. If they profit from it, why would they change? It will need to come from the people as a shock to the current status quo. In the absence of a human rejection of the status quo, we are convinced that Mother Earth and Father Sky will simply continue their communication breakdown, and an environmental shock will displace the status quo. When this occurs, only those with knowledge of how to manage their relationship with the four sacred elements will be empowered to continue with life as leaders for the Navajo people.

CONCLUSION

This chapter has attempted to only briefly redirect the dialogue on contemporary Navajo governance reform. In many ways, it is a demand that advocates of other non-Navajo models of governance truly investigate their own positions as we have here. We remain convinced that foreign models of governance will do exactly as they were designed to do. The Navajo Nation continues to engage in extractive economies such as the purchase of coal mines. In the process, the Navajo Nation purchased the mine and waived all liability the previous owner may have had for environmental damage and the risk they placed on workers forever.[51] They will extract resources from the Navajo people and deliver them to a few Navajo elites, and more generally serve the global political economy with little to no return on the Navajo peoples' investment. This will maintain the current imbalance of greed, jealousy, and hunger.

We encourage individuals to examine the validity of claims made here. We remain assured that foreign aid is a better way to critique current international relationships between all Native nations and the United States. It brings us to a precise focus on the relationship that current leaders have with their constituents and with special interests. We can continue to talk about equality, equity, and accountability, or we can fully explore how these principles are not present in the current interaction relationship. Current relations have not impacted the levels of greed, jealousy, and hunger. Elites remain wealthy, jealous of rivals, and hungry for power. The average citizen remains relatively impoverished, jealous of the elites, and hungry for fairness. On all sides, Navajo leaders have thoroughly failed their constituents, and we need not discuss how the U.S. government has failed in its trust relationship to the Navajo Nation. Yet, the "good governance" model is not a one-size-fits-all approach.

We further invite others to reexamine the inductive decisions they may have implicitly allowed to creep into their policies and discussions. At the heart of the matter is the access individual Navajos have to the four sacred elements. Without such elements, individuals cannot sustain their lives by growing corn and tobacco. But, as we argue, this is exactly what the United States wanted to occur. When we terminate our own political economy or when we alternatively fail to rebuild it, we invite further dependency on the global political economy. When we foster our peoples' proper access to the four sacred elements, we gain the potential to resolve our relationship with the six current-day monsters. Further, we gain the potential to displace the current status quo, enrich Navajo citizens more uniformly, and begin our path toward a better global relationship between the Navajo Nation and the environment. Our ancestors knew how to govern themselves, and still do today. Navajo people have never asked Window Rock for permission to do a ceremony. People just got together, assigned tasks, and carried out what needed to be done. We need to rediscover our own ability to set the agenda for today and tomorrow. *T'aa Akodí* (That is all).

APPENDIX

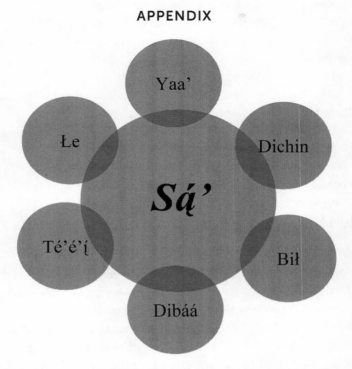

FIGURE 5.7. Original model for managing the six monsters with us today. *Sá'* loosely translates as wisdom, age, and knowledge.

NOTES

1. Eric D. Lemont, ed., *American Indian Constitutional Reform and the Rebuilding of Native Nations* (Austin: University of Texas Press, 2006).
2. Gary King, Robert Keohne, and Sidney Verba, *Designing Social Inquiry: Scientific Interference in Qualitative Research* (Princeton, NJ: Princeton University Press, 1994).
3. Gary Goertz, *Social Science Concepts: A User's Guide* (Princeton, NJ: Princeton University Press, 2006), 70–74.
4. AnCita Benally, "Dine' Binahat'a', Navajo Government" (PhD diss., Arizona State University, 2006), 1–39.

5. Michael Lerma, "Guided by the Mountains: Traditional and Contemporary Approaches to Diné Governance" (PhD diss., University of Arizona, 2010), 197–227. Also published under the same title in 2016 by Oxford University Press.

6. Garrick Bailey and Roberta Glenn Bailey, *A History of the Navajo: The Reservation Years* (Santa Fe, NM: School of American Research Press, 1999), 25–104.

7. David E. Wilkins, *The Navajo Political Experience*. (New York: Rowman and Littlefield, 2013), 151–55.

8. Ibid., 17–37.

9. Michael Lerma, *Guided by the Mountains: Navajo Political Philosophy of Governance* (New York: Oxford University Press, 2016).

10. John Stuart Mill, *A System of Logic Ratiocinative and Inductive: Being a Connected View of the Principles of Evidence and the Methods of Scientific Investigation* (London: Longmans, 1967), 185–205.

11. Evangeline Parsons Yazzie, Margaret Speas, Jessie Ruffenach, and Berlyn Yazzie, *Diné Bizaad Bináhoo'aah: Rediscovering the Navajo Language: An Introduction to the Navajo Language* (Flagstaff, AZ: Salina Bookshelf, 2007), 379–92. Although this is a book on language, there is a chapter titled "Diné Biwááshindoon," or Navajo government. See also Robert Yazzie, Avery Denny, Amber Crotty, Dana Eldridge, Moroni Benally, Michael Lerma, and Andrew Curley, *Recommendations for Restructuring the Navajo Nation Council* (Tsaile, AZ: Dine Policy Institute, 2011). See also Raymond D. Austin, *Navajo Courts and Navajo Common Law: A Tradition of Tribal Self-Governance* (Minneapolis: University of Minnesota Press, 2009).

12. Donovan Quintero, "With General Election Looming, Finality for Deschene's Chance to Remain a Presidential Candidate May Come Today," *Navajo Times*, October 17, 2014.

13. Chris Deschene for Navajo Nation President 2014, October 3, 2014, https://www.youtube.com/watch?v=iSglL3AvZ78.

14. Chris Deschene (Navajo Nation Presidential Candidate) discussing his yearning for patience with his learning his language at the First Navajo Nation Presidential Forum, July 2014.

15. *Colonial actor* is a term developed to represent at least three polities interacting with the Navajo Nation during its history. Spain, Mexico, and the United States have all interacted with the Navajo Nation in terms of diplomacy and

political economy. *Colonial actor* designates a general interaction between one of these three colonial nations.

16. S. James Anaya, *Indigenous Peoples in International Law* (New York: Oxford University Press, 2004); Vine Deloria and David E. Wilkins, *Tribes, Treaties, and Constitutional Tribulations* (Austin: University of Texas Press, 1999).

17. Bruce Bueno de Mesquita, *Principles of International Politics* (Washington, DC: CQ Press, 2009); Bruce Bueno de Mesquita, *The Dictator's Handbook: Why Bad Behavior Is Almost Always Good Politics* (New York: Public Affairs, 2011); Michael Lerma, *Indigenous Sovereignty in the 21st Century: Knowledge for the Indigenous Spring* (Miami: Florida Academic Press, 2014), 124–46.

18. Austin, *Navajo Courts and Navajo Common Law*; AnCita Benally, "Dine' Binahat'a', Navajo Government"; Tiana Bighorse, Gus Bighorse, and Noel Bennett, *Bighorse the Warrior* (Tucson: University of Arizona Press, 1990); David M. Brugge and J. Lee Correll, *The Story of the Navajo Treaties* (Research Section, Navajo Parks and Recreation Dept., Navajo Tribe, 1971); David Wilkins, *Diné Beehaz'áanii: A Handbook of Navajo Government* (Tsaile, AZ: Navajo Community College Press, 1987), 26.

19. Lerma, *Indigenous Sovereignty in the 21st Century*, 124–46.

20. Andrew Needman, *Power Lines: Phoenix and the Marking of the Modern Southwest* (Princeton, NJ: Princeton University Press, 2014).

21. Lerma, *Indigenous Sovereignty in the 21st Century*, 145.

22. Ibid., 124–47.

23. Goertz, *Social Science Concepts*, 27–67; Giovanni Sartori, "Concept Misformation in Comparative Politics," *American Political Science Review* 64, no. 4 (1970): 1033–53.

24. The word *Tó* is Navajo for water. Water can be named anything you want. For example, one may call water *aqua* in Spanish. The labels do not matter. The necessary conditions are the true essence of water.

25. John Hoffman and Paul Graham, *Introduction to Political Ideologies* (New York: Pearson Longman, 2006), 56–58.

26. Ibid., 23–27.

27. Ibid.

28. Linda R. Monk, *The Words We Live By: Your Annotated Guide to the Constitution* (New York: Hyperion, 2001); de Mesquita, *Principles of International Politics*.

29. Monk, *The Words We Live By.*

30. Ibid.

31. Vine Deloria and Raymond J. DeMiallie, *Documents of American Indian Diplomacy: Treaties, Agreements, and Conventions, 1775–1979* (Norman: University of Oklahoma Press, 1999); David H. Getches, Charles F. Wilkinson, and Robert A. Williams, *Cases and Materials on Federal Indian Law* (Eagan, MN: Thomson/West, 2005); Lerma, *Indigenous Sovereignty.*

32. James Mahoney, *Colonialism and Development: Spanish America in Comparative Perspective* (New York: Cambridge University Press, 2010); James Mahoney, "Long-Run Development and the Legacy of Colonialism in Spanish America," *American Journal of Sociology* 109 (2003): 50–106.

33. Steven T. Newcomb, *Pagans in the Promised Land: Decoding the Doctrine of Christian Discovery* (Golden, CO: Fulcrum, 2008).

34. Michael Lerma, "Indigeneity and Homeland: Land, History, Ceremony, and Language," *Indian Culture and Research Journal* 30 (2012).

35. Parsons Yazzie et al., *Diné Bizaad Bináhoo'aah: Rediscovering the Navajo Language.*

36. T. Sihasin Gorman-Keith, "Meaning of Graduation to Navajo College Students at Northern Arizona University: An Interpretive Case Study" (PhD diss., Northern Arizona University, 2004).

37. Nancy C. Maryboy and David Begay, *Sharing the Skies: Navajo Astronomy* (Tucson, AZ: Rio Nuevo Publishers, 2010).

38. Robert Yazzie et al., *Recommendations for Restructuring the Navajo Nation Council*; Austin, *Navajo Courts and Navajo Common Law*; Benally, "Dine' Binahat'a', Navajo Government"; Marianne Nielsen and James Zion, *Navajo Nation Peacemaking: Living Traditional Justice* (Tucson: University of Arizona Press, 2005).

39. Benally, "Dine' Binahat'a', Navajo Government"; Bighorse et al., *Bighorse the Warrior*; Wilson Aronilth, *Foundation of Navajo Culture* (Tsaile, AZ: Dine College Press, 1991).

40. Benally, "Dine' Binahat'a', Navajo Government."

41. Benally, "Dine' Binahat'a', Navajo Government"; Aronilth, *Foundation of Navajo Culture.*

42. Lerma, *Guided by the Mountains.*

43. Deloria and DeMiallie, *Documents of American Indian Diplomacy*; David Wilkins, "Governance within the Navajo Nation: Have Democratic Traditions Taken Hold?" *Wicazo Sa Review* 17 (2002): 91–129.

44. Benally, "Dine' Binahat'a', Navajo Government."
45. The authors acknowledge that there are differing positions on the actual number of monsters from the oral accounts. Some stories say there are seven monsters: see Benally, "Dine' Binahat'a', Navajo Government." Some suggest six monsters: see Yazzie et al., *Recommendations for Restructuring the Navajo Nation Council*. Still others suggest there are four monsters.
46. Robert Yazzie et al., *Recommendations for Restructuring the Navajo Nation Council*; Benally, "Dine' Binahat'a', Navajo Government."
47. Robert Yazzie et al., *Recommendations for Restructuring the Navajo Nation Council*.
48. Ibid.; Berard Haile, *Soul Concepts of the Navaho* (St. Michaels, AZ: St. Michaels Press, 1943), 91.
49. Lerma, *Guided by the Mountains*.
50. Lerma, *Indigenous Sovereignty in the 21st Century*, 124–46.
51. Alastair Lee Bistoi, "Done Deal: Tribe Officially Owns a Coal Mine," *Navajo Times*, January 2, 2014.

EMPOWERED SOVEREIGNTY FOR NAVAJO CHAPTERS THROUGH ENGAGEMENT IN A COMMUNITY-PLANNING PROCESS

MICHELLE HALE

I N APRIL 2016 a group of Indian planners gathered to discuss the future of community planning in terms of education about the process, need, and impact; training and tools for current and future planners; collaborative partnerships among those who do various aspects of land-use management or community development for Indian Country; and communication within and among the various federal, state, and tribal entities with vested interest in Indian community development. The participants brainstormed opportunities to use a strategic and comprehensive planning process to help Indian nations address issues of fractionation, to better manage community growth, and to sort out complex land-status issues that often impinge on community development when specially designated Indian lands—such as allotments—confuse investors and restrict the acreage available for community projects such as housing, public-use areas, and transportation corridors.

The Indian planners emphasized the need for an Indigenized planning process, one that empowers rather than disenfranchises Indian people. After more than a century of planning and community-development work done for us by the federal government through the Bureau of Indian Affairs (BIA) and various agencies, Indigenous planning presents an unparalleled opportunity for Indian nations to construct a process that honors Indian worldview and traditional values as they pertain to land and resources (Walker, Jojola, and Natcher

2013). Indigenous planning invites Indian nations to put their unique stamp on the tools of planning so that consultations with community stakeholders, visioning sessions, mapping, and implementation are done in culturally appropriate ways. The expectation is that a culturally driven planning process may have greater resonance with the community it serves, resulting in improved support and investment from the local citizens, and thus an enhanced chance of successful implementation.

What emerged from this discussion was a poignant assertion that Indigenous planning is a catalyst for empowered Indian sovereignty because it offers Indian nations an opportunity to take planning processes and tools and make them their own. It is a chance to take action to address long-held criticisms that BIA-driven development does not always match the desired outcomes of the community, or that off-reservation consultants fail to understand the unique cultural, historical, and political nuances of reservation communities. At times, reservation community development is driven by the availability and timing of federal grants, which means projects are not always part of an organized, large-scale, long-range plan, put forth by the Indian community; Indigenous planning facilitates a comprehensive, long-term, strategic approach to the federal grant process.

In the eyes of some Indian people, concepts of open space, the implementation of a zoning code, or creation of a land-use plan may seem like Western tools and bureaucratic processes that only serve to further regulate and assert BIA control over Indian resources. For some, planning is associated with a process, tools, and policy expected to only further dispossess Indian people of resources and infringe on governmental and cultural sovereignty as it pertains to our land. However, because not all Indian nations have comprehensive zoning codes, master plans, or even the internal resources such as trained professionals with the equipment and resources to realize planning, I contend that the blank slate is an invaluable opportunity to create tools and processes from the ground up and to integrate cultural values and norms where needed. The result could be tools and processes that galvanize people-driven community development. If Indian citizens take issue with the concept of "open space," Indigenized planning equips that community to replace that language and ideology with alternatives that better match the local community's mores. If an Indian nation values its members' privacy and protection for sacred spaces, it can employ a strategic zoning policy to keep unwanted development and foot traffic away from shrines, ruins, or ceremonial grounds. Often, Indian nations use zoning to focus retail, tourism, and development that invites high-volume traffic to the perimeter of their land so as to provide a buffer between the reservation residential area and commercially developed areas. Such practices demonstrate the assertion of tribal control over land use and access, and an orchestrated effort to build and maintain a certain quality of life for its citizens.

One example of tribally driven planning is the Salt River Pima-Maricopa Indian Community (SRPMIC) in Arizona, where community planning has been a work in progress since the 1950s. "The Community initiated a more formal approach to 'community planning' by utilizing public and private agencies in preparing a direction for growth, economically and physically" (SRPMIC General Plan 2013). SRPMIC adopted its first general development plan in the 1960s. "The 1970 SRPMIC General Development Plan documented past efforts and provided guidance for future growth; the 1978 General Development Plan Update included a growth factor by requiring periodic review; and 1988 amendments included increased number of home sites, water rights settlement, major roadway improvements, major enterprises established, and a regional shopping center developed" (SRPMIC General Plan 2013). SRPMIC has decades of experience with the language and tools of planning, and attests to the usefulness of the process to help assert political and economic sovereignty. As a Phoenix-area Indian nation adjacent to Scottsdale, Mesa, Tempe, and Fountain Hills and located along the Loop 101-Pima Freeway, the Salt River community has been able to capitalize on market opportunity to lease land and space and to grow tribal enterprise along the designated commercial corridor due to effective planning. According to Ruben Guerrero, director of corporate affairs for Salt River Materials Group, the community approved an expansion of the commercial corridor along the western edge of the reservation using a zoning ordinance that amended the 2006 plan; it took effect in July 2015 (2016). That action was made possible by the review and amendment option articulated in the 1978 plan, and demonstrates the efficacy with which SRPMIC has employed planning as useful and flexible to enhance ongoing community-development work. Although the change expands the reservation's commercial-use area, it also maintains a comfortable buffer between the enterprise zone and the residences at SRPMIC. A final aspect of the Salt River plan that resonates with cultural sovereignty is the designation of 19,000 acres of the 52,600 acre reservation as a preserve—an action that protects land and resources that hold cultural significance for the people, and also sets aside this valuable resource for future generations.

The aforementioned Indian planning meeting—National Tribal Planners Round Table and Strategic Planning Session—convened in Phoenix, Arizona, in April 2016. The gathering coincided with the annual meeting of the American Planning Association (APA). Participants included tribal planners, educators, consultants, and technicians who work for the federal and tribal government or who own their own businesses and do regular consultant work with Indian nations. Most of the participants are American Indian, and several work for their own nations. SRPMIC serves as an example of where Indian people want their communities to be in terms of tribal ownership and control of a planning process and the creation of plans, codes, and ordinances that accurately reflect the local community's history and culture. There were many calls to action to put Indian nations in the driver's seat of reservation community development. Participants see planning as critical for helping Indian nations to better actualize their powers of self-governance and for the realization of a very practical exercise of Indian sovereignty. The group admitted that a necessary first step is education: for reservation community members; tribal employees; contractors and consultants; staff in local, tribal, and federal government (Indian and non-Indian); and others who provide technical assistance for planning (2016).

IMPLICATIONS FOR THE NAVAJO NATION

As I listened to the discussion at the National Tribal Planners Round Table, I could not help but think of my own community on the Navajo Nation and the impact that a Navajo-driven planning process could have on Navajo community development. In 2015, the Navajo Nation hired more than a dozen Navajo planners to work directly with local people on the chapter level—the 110 chapters across the Navajo Nation being the bodies of local government. By hiring Navajo people, the hope is that they will be more effective in getting people engaged in crafting a process that is not seen as dubious, and in developing tools that equip and empower rather than marginalize and dispossess. Since many of the newly minted Navajo planners speak the language of the people, were born and raised on the reservation, or have at least lived on the nation for many years, they have a powerful understanding and appreciation for existing cultural norms and practice, politics, and local history. They are able to relate to the people in a way that hired consultants cannot. When the round-table planners assert that Indian Country needs homegrown planners to do effective planning, the Navajo planners fit the bill. The challenge, however, is few members of this group have formal training or education in urban design, planning, natural resources, law, design and architecture, environmental science, or sustainability.

In 2015, the Navajo Nation partnered with Arizona State University's School of Geographical Science and Urban Planning to provide technical training and education in tribal planning (ASU Now 2015). Students learned how to use geographic information systems (GIS) to gather, manage, assess, and use data to help them with reservation planning. They were exposed to tools and technologies in mapping, informed of methods and approaches used in community planning, and provided with a primer on Indian law as it pertains to land use, regulatory authority, and management. Presenters shared case studies and examples of how Indian and non-Indian communities address issues of land use, zoning, sustainability, environmental regulation, transportation, and jurisdictional authority. Issues specific to the Navajo Nation included grazing rights, small business, and limits of central and local authority and jurisdiction. Participants had opportunities to reflect on the new tools and information and brainstorm ways in which they could employ those tools and ideas as they embark on the work of community planning. As Navajo community members, they have the ability to decide which tools will work at the grassroots level and which should be discarded. Their knowledge and experience as Navajo people enable them to efficiently pick and choose which case studies or information have relevance to their work and which can be used as a springboard for Navajo approaches, models, or thought processes on planning issues.

For Local Governance Act (LGA) certified chapters, the responsibilities to manage community planning are immense. The Navajo Nation Division of Community Development expects that chapters develop land-use and strategic plans, conduct community-needs assessments, prepare infrastructure capital-improvement plans, prepare proposals for various funding sources, and complete Pre-Procurement Activities (PPAs) (2016). Moreover, to complete the infrastructure capital-improvement plan, chapter leadership must possess the skills to inventory existing capital, add proposed new capital, prioritize projects, and develop a six-year plan (Navajo Nation Division of Community Development 2016). The development of a six-year plan requires planning education to familiarize community members with the tools and process of planning. The lack of internal know-how is typically what prompts the hiring of outside experts. With improved internal capacity for planning, this scenario may be dramatically changed in the future.

Although only 43 of the 110 chapters are LGA certified, there remains ample opportunity for those chapters who choose LGA certification to secure it. For would-be certified chapters that struggle to meet minimum required skills for the five management system policies and procedures, the Navajo Nation offers support through the administrative service centers, previously established as local governance support centers (Navajo Nation Division of Community Development 2016). Several of the Navajo planners previously or currently work with the service center or with other departments within Navajo administration that work on community development.

WE HAVE ALWAYS BEEN PLANNERS

The Diné people have always been planners. Effective planning meant survival. Navajo leaders led the people and maximized opportunities for survival by strategically planning war parties, peace negotiations, land use, and access to resources.

Modern planning has largely been the purview of the federal government and Navajo Nation administration. Since the 1868 establishment of the Navajo reservation, the BIA has been largely responsible for the design, implementation, and maintenance of reservation infrastructure that includes roads, housing, utilities, and facilities.

Upon passage of the 1975 Indian Self-Determination and Education Assistance Act (PL 93-638) the Navajo Nation has increasingly used 638 funding opportunities to assert Navajo control over project selection and prioritization, input on design and userability, and responsibility for contractual agreements for development. One example of this is the Tsehootsooi medical center in Fort Defiance. The $18 million, 43,000-square-foot facility is largely funded by 638 monies (Johns 2016). In the spirit of Diné self-determination, the Navajo Nation acts as partner on the project instead of mere beneficiary of a federally funded initiative. Navajo architect Cliff Johns incorporates elements into the design of the hospital that hold cultural and historical significance for the Navajo people who will use the facility. In the design process Johns consulted with Navajo traditional leaders to create a patient-based facility where healing benefits mind, body, and spirit. There is space available for traditional ceremonies. The facility will reflect a unification of traditional and modern concepts (2016). The hope is that Navajo patients and doctors will recognize their cultural identity in the facility, feel a sense of ownership in the space and use it as a comfortable and powerful place for healing. Making the hospital recognizably Navajo is indeed a progressive assertion of sovereignty within the built environment and an innovative alternative to the Indian Health Service (IHS) hospitals that are ubiquitous across Indian Country.

Johns lauds 638 as the catalyst for Indigenizing the Navajo medical facility; the Navajo footprint is unmistakable on this project funded by the federal government. However, the open door for empowered development is only half the battle for Indian nations. The other half is the ability to step up to plan, build and maintain for future generations. With an expanded role and responsibility in community development, especially in the realm of infrastructure improvement and maintenance, never before has there been an urgency and need for useful planning tools and processes. If those tools and processes can also be culturally grounded and community driven, the future may well hold a more positive and emboldened experience for Indian communities.

Optimism surrounds the prospect that the Navajo planners of 2015 will secure proper training expeditiously and embark on work that will facilitate positive growth on the local levels on the Navajo Nation. It is an opportunity to build safe and prosperous communities on the nation, from the ground up. It is a chance for chapters such as Lupton, Leupp, Teesto, Naschitti, and Shonto to be in the driver's seat of their homegrown community development plan, rather than having that plan dictated by Window Rock. Time will tell, and there are sure to be bumps in the road linked to funding, politics, and attrition among planning professionals, but with strong support from the citizenry and Navajo government, community-based planning may hold the key for practical and effective sovereignty on the Navajo Nation.

CREATIVITY AND VISION

NAVAJO SOVEREIGNTY THROUGH THE LENS OF CREATIVITY, IMAGINATION, AND VISION

COLLEEN GORMAN

INTRODUCTION

Y A'AT'ÉÉH (GREETINGS)! I was asked to write about Navajo sovereignty and its challenges in the future through the lens of creativity, imagination, and vision. We each have an idea of what sovereignty, power, and autonomy mean for Diné. What I share with you is my background, knowledge, and understanding of this space, our place in the world and universe. There is power in thought, intention, breath, and spirit, and my intention is to inspire reflection, ideas, and action. My vision is to remind people that we create our own sacred space to exist in.

The foundation of who I am comes from my name, clan, and family. Colleen Gorman, dashijiní. Hazbaa' yinishyé (my name is Escapes the Enemy; like a bird that flies up above a rock). Naaneesht'ézhí Táchii'nii nishłį (I am Red Running into the Charcoal Streaked Water). Bįįh Bi Toodnii Tódích'íinii báshíshchíín (I am born for Deer Springs Bitter Water). Kínłíchíí'nii dashicheii (Red House is my maternal grandfather's clan), 'áádóó Dibé Łízhin dashinálí (and Black Sheep are my paternal grandparents). Faye and Tyrone Gorman are my parents. Canyon de Chelly, Canyon del Muerto, the Little White House Canyon, and Bear Springs are in my memory and heart. I will share some names and places because they have influenced my life as a Diné.

Shi másání (Grandma Alice Clah) is 103. She is from Díwózhii Bi' Tódí (Greasewood Springs, aka Lower Greasewood). One of our ancestors was Naaneesht'ézhí (Zuni), one of two sisters. When family returned to Zuni due to war, she remained with Diné relatives, and became Táchii'nii when she had her *Kinaaldá* (Puberty Ceremony). Hastiin Shash Bí Toodí (Mr. Bear Springs) was Grandma Alice's father. He was *hataathli* (a singer/medicine man) from Shash Bí Toodí (Bear Springs) in the Toyei/Steamboat area. Haskay Yah Néyáh (He Went to War and Came Back Again), Harrison Begay was Grandma Alice's brother. He taught me how to draw and paint. I grew up knowing Slim Clah as my *cheii* (maternal grandfather), although he wasn't, and my actual cheii died long ago. Grandma Alice's sister Mary Brown, an herbalist, raised my mom. Half of my life came from my mother, Faye Gorman's, sphere of life and influence, and it was full; a lifetime of Blessingways, *Yeibichei's* (Nightways), *Ndaa'* (Enemy Way), fire dance, and late-night prayers. In addition to traditional ways, we followed Native American Church and Catholic Church ways.

Chinle calls to me like daily *tádídíín* (corn pollen) prayers left by parents in the footprints of their beloved children last seen in the cornfield. Canyon de Chelly and Canyon del Muerto junction is where my dad's family came together. We call the land on the del Muerto side of junction Asdzáá' Łághai (Mrs. White) for the name of our relative who hid from Kit Carson and remained behind. She gathered lost animals and replanted. Family came back to her. This is why we have land in both canyons near the junction. Gorman Ranch life revolved around the Dave Gorman Memorial Rodeo Club and my dad's immediate and extended family. This is where I grew up. *Shinálí ndéé* (my paternal grandparents) were Dave and Jessie Gorman. My great-grandmother nálí was Ch'idíneezbaa' (Warrior/Prepared for War That Didn't Happen), Mary Brown. She was a *Ndilniihii* (Hand Trembler) and could speak English, but never deigned to; everyone had to talk to her in Navajo. Until somewhere between the ages of 107 to 113, her presence centered our family. Mary's siblings were Grey Eyes, Benjamin Stuart, Benedict Stuart, John Long, Navajo Johnnie, Grace McRae, and another sister (name unknown, whose sons are known as the Bennet brothers in the Kaibeto, Cow Springs, area). Jake Brown was her husband. Her daughters were Jessie Gorman and Lucy Jones. K'é Hazbaa' (A Warrior/Lady with Greetings) was Mary's mother. K'é Hazbaa' was a child of Hwéeldi ("The Place of No Hope" (aka Bosque Redondo and Fort Sumner). K'é Hazbaa's father was a soldier. She walked back from Hwéeldi when she was four. K'é Hazbaa' died pregnant, crushed by a crowd when food rations were being issued at Fort Defiance. Mary Brown and the love of family kept us together. Grey Eyes traveled often to maintain family relationships and bring news back to her. When she passed away, there were five living generations from her. Our family grew up helping Grandma Brown herd sheep, pick fruit from the orchard, and climb Anasazi trails to enter and exit the canyons.

Today I live in Albuquerque with Carlos Barros and our children—Táchii'nii Gorman, Phillip Bailey, and Salvador Barros. I am a teacher, an artist, a performance poet and singer, and a media maker. I consider myself a creator because I am a mother. Creating in many forms is how I become a vessel for Creator. I co-created the first statewide and state-authorized charter school in New Mexico, the Media Arts Collaborative Charter School (MACCS). Teaching Indigenous peoples, youth, and unheard voices how to tell their own stories using media is a lifelong endeavor. I cofounded the Indigenous Research Center (IRC) to be a resource for sacred calendars and geometry. Creator comes in many forms. Sacred forms reveal themselves through these tools. Spiderwoman Web Productions is a personal venture.

REFLECTIONS ON NAVAJO SOVEREIGNTY

What I see for Diné in the future are battles on multiple levels. Brandon Benalli, partner to my childhood friend Radmilla Cody, provided an apt description of two viewpoints on Navajo sovereignty: "Some people see sovereignty as the treaty of 1864, where we are wards of the federal government, and there are others who view sovereignty as complete autonomy, where we are free to be Diné on our own terms" (February 2014). I foresee struggles for existence that will take place within the gray areas of the spectrum described by Benalli; the spectrum from sovereign dependent Navajo Nation to sovereign independent Diné.

For the purposes of this discussion, the sovereign dependent Navajo Nation is the tribal government, and a sovereign independent Diné is the individual who is a child or a descendant of those indigenous to Dinétah before European colonization and who referred to themselves as Diné (The People) whether or not they have been raised in modern times according to Diné traditions due to circumstances of colonization, and whether or not a Certificate of Indian Blood has been issued to them. The reference to a child of Diné in this definition is deliberate because this includes children who have been adopted as family and raised by Diné. Clan expresses my origins and lineage. Diné have always adopted and intermarried with people of other cultures. My descendants will be Diné. The government created the CIB to breed of us out of existence on paper for reasons of colonialism.

During World War II, the Double V meant two victories for African Americans (and other people of color) who fought in the war: victory over racism and discrimination at home, and victory over enemies abroad—a Double Victory. For Diné, I see victory at home over "isms" such as internalized "isms" of racism, sexism, and colonialism, which lead to self-oppression, and perpetuate cycles of anger, fear, shame, and guilt and violence against ourselves.[1] As Diné, we are first and foremost children of Mother Earth. Our brothers and sisters are still the plants and animals of our mother. Diné must consider global issues as individual, sovereign, independent Diné and as a collective, sovereign, dependent Nation. We must analyze our strengths, weaknesses, opportunities, and threats, taking into special consideration our first mother, Nihimá Náhásdzáán (Mother Earth).

As individuals and as a nation, the battles we have to face are also spiritual battles, and so we must ask ourselves the following questions: What path have we chosen for ourselves? Where do we center ourselves? Is our path to create light or to spread negativity? How do we make ourselves sacred, or create a sacred space around us? Are Holy People a part of our daily lives in thought and in prayer? Do we bring them forth to life with our breath? What is our *Nitsáhákees* (thought/intention), when we approach our *Nahat'á* (planning and preparation) for *Iiná* (life)? *Siihasin* (reflection) should also be a daily habit in this.

We will continue to battle racism, hatred, ignorance, greed, fear, and white privilege that have motivated institutional forms of disenfranchisement. Corporations with no heart or soul have their ideas about how we should move forward as a sovereign nation. Usually this means giving up land and resources. Benalli discussed the idea that we must always return to and have full control of the land, "otherwise we will have sovereignty on paper, but we won't really have it. Some consider [that] sovereignty is for us to have full and complete control of our land back." Politicians and corporations have their ideas, therefore transparency and accountability from the Navajo Nation government is crucial.

It is important for us to return to the land and to sacred places, wherever we are, to recenter. We have generational traumas to heal from. Circumstances and economics have led to many of us living outside Dinetah, our traditional homelands within the sacred mountains. It's important to create a sacred space for ourselves as a matter of habit, and this means Indigenizing ourselves to the land wherever we are. Tom Edison, a medicine man, said in a family prayer meeting, "Just because I stopped going to church doesn't mean I stopped having faith. I can pray from my home. I have that personal relationship with God, Creator, the Holy People."

When I was little, my mother told me that if you know the stars, you can always find your way home. Since then, orienting myself with the stars was one way for me to stay centered. In 2001, I learned a new, yet ancient way of orienting myself to the stars—through sacred calendars that map planets and the stars to large swaths of time. I also learned how to use symmetry as a tool to bring forth balance and life, and the ancient visual language of sacred geometry. In our creation story, we traveled through Mother Earth and five worlds' time. The Twins led us to Spiderwoman, to faith in the form of a baby eagle plume, and to Mountain Way songs that bring us back home. Morning Star/ Big Reed (Be'egoch'idi) led us through a hole in the sky at different times and to different worlds. According to "Indian time," the beginning and end cycle like a clock. In the book *Black Elk Speaks: Being the Life Story of a Holy Man of the Oglala Sioux*, Black Elk's words that everything tries to be round appears to holds true when looking at patterns of time and space. It has set a foundation for one of my personal life endeavors to teach others this circular understanding of the universe.

FRONTLINES IN THE FIGHT FOR SOVEREIGNTY

MEDIA AND ART AS A MEDIUM FOR EXPRESSING SOVEREIGNTY

As Indigenous people, we have the right to communicate. We have the right to access the tools necessary to communicate our ideas and values to the world through our art and media. That right is part of our sovereignty. Article 16 of the Declaration of the Rights of Indigenous People states:

> Indigenous peoples have the right to their own media in their own languages. They also have equal access to non-indigenous media. Government owned media must reflect indigenous cultures.[2]

Community access to media tools and centers should be part of a democratic process to arrive at community solutions. Media can and should be used as forums to explore themes, problems, and outcomes, as well as ensure transparency.

Freedom of expression is essential to Diné sovereignty, and there should be opportunities for our youth to learn to create media and content to be involved and participate. Grassroots sovereignty for Diné could take place through the combination of media and initiatives like "Art Attacks." As a collective, our nation needs to have an art explosion to use mediums to identify and address issues plaguing our communities such as drug abuse, alcohol addiction, domestic violence, child neglect, abuse, etc. In 1997, Klee Benally (an activist and musician) and I envisioned an Indigenous Action Media (IAM) as a form of grassroots activism to counter information poverty. Community media can and should be used for community development. I seek ways to create opportunities for youth to learn how to create media. As an employee of a nonprofit community media center, Quote Unquote, Inc. (QUQ), I co-founded a media-arts school and helped launch its second TV channel. As board president for QUQ, I'm helping to launch a low-power FM radio station.

As a media producer and activist, I seek to support democracy and the First Amendment. A big question that I have is: where in Indian country do we have a television or radio station that provides the opportunities and means for responsible expression of political, cultural, spiritual, and individual beliefs through free speech? On the reservation, KTNN includes Native and non-Native music, and covers local sports, news, and cultural storytelling in Navajo and English. A newer radio station in Gallup caters to younger Navajos because it interweaves hip-hop, pop, Navajo, and Native music with Navajo-language advertising. However, the big question still remains: where in Indian country today is there a true inclusion of opinions that brings a wide range of perspectives not watered-down by fear? More specifically, where is there Navajo or Native media that does not just spout mainstream news and views in the Navajo language? I'm talking about diverse *forums* for the expression of freedom of speech by and for our people. Koahnic Broadcast supports Indigenous views through productions such as *National Native News*. Yet live show protocols appear to ensure "tourist-friendly" opinions and questions when addressing critical issues. If we are going to exercise our sovereignty, we are not going to ask permission about what to say, how to say it, or go about censoring ourselves so we don't really say what is on our minds. Certainly, some rules are necessary in order to moderate forums to ensure compliance with FCC broadcast rules. However, what we need, and what I feel like we do not really have yet, is the use of media for community dialogue through forums as well as various formats for Diné free speech. Social media might provide some of this, but even Facebook has censored live streams from Dakota Access Pipeline protestors.

Indigenous people have the right to information about how our lives are being decided upon. Various barriers prevent us from gaining access to tools to create and distribute mass media. Media has an important role because it can ensure accountability. Ann-erika White Bird, a freelance journalist, was falsely accused of being ISIS by the Rosebud Sioux Tribal Treasurer after she sought information and asked for accountability. She's been cleared by tribal police and has the document posted on the "Lakota Voice" news blog. The treatment that she was given due to her work as a journalist seeking accurate public information and accountability brings to light the shenanigans politicians go through to hide actions that may be less than ethical.

Cultural preservation is also tied to our sovereignty. Preserving culture can take place through grassroots media efforts. A big question is: can we get to our elders in time, before it is too late to preserve their knowledge? My uncle Francis Begay, a medicine man from the Steamboat area, recently passed away. So did my great-aunt Mary Brown, living in Albuquerque, at the age of 103. We don't need fancy cameras or Hollywood producers to filter how we document our stories. A growing number of us have smartphones and tablets, and can use these to record audio and video. After communicating with my relatives about the history shared at the beginning of this chapter, I plan to record family history through interviews using multimedia. These are tools that we should already be using to preserve our stories and songs so that we, our children, and future generations can better understand our history and culture.

OTHER EXTERNAL CHALLENGES AND THEIR IMPACT

Major external challenges to Navajo Nation sovereignty will result from global population growth and climate change. It is estimated that Earth, in its current state, can support a maximum of ten billion people where food is concerned.[3] Currently the global population has reached seven billion and is increasing at an exponential rate. When rats increase their population in a closed environment, resources become scarce, and conflict increases. Additionally, according to *National Geographic*, a megadrought is slated to hit the Southwest and the Great Plains. As a result of global population growth, climate change, and decreasing resources and access to water, I foresee the country and the world polarizing and radicalizing.

EXTERNAL CHALLENGES SURROUNDING WATER:
TÓ 'ÉÍ 'IINÁ 'ÁTÉ (WATER IS LIFE)

In 2001, Dr. Gary A. Smith at the University of New Mexico taught a course entitled "Albuquerque's Water Future." In this course, I learned that the Rio Grande Water and the Colorado River Compact assumed a certain amount of annual rainfall and river flow.[4] According to studies of tree rings, annual precipitation was at its highest in a thousand-year cycle when Anglos arrived in the Southwest. Thus, the allocation of water in these compacts is based on precipitation rates at its highest in a thousand years. Population growth as far back as 1884 (twenty years before the 1904 National Irrigation Congress) resulted in decreasing water supplies. During this time, Rio Grande water supplies and allocation in southern New Mexico and around El Paso and Juarez also became critical.

CLIMATE CHANGE

Climate change is an issue no one can avoid. During the water class, I learned that due to the thousand-year natural cycle of rainfall, annual precipitation is decreasing in the Southwest. Additionally, according to an article published by *National Geographic* in February 2015, the worst "megadrought" (thirty-five years or longer) is expected to occur within the next seventy-five years in the Southwest and central Great Plains, and chances of this drought occurring for the rest of the world are above 80 percent.[5] A major factor besides the natural cycle of precipitation is greenhouse gas emissions. Reducing emissions to a "middle of the road" target might lower chances for the Great Plains from 80 percent to 60 or 70 percent, yet will have no effect on the megadrought to occur in the Southwest.

Large fossil-fuel industries influence media and politicians to diminish and discredit independent findings made by hundreds of climate scientists on global warming. These politicians take measures to prevent and limit voices speaking out on this issue. Florida's republican governor, Rick Scott, went so far as to ban the use of the phrase *climate change* when he took office in 2011.[6] We are also witnesses to actions taken by government agencies—for example, the EPA's toxic spill in the Animas River. Dave Taylor predicted the spill in an op-ed published a week prior to the spill.[7] Now they have a Superfund site.

During the Great Depression, when resources were scarce, those who lost out the most were minorities. As water becomes polluted due to practices like fracking and pesticide use, and clean, fresh water becomes scarce due to drought, challenges to our sovereignty will come from corporations and politicians focused on gaining access to our resources and water rights. Politicians often seek to limit Indigenous voices and power due to racism, colonialism, and ignorance, and because we speak up for Mother Earth. Imperialistic foundations of corporate charters since colonial days are institutionalized and reinforce their power. Economic and business models taught in schools worldwide also assume unlimited resources.

Colonialism by another name, globalism, is going strong. At the beginning of 2015, Arizona senator John McCain and his cronies managed to open up White Mountain Apache Indian lands for mining by an Australian copper company.[8] Measures such as the Trans-Pacific Partnership (TPP) support extraction of raw materials from Mother Earth for economic purposes, at the expense of human health, safety, and the environment. With a right-wing Congress in power, a lame-duck president on his way out, and a Supreme Court ruling that legitimizes unlimited funding to Super PACs (Political Action Committees) by individual billionaires and corporations to support elections, the principles of democracy in the U.S. are being undermined.[9]

Navajo sovereignty, Indigenous sovereignty, and humanity's rights are going to get their cans kicked to the side of the road unless we get off our rear ends, and stand up for what we are here for. As Diné, as Indigenous people, we need to recognize our role in reminding the world about the importance of balance, and the importance of our brothers and sisters—the plants, animals, water, mountains, and even other planets. We are going to have to fight Manifest Destiny, imperialism, colonialism, racism, ignorance, hatred, greed, and massive superiority complexes on global and interplanetary scales. This reemphasizes why Diné and Indigenous peoples worldwide need to own and create their own media. We can and should speak up for Mother Earth. We are the voices of the unheard speaking out against oppression.

REFLECTION ON SOVEREIGNTY THROUGH TRADITIONAL KNOWLEDGE

Years ago I found Diné Beehaz'áanii in a book on Navajo government, and I wrote it down in a poetry journal so that I could read it, hear it, and feel the words in my mouth, heart, and thoughts. I'd almost forgotten these words because like so many others, I've been busy just trying to survive day to day as an urban Indian.

Diyin Dine'é sin dóó tsodizin bee nahasdzáán dóó yádiłhił nitsáhákees yił hadeidiilaa	The Holy People ordained through songs and prayers that Earth and Universe embody thinking
Tó doo dził diyinii nahat'á yił hadeidiilaa	Water and sacred mountains embody planning
Niłch'i dóó nanse'ałtaas'éí iiná yił hadeidiilaa	Air and variegated vegetation embody life
Kǫ' adinídíín dóó ntł'iz náá dahaniihjį' siihasin yił hadeidilaa	Fire, light, and offering sites of variegated sacred stones embody wisdom
Nitsáhákees 'éí nahat'á bitsi silá	Thinking is the foundation of planning
Díí ts'idá 'aląąji' nihi beehaz'áanii bitsi siléí nihá' ályaa	These are the fundamental tenets established
Iiná 'éí siihasin bitsi silá	Life is the foundation of wisdom
Hanihi' diilyaadi díí nihiihdaahya' dóó bee hadíniit'é	Upon our creation these were instituted within us and we embody them.
Binahjį' nihéého' dílzinígíí 'éí	Accordingly we are identified by
Nihízhi'	Our Diné name
Ádóone'é niidlíinii	Our clan
Nihiinéí	Our language
Nihee ó'ool'įįł	Our lifeway
Nihi chaha'oh	Our shadow
Nihi kék'ehashchíín	Our footprints
Díí bik'ehgo Diyin Nohokáá' Diné nihi' doo'niid	Therefore we were called the Holy Earth Surface People
Kodóó dah 'adíniisą' dóó dah 'adiidééł	From here growth began and the journey proceeds.
Áko díishjįįgi 'éí nitsáhákees nahat'á, 'iiná, saad, oodlą' beehaz'áanii nihita hólǫ́	So different thinking planning, lifeways, languages, beliefs, and laws appear among us

Ákondi Diyin Dine'é Diné bi
beehaz'áanii bitsi siláí nihá
haidiilaaígíí doo łah 'ánáá'níił da

Áko 'iiná bee hanihi'diilyaa dóó nihiih
yilyáhígíí bee hod'áágóó Nohokáá'
Diné daniidlį

But the fundamental laws placed by
the Holy People remain unchanged

Hence as we were created and with
living soul we remain Diné forever

Brandon Benalli said, "Diné Beehazáanii teaches us to be resilient . . . it's
not rigid. It's all about growing. It's not about following a strict set of rules. It's
about learning, moving forward. Having a balance." Benalli acknowledged the
fear of loss of culture through the death of our elders with the following thought:
"It's true that a lot of people are afraid of losing songs and language. Language
is essential to Diné sovereignty and identity. That doesn't mean we can't continue on in our own terms. It's essential to that process of cultural sovereignty."

CONTROL OVER AND DEVELOPING
OUR CULTURAL HERITAGE

Songs and prayers are a core part of our culture. These tools create a sacred
space for one to recenter, strengthen, and protect. They help one to cope during
hard times and are a way to celebrate blessings. I've been lucky to have learned
some of these songs and prayers. The deliberate intention and initiative to
seek these out and make the effort to learn, understand, and carry them out in
one's own time and space brings many blessings and a deeper understanding
and knowledge of self and culture. There are many levels of understanding in
these aspects of our culture. It is important to learn our songs and prayers using
the different means and tools available to us. I am lucky to have been allowed
to record some of these songs and prayers because they came from my great-
grandpa Hastiin Shash Bítoodí.

Radmilla Cody, who sings many beautiful songs, made a point that "beyond
preservation is revitalization." I interpret the idea that new songs and prayers
also have to be created. As Indigenous people, we do have the right to develop
our culture: "Indigenous peoples have the right to control and develop their
cultural heritage, traditional knowledge and sciences and technologies, including seeds, medicines, knowledge of flora and fauna, oral traditions, designs, art
and performances. Governments shall take measures to protect these rights."[10]

Songs and prayers that are old now were once new. Our breath makes the language move, alive, and with the life that we have, we should create new songs and prayers.

A new prayer song came to me and helped me when I was starting the school for media arts. That was a hard journey. The work was time-consuming, thankless, and a source of much stress personally and professionally. In singing this prayer song, and in remembering and invoking the names of the Holy People, it gave protection and blessing to the work that I was doing.

"Nahadzáán Shimá (Mother Earth), Yádiłhił Shitáá (Father Sky), Háyoołkááł Shichei (Grandpa Dawn), Chahołhééł Másání (Grandmother Darkness), Dził Asdzą́ą́ (Mountain Woman), Tó Asdzą́ą́ (Water Woman), Yoołghai Adzą́ą́ (White Shell Woman), Adzą́ą́ Nadleehé (Changing Woman), Haashch'éé Yáálti'i (Male Talking God), Hashch'éhowaan (Female Talking God), Jóhónaa'ei (Sun), Nihotsoi (The Evening Yellow Light On Top of the Earth), Nadą́ą́' Áłghai (White Corn), Nadąą' Łitsoi (Yellow Corn), Tádídíín Ashkii (Corn Pollen Boy), Ánłt'ánii At'ééd (Corn Beetle Girl), Sa'ąh Naagháí Bik'eh Hózhǫ́ (Corn Pollen Path). *Nihił hónlóodoo dóó nihaa 'áholyą dooleeł* (Walk with us and help us). *Nihá'áłchíní ba 'áhoolyą dooleeł* (Take care of our children). I sing to you a prayer for the children to learn a circular understanding of the universe. You see in dreams, releasing gravity allows one to become a multidimensional being. Using symmetry, from Chaos comes balance and life, and a visual language of Sacred Geometry. I sing to you a prayer for the children to learn a circular understanding of the universe in motion. I sing to you a prayer for the children to learn a circular understanding of the universe and all creation." *Nihá 'áłchíní hozhǫ́ nohokáá danohséł dooleeł* (Our children will grow up on this earth in a good way). *Nihitsídjį́' hozhǫ́ dooleeł, nihikéé'dę́ę́ hozhǫ́ dooleeł, nihikáhdę́ę́ hozhǫ́ dooleeł, nihiyáági hozhǫ́ dooleeł, nihizahdę́ę́' hozhǫ́ dooleeł, t'aa'áłtsxo hozhǫ́ dooleeł. Hozhǫ́ nahasdlį́į', Hozhǫ́ nahasdlį́į', Hozhǫ́ nahasdlį́į', Hozhǫ́ nahasdlį́į' dooleeł* (With beauty before us, behind us, above us, below us, from our mouth/words and all around, it will be beautiful).

My Navajo isn't perfect, and I may need to reconjugate verbs, but this prayer song helped to give me purpose. It created a sacred space for me to work by invoking the names of the Diné Holy People. It also reminded me at every step whom I was doing this for—my children and the next generations. It is a Diné worldview.

FROM SACRED SONGS TO SACRED GEOMETRY

As Diné, I've learned that Creator is in all things, and this makes our journey okay, the right one to be on, whatever it is that we are doing because all our mistakes, failures, and successes are part of life's path to find balance. The song I shared about a circular understanding of the universe in motion originally came to me while I working on a project to open people's eyes to a sacred understanding of time, space, and the universe. That project, "Celestial Beings in Indigenous Skies," took two years to complete, and the end product was a large-scale full-dome animation for the New Mexico Museum of Natural History's Lodestar Planetarium. To see the universe in balance is Diné. The sacred geometry techniques used were learned from a fellow Athabaskan, Roger Cultee, of the Quinault Nation.[11] "Celestial Beings in Indigenous Skies" presents the universe perfectly balanced through sacred geometry. The purpose was a study of sacred geometry in motion and to help others to see celestial bodies in an entirely different light.

Sacred geometry is an ancient art form. "Celestial Beings in Indigenous Skies" animates the planets to tell their story using the language of math and symmetry. The large-scale full-dome format and the online video animation are new mediums for the application of sacred geometry. As "Indigenous beings" of the universe, the planets and stars tell their stories and are revealed through movement. One can interact with them three-dimensionally using a clear crystal sphere. This tool allows one to see the moving images in three dimensions and "crystal clear." A tablet or iPad works great for viewing sacred geometry through a crystal sphere because the images can be seen from different points of views and the images are a fairly good size. Time brings the work into the fourth dimension.

This approach to viewing the universe in a balanced and animated manner is completely different from mainstream society's perception of planetary bodies and the universe. Western culture views planetary bodies as objects, things to mine for wealth, a resource to exploit. That view extends Manifest Destiny on an interplanetary scale. After viewing this animated work, some people may come up with excuses to fear and discredit using sacred geometry to view the animated spirit of planets as well as people and places. As Indigenous people, we have the right to create our own art and interpretations. Sacred geometry is ancient, and it is a tool that allows the spirit of a rock, a tree, a mountain, or a planet to reveal itself. The shape and clarity of a crystal sphere brings the revealed spirit into three dimensions. Considering that my great-grandmother Mary Brown was a Hand Trembler, and that *Dest'įį* (Crystal/Star-Gazers) are part of our Diné culture, I feel that the use of crystals to view sacred geometry extends gifts from the past with those who are here now.

FROM SACRED GEOMETRY TO SACRED CALENDARS

Ancient calendars and stars relate to sacred geometry and Diné sovereignty because they are tied to Spiderwoman (the First and Perfect Weaver of Time), the Diné Twins, and Big Reed (brought Diné into this world). The practical aspect of the 260-day sacred calendar and the year-count calendars is that they relate to seasons, to planning human conception and birth, and to mapping time in earth year cycles, planetary year cycles, and stars' (including our sun's) cycles, and transit around the Milky Way. The sacred calendars present a structure of time that resembles the structure of DNA, if you look at it using sacred geometry and view it in three dimensions. The calendars relate to our "prehistory," our future, and our survival in the past, present, and future. The patterns of time can be visually portrayed, and one can literally see the patterns. The sacred calendars reveal the cyclical, spiral, double helix, and other patterns of time that range from small to large swaths of time. These patterns impact us in the present world and the next world.

STAYING CENTERED WHEN IT COMES TO SACRED KNOWLEDGE

Right before I became aware of sacred calendars and sacred geometry, I was in a deep depression. I was literally struck by lightning while singing a prayer song to lift my spirits. I considered that particular event to be a proverbial kick in the butt by Universe to help me get over the pity party I was having. I recommitted myself to the Creator and what path arose from that. After getting struck, I eventually had a "doing" (the Lighting Way ceremony) to become grounded again. Learning about sacred calendars and keeping time actually interfered with staying grounded and present. I realized that I couldn't use spiritual knowledge as a form of escape. I still had to live in the present and deal with realities of life. That realization is crucial when it comes to learning about, using, and sharing sacred knowledge. I will share some basic understandings with you now so that you can understand how the calendar works, and what I foresee based on patterns of time.

SACRED CALENDARS AND PATTERNS OF TIME

For more than a decade, I've learned from and helped Roger Cultee and Tracy Greer to teach people about the sacred calendars. We established the Indigenous Research Center for this purpose. Roger has studied the calendars longer than anyone else in the group, and has made some huge leaps in understanding time. He's mathematically shown that planetary cycles in the solar system adhere to their year-count cycles in patterns that mirror Earth's year-count calendar. Their cycles proceed in a similar and orderly manner. His mathematical description of the calendars tied to the Eagle Sun Bowl[12] breaks down the solar system's movement in time and space around the sun and the Milky Way. The calendars also describe world cycles. All this information is too much to cover in a few pages, but I will attempt to provide some basics.

FUNDAMENTALS OF THE 260-DAY SACRED CALENDAR

The 260-day sacred calendar is essential to understanding how "Indian time" works. The calendar is used by many Native peoples in the Americas. It's time up north where the medicine wheels are, and it's time down south in Mexico, Central, and South America. After studying it for years, I've come to realize that it's also Diné time. The most practical aspect of the calendar is that if you understand it, then you know when to plant. It's the only calendar that divides that year into four equal parts. It's more accurate than the Gregorian calendar used today.

The 260-day sacred calendar can help one to gain a deeper understanding of Venus as the Morning Star and Evening Star, the Pleiades, the solar year, leap days and years, medicine wheels, as well as the forgotten thirteenth Navajo month.[13] I learned from Francis Begay that our Diné thirteenth month translates into a word for tarantula. In this way, the Diné Holy Person Spiderwoman is recognized in the sacred calendar. As Weaver of Time, this makes sense.

Our emergence from the First World to the Fifth World gains new layers of meanings, as does one's understanding of the Diné Twins. Our creation stories are multidimensional.

The 260-day sacred calendar is entirely based on numbers. It's a mathematical equation based on the numbers thirteen and twenty. There are twenty day names on the calendar. Then there are thirteen cycles of these twenty days in the calendar before the end is reached. Like a clock, time repeats on the calendar. Twenty days times thirteen equals 260 days. Physically examining the calendar reveals time patterns. Some are circular, a spiral, and even the double helix pattern of chromosomes. Each day is associated with a cardinal direction. Different tribes came up with the twenty different day names in their own language. Solar years can be derived from the 260-day calendar. Deriving and mapping solar years results in a year-count calendar. The year-count calendar helps to provide a view of larger cycles of time.

THE YEAR-COUNT CALENDAR

There are larger cycles of time, and by moving through time in 365-day segments, each solar year is derived from the 260-day calendar. The name of each year on the year-count calendar is derived from the day names and numbers on the 260-day calendar. After fifty-two years are mapped out, time repeats on the year-count calendar in terms of year and day. In effect, one's birth day and year occurs once every fifty-two years.

Leap days are accounted for, and they realign the calendar to the stars. The Gregorian calendar adds one leap day every four years (.25 day/year × 4 years = 1 day). Earth's year-count calendar has thirteen leap days (.25 day/year × 52 years = 13 days). These leap days are unnamed (not named on the 260-day sacred calendar), and are added at the end of fifty-two years so that Earth's planetary cycle is realigned in time to Venus and the Pleiades.

Even larger cycles of time patterns are revealed through mapping fifty-two-year cycles. The beginning of a fifty-two-year cycle begins on the day and year called 1 Reed. During the 1 Reed year/day that takes place once every fifty-two years, Earth, Venus, and the Pleiades are in alignment. On Earth, Venus sets as the Evening Star while Pleiades rises. The Pleiades is at its highest point at midnight. Each year thereafter, this event occurs a little bit off in time, until the fifty-two-year cycle is completed. When the thirteen leap days are added to adjust the calendar, then the calendar, planets, and stars are back in alignment.

On the year and day 1 Reed Venus rises as the Morning Star. Thus the Pleiades, Morning Star, and Evening Star (or "Twins") have their place in the calendar.

INTERPRETING PATTERNS OF TIME

The sacred calendars are critical for one to understand large cycles of time through an Indigenous worldview. A page from the Codex Vaticanus (see figure 7.1), which is included in *Archaeo-Astronomy in Pre-Columbian America*, is a good "NDN meme" from hundreds, if not thousands, of years ago. It portrays fifty-two-year cycles of time as cycles of the heavens and underworld. IRC members prefer to call the cycles shown here as the Indigenous Age of Reasoning (or Heaven Cycles) and the Indigenous Dark Ages (or Hell Cycles). Cultee concluded that because "Indians think in circles," it appears to be labeled incorrectly with Roman numerals, due to the European hierarchical mind-set.

The glyphs on the page depict thirteen fifty-two-year Heaven cycles. Columbus arrived in 1492. This was the beginning of the last twenty-six years of the last Heaven Cycle/Age of Reasoning (labeled I). At this point in time and history, he found peaceful, beautiful peoples and cultures flourishing. After his arrival, Indigenous peoples began the transition in time out of the Heaven Cycle.

The glyphs on the page also depict nine fifty-two-year cycles of the underworld. Blond-haired, blue-eyed Cortez arrived in that first Hell cycle's 1 Reed year. This was the beginning of nine Hell Cycles, or Indigenous Dark Ages. His role as the dark twin, Evening Star, came into play as the powerful Aztecs mistakenly heralded him as Morning Star (Quetzalcoatl) and were swiftly conquered. During the Indigenous Dark Ages, each cycle was worse than the one before. Indigenous people of the Americas experienced hell on earth. In this age of darkness, we forgot ourselves. We fought mass genocide, but to no avail. As survivors we've ended up lost, coping with the effects of genocide.

THE BEGINNING AND END OF TIME
. . . AGAIN AND AGAIN

Indians think in circles, and time cycles like a clock. The pendulum is starting its swing back, and according to Indian time, we are moving back into the Heaven Cycle, the Indigenous Age of Reasoning. According to patterns of time, a transition will occur over the next twenty-six years. On Earth's

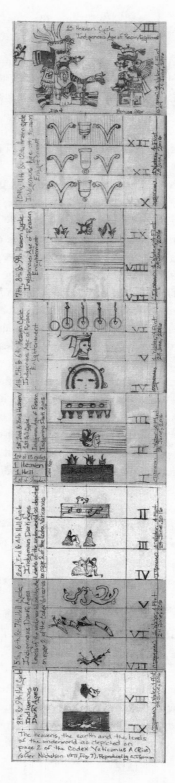

FIGURE 7.1. The heavens, Earth, and the levels of the underworld as depicted on the Codex Vaticanus A (Rios). Reproduced by C. T. Gorman.

year-count calendar, the beginning of the last fifty-two-year cycle started in 1986. The year 2012 correlated with the year 1492 on the year-count calendar. We are now progressing through the last twenty-six years of a cycle that is transitioning us out of the age that began when the Dark Twin Cortez arrived. The next 1 Reed Heaven Cycle starts in 2038, after thirteen leap days have passed and the Pleiades, Earth, and Venus realign in space and time.

A DINÉ INTERPRETATION OF TIME

The connection of the sacred calendar to Navajo culture wasn't clear to me until I read about Be'egoch'idi (Big Reed) in our Emergence story. I read about him during my dad's wake in November 2012, when family stayed up all night, the fourth night after burying him. Reading out loud from the Navajo culture publication sold at gas stations on the reservation, I read that Be'egoch'idi was blond-haired and blue-eyed, and that he brought us up from previous worlds into the succeeding one. We came into this fifth "Glittering World" through a reed, the "Big Reed." His number and name is 1 Reed.

The calendar shows on many levels that Creator is everywhere and within us. We can see this through sacred geometry and through sacred time. In our oral stories, it is said that when we reunite with other Diné people, this world (cycle) will end. I believe that time is coming. We and our children are like Be'egoch'idi. Our role as Diné, as Indigenous people, is to help bring everyone into the next world. We have to teach our children to save seeds, to plant, to harvest, to store water, and seek balance. Like the Diné Twins, Spiderwoman, and Holy People, we will fight the new monsters that have been created. We can do so with faith in *Hózhǫ́* that we keep close to our heart with a baby plume feather as Spiderwoman directed the Twins to do when they sought out their father, the Sun, for help and weapons to kill the monsters that were killing Diné. If our children are challenging to raise, that is a good thing. They will need to be strong to fight and challenge a system and paradigm that destroys, rather than creates and exists in balance.

CONCLUDING THOUGHTS

Exercising our Diné sovereignty in the future needs to be made on our own terms. In exercising sovereignty, art and expression through media is important for addressing politics and colonization's impact. Community access to media tools and centers should be part of a democratic process to arrive at community solutions. Since culture revolves around language, learning songs and ceremonies is essential. Creating new songs is important. Our language is flexible, and so is our culture. Most importantly, recentering ourselves and "re-Indigenizing ourselves to our land" wherever we are is critical. Everything ties us to Mother Earth.

Looking to the past, present, and future, to Mother Earth, the planets, and the stars, I believe that in the next few decades, battles are going to be waged on many levels. I believe that many will re-Indigenize themselves as children of Mother Earth. Those in power will fight the change. Our sovereignty will be put to the test, as will our understanding of who we are as Diné. As Diné, our role has been the same since the beginning of time. During a Sihasin performance, Clayson Benalli stated: "We must recognize that we are brothers and sisters on this world. Our traditional teachings share with us . . . everything has four sacred colors . . . every plant . . . animal . . . honors, it recognizes the four sacred directions . . . before colonization, before America, Turtle Island, this land . . . the place that we were given as people was to care-take, to protect it, to preserve it, to collect and gather medicines . . . the balance that we held as people was very important. And now we see those imbalances, we see walls, and fences, poverty, things that are dividing. Division. Competition. Those are alien concepts to us. . . . These people from the top of Alaska and Canada all the way down to Chile, these are First Nations Indigenous Native Americans. These are our brothers and sisters as well as . . . all of us, this entire world, we are all brothers and sisters."[14] Sacred geometry and sacred calendars are tools that can help us understand out place in this world and the next. Our role as Diné is to remind the world of Hózhǫ and balance in the universe.

NOTES

1. I write a line in a poem that states that the only "ism" that isn't negative is a prism, and that's because it reflects light. I have found additional "isms" that are positive but will leave that for the reader's reflection.
2. http://www.un.org/esa/socdev/unpfii/documents/DRIPS_en.pdf.
3. Natalie Wolchover, "How Many People Can the Earth Support?" *Live Science*, October 11, 2011.

4. Ibid.

5. Brian Clark Howard, "Worst Drought in 1,000 Years Predicted for American West," *National Geographic*, February 12, 2015.

6. Tristram Korten, "In Florida, Officials Ban Term Climate Change,'" *Miami Herald*, March 8, 2015.

7. Michael Patrick Leahy, "Geologist Predicted EPA Project That Caused Toxic Spill Would Fail 'Within 7 to 120 Days,'" *Breitbart News Network*, August 13, 2015.

8. http://www.diversityinc.com/news/stealing-indian-land-copper-mine/.

9. Adam Liptak, "Supreme Court Strikes Down Overall Political Donation Gap," *New York Times*, April 2, 2014.

10. Article 31 of the Declaration of the Rights of Indigenous Peoples on Cultural and Intellectual Property.

11. Quinaults are an Athabaskan Northwest Coastal tribe.

12. Also known as the Aztec Calendar Stone.

13. I learned that bit of information from my uncle Francis Begay during the reception at my Grandpa Harrison Begay's funeral in the fall of 2012.

14. Siihasin performance at the South Broadway Cultural Center in Albuquerque, New Mexico, March 17, 2015.

DINÉ SOVEREIGN ACTION

Rejecting Colonial Sovereignty and
Invoking Diné Peacemaking

LARRY W. EMERSON

OVERVIEW

N EW PERSPECTIVES ON Diné sovereignty are much needed because Diné scholars and activists are actively reclaiming, restoring, and reframing Diné identity, culture, language, history, and self-governance with many writers incorporating theories regarding decolonization, healing, transformation, and mobilization.

It can be argued, too, that Diné activist and scholar perspectives are so old, they look new. This is because the scholars and activists draw from Diné traditional knowledge. They are evolving a precolonized sense of sovereignty while rejecting settler colonial versions of sovereignty. They are actively critiquing Western, modern, capitalist, and colonialist frameworks.

Through this kind of inquiry, new perspectives are emerging and applied to areas such as nation building, self-determination, policy and law, language revitalization, intergenerational and historic trauma and healing, schooling and education, critical theory, research and evaluation, development, views on natural resources, and activism itself. Variables like gender, class, race, democracy, social justice, and non-Western Indigenous studies are often added to the Diné traditional knowledge lens.

According to Diné leader and activist Duane "Chili" Yazzie, "the condition of our Navajo Nation is greatly troubling, we are in a state of shifting situations. There are erratic changes happening that are not positive that could have lasting detrimental impacts. Before it gets worse, we should slow down, perhaps stop and see where we are and where we are going. Looking around in this chaotic scenario; we see our relatives, those of us who call our beloved lands our home, we who are not going anywhere. And we would be remiss if we did not acknowledge that there may be external non-Diné forces interfering and helping create the chaos."

In April 2015, I interviewed two Northern Diné community-based thinkers to understand their perspectives regarding the term and concept of *sovereignty*.[1] By "community-based," I mean folks who live and work in their communities and do not necessarily work at the macro political level in Window Rock, Navajo Nation, headquarters. They spend most of their time working with families, extended families, elders, and youth at the local level. The interviews reveal two Diné-based themes that show a distinct difference to dominant society's views and practices regarding sovereignty.

The first theme is the recognition that the present form of Diné self-governance must be completely rejected and replaced by a decolonized, Diné culturally and linguistically relevant self-governance model.

The second theme is that the Diné *hozhóójí naat'á* (peacemaking) methodology offers us a distinct non-Western, Indigenous-centered way to engage and Indigenize the sovereignty concept.

Lastly, I offer a reflection on the two themes.

STORIES AND PATTERNS

In my reading of the history of the term and concept regarding sovereignty, I find a distinct pattern of interaction or story between the Indigenous and Western. Indigenous people describe a clear distinction regarding the sovereignty concept that conflicts with settler colonial views. Diné history tends to wind through a heavy context of colonial control, and in recent years (e.g., 1970s–present) moves away from such control so as to restore Diné ways of knowing and self-governance.

The term *sovereignty* has *Bilagáana* origins rooted in imperialism, conquest, control, power, and wealth, and therefore is detrimental to Indigenous ways of knowing, being, and becoming (Nálí 2015; Yazzie 2015).[2]

The term also has origins in Eurocentric notions of royalty, hierarchy, church, and state. One phase of its evolution concerns the notion of a people's sovereignty versus monarchal sovereignty. At one point, the church also claimed sovereignty as well (Alfred 2005; Barker 2005).

The term is a Bilagáana settler colonial import into the lands we know as Dinétah, that includes our six sacred mountains (Yazzie 2015). This imperialistic term, embedded and often hidden in the term, has been used to legitimize and justify the colonization of Indigenous people across North and South America—indeed, across the world (Alfred 1999). The concept is used to legitimize, marginalize, or extinguish Indigenous self-governance (Alfred 1999; Alfred 2005; Porter 2005).

The contemporary "federal-Indian" law concept is steeped in the assumption that the settler colonial sovereignty model must necessarily subordinate, rule over, marginalize, and subjugate Indigenous rights (Porter 2005). Many tribal leaders have accepted the colonialized model of sovereignty to the detriment of Indigenous philosophy, despite the fact that Eurocentric models of sovereignty directly contradict and threaten Indigenous peoples and lands (Barker 2005).

There is a serious problem with Western industrial civilization because of its self-destructive practices that have negatively contributed to global warming and climate change. Therefore, when Indigenous leaders assimilate to Western industrial civilization values and sovereignty, they place Indigenous people in serious jeopardy. This amounts to a self-destructive form of Indigenous self-colonization (Jensen 2006).

Indigenous people have the option of creating a legitimate postcolonial relationship with colonial settlers, but this involves both sides abandoning notions of European superiority, colonial authority, and industrial civilization (Barker 2005).

There is a growing collective story of Indigenous nations who have sought to incorporate sovereignty into their constitutions and unwritten laws. Indigenous nations thus redefine and restructure the relationship of a government to its people by including its customs and traditions to define those relationships (Tatum 2014).

Despite efforts by the Bureau of Indian Affairs (BIA) to define and control Navajo justice, Diné judges have relied on Diné values critical to their survival (Austin 2009).

Since the early nineteenth century, Diné have been struggling to define democracy for itself in a very complex context of federal, state, and tribal law (Wilkins 1999).

Indigenous people have recognized that to restore peace, harmony, balance, and wellness, they must recognize notions of colonial sovereignty as obstacles and obstructions (Barker 2005).

Indigenous traditional teachings and practices offer colonial settlers a peaceful way out of the notion of sovereignty as conquest, power, control, domination, and superiority. Indeed, many settler colonials are listening, too (Barker 2005).

Intrinsic to Diné language, culture, identity, history, and values are ways and solutions regarding how to view, understand, and practice the concept of sovereignty. We need not import foreign and alien concepts of sovereignty whose fundamental purpose is to invalidate who we are (Yazzie 2015).

THE WRITINGS OF DUANE "CHILI" YAZZIE: REJECT, REDEFINE, AND TRANSFORM THE BILAGÁANA CONCEPT OF SOVEREIGNTY

The following are excerpts from Duane Yazzie's writings, who offered these perspectives in regard to the Diné sovereignty question:

SOVEREIGNTY—A MOST TREASURED POSSESSION

Sovereignty is one of our most treasured possessions, it defines who we are as a Nation of People. Indigenous People have been sovereign since the time of our creation, we were gifted with it at our birth; this constitutes what is meant by "Inherent Sovereign," we already had it. Our sovereignty is not "manmade," therefore it is not subject to being blessed or ratified by any earthly power.

There is no adequate basis for comparison between our Indigenous Sovereignty and that of the states or the federal Government, because of their different origins. However, in today's political terms, our Sovereignty is at least equal to that of the states, it is certainly not inferior. Our Sovereignty is considered lesser than the Sovereignty of the US Government, only because the Native Nations were subjugated into forced submission by the might of the United States Federal Government using various means of conquest.

To be Sovereign means to have the absolute freedom to think freely, to believe and practice the ways we choose, to fend for our family and people on our own terms. Sovereignty is a matter of life and soul. It is a matter of attitude; it is what we make it. The essence of a peoples' Sovereignty is defined by the heart and will of the people. We were empowered by the Creator to have these beliefs and to be Sovereign in these ways. Indigenous Peoples of the Western Hemisphere immensely enjoyed this life of Sovereignty through the centuries, advancing civilization and democracy to unprecedented heights.

SOVEREIGNTY—IN THE BEGINNING

Seems to me in the beginning when we as five-fingered humans came into being, there were 4 original levels of Sovereignty. The foremost is the indisputably omniscient Sovereignty of the Creator and second is the Sovereignty that was blessed to the Earth Mother in her creation. Third is our individual sovereignties as children of the Holy Breath and our Earth Mother and lastly is the Sovereignty of the collective people which is a fusing, a binding together of our individual sovereignties. This collective Sovereignty forms the foundation of society and governance of a people.

SOVEREIGNTY—WESTERN WORLD DEFINITION

What does the word sovereign mean? Webster's dictionary says it means the head of state in a monarchy. *adj.* 1. Supreme: paramount. 2. Supreme in power or rank. 3. Self-governing: independent. Mr. Webster goes on to say that sovereignty means 1. Supreme of rule or authority. 2. The rank, authority of a sovereign. 3. Political autonomy.

Of these definitions, the ones that fit closest to what we think we mean when we say Sovereignty are self-governing, independent and political autonomy. Even so, these bilagaana words do not do justice to our sense and concept of Indigenous Sovereignty. Bilagaana's idea of sovereignty is linear and concrete, whereas our concept is spherical and abstract. The reason is simple; US sovereignty is man-conceived, as in being defined by a bunch of colonial bilagaana guys wearing white powdered wigs. Indigenous Sovereignty is a gift direct from the Almighty Creator, it is innate, it is inherent, it is our birthright.

We might design a new word in bilagaana bizaad, one that is adequate, one that would do justice to what Indigenous Sovereignty truly means. If that were possible. It is doubtful, as there are no parallels.

SOVEREIGNTY—IN PRACTICE, IN REALITY

A people true to its roots in the preservation and practice of those roots would remain truly sovereign. Within the modern day discussion of what Sovereignty means as it relates to government, our concept of Sovereignty has been subverted leading us to question, whether it is the people who are sovereign or is it the Tribal Government? Tribal government is referred to as a quasi-sovereign, which would means it is sort of sovereign, but not quite; it is sovereign only to the extent the federal government allows. Definitely that is not Sovereignty in the context that we think it should mean or want it to mean.

As a people we are not as sovereign as we think, we are confused as to what it should mean. This condition of confusion is of a deliberate intent, perhaps as a tool of the colonizer. Makes one think that they had this thing figured out over the centuries, after all, paleface has been committing war against and subjugating Tribal peoples for centuries. Nevertheless, even with outright genocide that annihilated many Tribes, disease blankets, our Trails of Tears, concentration camps, forced assimilation and the handouts, relocation, cultural genocide, federal government control of our lands, destructive exploitation of our lands/resources with or without sham consultation, some of us are STILL here. We continue to have pride in who we are, we have the audacity and the roots enough to question our oppressed condition. Though we may not be physically sovereign, we are sovereign in mind and spirit.

A LOST NATION

We are a lost Navajo Nation whether we realize it, accept it, or whether we reject the notion. We are Diné—we have original teachings, original thoughts, original values, and original lifeways that contain original concepts of governance. We have been wrested away from those original paradigms, so here today, we are somewhere between our roots and the fleeting promise of the American dream, whether by forced assimilation or by choice. Yes, physically it is not possible to live again on the sheepskin; that's a given, and no one is saying for us to go back to that lifestyle. Although for some of us chizzie rez kids, it is a romantic, idyllic life condition that we might prefer, if we could, over the rat race of today, with its myriad rat-race ills.

Those who want to be true to our original Dinéness, the spherical and abstract form of it, need only to have that desire to be—whether we live in the shadow of skyscrapers, struggling paycheck to paycheck, or herding sheep, whether we are fluent or not. Just the desire and faith to stay Diné is enough to lay claim to our Indigenous birthright and keep us tethered to our originality. On an individual basis, that may be enough for us to make our way through our personal worlds with all its challenges; we have little choice considering the overwhelming forces of the modern world. But on a national basis, as in the Navajo Nation government, it is not enough. For us to achieve greatness as a people, as a nation, we must recognize our roots and defer to them for guidance; it is unfathomable for us to be a strong, vibrant, independent sovereign nation pretending to be something we are not and could never be.

HONOR OUR ORIGINALITY

It is a mistake for politicians, bureaucrats, academics, or anyone to dismiss the validity of our Indigenous life story and all that is interwoven with it. That is not saying that all have to respect it or hold it sacred; that is not possible with our seemingly divergent belief systems and ways of worship. Some of us believe our collective good-intent worship is channeled to the same Almighty Creator, but even that notion is rejected by some.

In comparison to the fanatical (ugly) and fantastic (glittering) world of today; the good-intentioned-traditional Indigenous world is, and was, simple, calm, orderly, strong, and happy. Our Creator Maker did not make a mistake in our creation; we were made a unique and special people with unique and special ways—our values and life principles. (All peoples were made special at their origin—after all, we are all children of the same Creator.) As Diné, we were molded and set on Earth with our special ways; our ways remain valid, intact, and very relevant, even now, and perhaps especially, in today's chaotic world. In these original roots, our values remain vibrant; they have compassion, humbleness, honor, and courage. They embrace teachings and guidelines on how we should carry on and survive in this chaos, and there are reflections in these roots that would bring into perspective the truth and validity of "our" colonized Navajo government. We must return to our roots if we are to regain our true identity as Diné and grasp on to the fundamental essence of our Indigenous sovereignty.

OUR IMPRISONED SOVEREIGNTY

Up until the time we were made prisoners of war in 1864, we lived a life of sovereignty. Physically it may have been a hard life, but we were who we were supposed to be, and we had freedom. At the end of our years of imprisonment,

General Sherman tried to convince our chiefs to take a trip to Oklahoma Territory—the general wanted to relocate the Diné there. Barboncito and the chiefs said, "No, we want to go to our home within our four mountains." The Treaty of 1868, as a revered contract between two nations, recognized our sovereignty.

We started our lives over and became strong again, though somewhat less sovereign, because we had to live with the U.S. federal government's heavy hand: overbearing BIA agents, the kidnapping of children into the treacherous boarding schools, the cruel and unrelenting program of assimilation, the livestock reduction, etc. In 1922, oil was discovered, and the feds imposed on us the first form of the Navajo government system. The elementary intent was to make a centralized government, so there would be a formal, "legal" entity with whom oil companies could form contracts. The government idea was a strange and foreign concept to our people at the time, and we rejected it several times before it was finally forced on us. Adopting it and adapting to it over time has not changed the fact that it remains a foreign concept.

The imposition of the colonial concept of tribal government was a great intrusion, where the man-conceived sovereignty of the U.S. federal government with its "I-know-better-than-you-so-I-know-what's-best-for-you-whether-you-like-it-or-not" paternalism "gave" us our government. They decided that tribal government sovereignty was inferior to the Great White Father's and relegated the tribal government to quasi-sovereign status. We will never regain a meaningful semblance of our original sovereignty, so long as we are satisfied with our tribal government and believe it to be good enough.

HISTORY AND WHAT WE MUST DO

There were times in our history when the Spaniards, Mexicans, and early Americans were trying to deal with us, and our great-grandparents refused to be one tribe under one leader. As a tribal people, we will mandatorily introduce ourselves by clan to establish family and clan relationships. In the not too distant past, these introductions also gave indication of where, physically, the individual's family was from. This corroborates the recognition that certain clans predominantly populated certain regions. In the olden days, clan matriarchs and patriarchs "ruled" their regions where the extended clan families kept within chimney smoke sight. For many, many reasons this scenario is not possible today.

However, with prayerful focus, a strong retelling of our story, and a respectful, objective, and realistic analysis of our situation, we can design a viable option to "right our wagon" for the remainder of our life journey. The first decision is to decide if we actually think we can or should even try to fix our chaotic government. It wasn't intended to take care of us—it was intended to approve an oil lease. This imposed government structure and process is not our way as Diné—it clashes with our original perspective—there is a better way. We have the reason, the roots, the land, the resources, the wisdom, and the courage to find that better way that will honor our great-grandparents. And there is a way to that better way.

CONFINED WITH OUR IMPRISONED SOVEREIGNTY

We will never achieve optimum sovereign status within the parameters of the current Navajo government structure. The Navajo government system is actually a condition of subjugation—it has its too many restrictions and limitations; it lets us do only within the constrictions of what the feds will allow. Tribal rules and laws are subservient to federal rules and laws. Tribal leadership is obedient to federal law—it does not dare challenge it. Our "leaders" might say, "Declaration of Diné sovereignty is not a realistic option, it will threaten our federal relationship, *Washingdoon* will withdraw the contract dollars, it will injure our treaty status."

Even if the feds withdrew the dollars, would that be the end of us? If we declared our sovereignty, would the U.S. government accuse us of subversion and try to "terminate" us? Yes, those would be undesired results; we do not want to do something that would unleash negative consequences. After all, our main concern is to situate the best opportunity for the utmost survivability of our Diné Nation, for the sake of the future of our children.

BREAK THE CHAIN OF OUR IMPRISONED SOVEREIGNTY

Change is difficult, yet we must have the audacity to believe a paradigm shift is possible—a paradigm shift that will be precipitated by deciding to put aside the current Navajo government structure for something better. No doubt it would be a major undertaking, one that would be permeated with uncertainty and risk. Some will oppose the idea without a second thought—even people who are objective will reject the opportunity to hear out the discussion. Some will say we can never go back to what we once were, or that to challenge the system would be unpatriotic, or that they prefer the difficult pursuit of the elusive American dream, which seems to require a surrendering of a part of one's Indigenous soul in order to become a capitalist. Nevertheless, the reasons to consider the change are clear.

Our truth is, we are made with Diné values and unique life perspectives—an original thought process. We are a special people with an indisputable history and roots. The great Creator did not place us on this earth to flounder and wait to be rescued by the paleface. We were given the creativity, ingenuity, intellect, and common sense to live and survive. We deserve to live and survive in a strong way on our own terms—this is our land, this is our life. We have the solemn responsibility to fight to protect the future of our children and our earth. Shedding this colonial Navajo government will make that paradigm shift—we could start all over and be who we supposed to be, while we can.

THE FALLACY OF GOVERNMENT REFORM

There is no point to trying to decolonize the Navajo government—it was not right for us from the start. Its structure and process is a replica of the American system, and the American system appears to be edging toward the possibility of failure, like the great Roman empire.

The Diné Fundamental Law is representative of a true form of Diné governance. It should not be in the Navajo Nation Code, as they are elementally different. The Diné Fundamental Law (Council 2002) is the logical foundation on which to build. To change the Navajo government is a scary and risky proposition, but we have come through scary, risky times, and it is clear that our future times will be even more difficult. Our best option is to be who we were created to be—Diné. Our stories, our values, our intellect, and our courage are our best opportunity to make a comfortable survival on our terms. In the long term, there is no point in trying to "fix" the Navajo government; we must rise above that—we are better than that. Why would we want to try to fix something that is foreign, colonial in essence—a system that does not comport with our Dinéness and is absent of *ajooba* and *k'é*? The existence of the Navajo government is inextricably intertwined with and dependent on the exploitation of our Earth Mother, against our nature.

It is a fallacy to think that the development of a constitution for Diné is the right course. The concept of a constitution is as foreign as the structure and process of the Navajo government. It is proper and incumbent on us to return to and consult with the elders and those who maintain our life story and who can advise us on what our proper course of action should be. Without this prerequisite consultation it would be an ill-fated effort, no matter what we endeavor on and how well intentioned those efforts are.

WHY RECLAIM OUR SOVEREIGN AUTHORITY?

We are Diné. We have k'é and values intended to provide us a life of *Hózhǫ́*. Our Diné life principles with our language and culture remain intact, vibrant, and relevant. These principles form a pathway we were to follow, to assure our comfortable survival. We must reaffirm our values and rely on our divine gift of *nitsáhákees* and our innate concepts of leadership to reclaim our identity and sovereign authority.

The Navajo Nation government structure is not able to meet our myriad needs; we are in a state of welfare, a condition that only worsens into the future. This demands a rebuilding of the government. We have the reason, the brains, and the courage to form a new government rooted in our life principles, one that engages the authority contained in our inherent sovereignty.

Rebuilding the government will require the consensus of all concerned in an all-inclusive process. In this great exercise of *nahat'á*, we can form a government that truly meets our *iiná* life needs now and into the future. It is necessary to regain complete control of our lands. All matters of government must be done on our Diné terms. We must do this to protect the future of our children, as they are, our *sihasin*.

Only then will it be possible to see, understand, and live the true essence of our sovereignty.

A CONVERSATION WITH HASTIIN DÍÍL BI NÁLÍ: DINÉ HOZHǪ́ǪJI NAAT'Á (PEACEMAKING) IS A METHODOLOGY TO ATTAIN DINÉ SOVEREIGNTY

Over an April 2015 lunch in Shiprock, Hastiin Dííl Bi Nálí and I talked about what he was learning about the concept and practice of sovereignty through his work as a Diné Nation Peacemaker in the Northern Navajo region. From the large restaurant window, we could see the tops of Dził Dibé Nitsaa (Mount Hesperus) situated near Durango, Colorado, and the northernmost sacred mountain of the Diné. He stressed certain very critical themes that I will outline here. "We now have many Diné demanding to go against who we are." While certain non-Indian groups appreciate and advocate Diné ways of knowing, many Diné do not.

Hastiin Dííl Bi Nálí described how a certain New York–area non-Indian attorney group, interested in nonadversarial court mediation and Diné peacemaking, over the past three or four years, have come to openly understand, appreciate, and advocate the validity, legitimacy, and value of Diné peacemaking. They speak of the necessity of Diné-style peacemaking as valuable for non-Indian populations. They do not carry any doubt of Diné peacemaking's validity. They openly discuss its merits in the context of justice for all Americans and are more than willing to work with Diné peacemaking principles to assure justice for their clients.

Hastiin Dííl Bi Nálí then described the irony that many Diné no longer appreciate nor understand Diné ways of knowing. Many have no interest in doing so. "Why is it that our own people don't believe in ourselves as Diné? We now have many of our own people demanding to go against who we are. This is the biggest obstacle to sovereignty. This is because we no longer speak our language or practice our ceremonies. We no longer think much about who we are. This has to do with our loss of our Diné language. We are our language," he said.

I pressed him to answer his own question. He responded, "We already have ways to understand ourselves through our songs, prayers, ceremonies, and language. Yet, for some reason, we tend not to appreciate it nor believe in them. Sovereignty is a process of achieving a state of being called *hózhǫ́*." He described this state of being as volitionally attained, or a *t'áá hwó ájít'é* sense of self-determination, in which the individual and group "take charge" of their destiny. They willingly discard the negative self-concept layers that obscure self-determined action and practice. In a sense, these negative layers are infested with historic trauma.[3] It requires healing and decolonization to transcend and transform this illness into wellness.

Diné peacemaking processes, he said, offer Diné an opportunity to embark on a healing journey that restores and revitalizes a sense of hózhǫ́ and k'é. It is in this process and attainment of hózhǫ́ and k'é that sovereign action is realized. Diné sovereign action is a beautiful process, he said.

The Nihigáál bee Iiná walkers,[4] he said, are trying to put something vital back into Diné thinking: "Why doesn't it rain anymore? Did we plant our crops this season? What are we doing about our land, the on-going drought? Are we taking only what we need from the land and are we stopping ourselves from profiting from our mother earth? *Hozhoogo náhodoo dleeł* means to prevent depleting our mother earth's products. We are rushing and doing things too fast, trying to get somewhere. Are we ever going to get there? Where's 'there' anyway? [laughter] Deadlines in our modern world never end, there's really no reason to rush. By putting mother earth back into our thinking, we attain *hózhó nahasdlii'* over and over again."

THE HOZHǪ́ǪJI NAAT'Á (PEACEMAKING) PROCESS IS A WAY TO UNDERSTAND AND ENGAGE DINÉ SOVEREIGNTY

Diné peacemaking is an ancient, precolonized practice of maintaining social harmony amid social disharmony that characterizes any society. The Diné peacemaking process was marginalized or disregarded when, in the mid-1900s, the U.S. Department of the Interior, Bureau of Indian Affairs judges began to train Diné judges in the newly structured Diné court system to use Western law. In the 1980s and 1990s, the Diné government began to retrofit Diné peacemaking into a Westernized court system.

However, Diné court judges never really abandoned important Diné principles regarding k'é and hózhǫ́ (Austin 2009), and today Navajo Nation peacemaking is being integrated more fully into the Navajo Nation Judicial Branch as an act of Diné decolonization.

According to the Navajo Nation Peacemaking Program,

> Traditional Diné Peacemaking originates in a place of chaos, *hóóchxo'/anáhóót'i'*, whether within an individual or between human beings. Perhaps due to historical and colonial trauma, Navajos shy away from face-to-face confrontations. However, such confrontations are vital in order to dispel *hóóchxo'/anáhóót'i'*. The Peacemaker has the courage and skills to provide the groundwork for the person or group to confront *hóóchxo'/anáhóót'i'* and move toward skills and competencies inherent in mastering harmonious existence. Life value engagement with the Peacemaker provides the sense of identity and pride emanating from our cultural

foundations. *Hóóchxo'/anáhóót'i'* can block and overwhelm clanship, *k'é*, which is normally what binds loving and interdependent human beings together in mutual respect. Through engagement, the Peacemaker educates, scolds, persuades, pleads and cajoles the individual or group toward a readiness to open up, listen, share, and make decisions as a single unit using *k'é*. When *hóóchxo'/ anáhóót'i'* is confronted, people may learn there is a choice to leave it or let go of it. When harmony, *hózhǫ́*, is self-realized and manifested, sustaining it will have clarity and permanent *hózhǫ́* will be self-attainable and sustainable, *hózhǫ́ǫ́jí k'ehgo nįná'íldee' ilhááhodidzaa ná'oodzíí'*.

Through stories and teachings, the Peacemaker dispenses knowledge, *naat'áánii*, in order to guide the whole toward a cathartic understanding of *hózhǫ́* that opens the door to transformative healing. The flow of *hózhǫ́* is a movement inwards toward the core issue or underlying truth. Recognition of this truth and the ending of denial provide the opportunity for healing or mutual mending. Realization of the truth occurs when individual feelings are fundamentally satisfied. The resolution of damaged feelings is the core material of peacemaking sessions, *hózhǫ́ji naat'aah*. Depending on the skill of the Peacemaker, *hózhǫ́* may be short or may take several peacemaking sessions.

A peacemaking case may occur like this: when social order is violated, an individual may be "sentenced" to a peacemaking process provided that their family, friends, spiritual advisors, and other associates are present. The other half of the circle is people who have, let us say, alleged that the individual has violated some form of social order. The group as a whole discusses the issue within the context of Diné lifeway principles of k'é, hózhǫ́, and other principles described earlier. The group—not a judge, attorney, or jury—eventually makes a consensus decision regarding the most healthy and wholesome outcome for the violator and the group.

Hastiin Dííl Bi Nálí said that Diné peacemaking needs to be widely known because it is a process to let people be in harmony with the life we are given. As examples of Indigenous traditional sovereign action, he described the manner in which traditional people gift one another through a process called *k'é hwiindzin*, or to be relational, to know and practice kinship compassionately and interdependently. Traditional Lakota and Kiowa have given him songs and dance regalia as ways to share themselves and their ways of knowing. "I have accepted these gifts," he said. "Our rituals have a similarity and we have ways to receive gifts from different cultures and to integrate them into our culture.

This is an example of how Diné sovereignty is practiced. . . . Diné sovereignty in this sense is walking in beauty." "There are two sovereignties: one to conquer, control, and manipulate and one to walk in *hózhǫ́* ceremony," he also said.

Hastiin Dííl Bi Nálí was clear that when we Diné lose our sense of identity, language, culture, history, and politics, we lose grasp of the very processes that will restore individual, family, clan, and community harmony, balance, peace, and happiness. There is no Diné relevant sovereign action when we adopt unhealthy recolonizing forms of identity, language, culture, history, and politics. In such cases, we only stand to destroy ourselves.

On the other hand, Diné peacemaking embodies harmony, balance, beatitude, happiness, love, and peace. Peacemaking processes do not use self-destructive and separational processes to better a person. Peacemaking, too, understands kinship as an embrace of the living natural world as our relatives. It is not just a human-to-human process.

Hastiin Dííl Bi Nálí summarized his thoughts by saying, "We have strayed away from an understanding of our language and identity. Some Anglo people recognize and appreciate the critical importance of Navajo traditional knowledge. They see a lot of good in who we are. My confusion is why our own people don't get it when our knowledge and identity is rooted in harmony and balance. Navajos can take our language and knowledge, where our identity is, for granted."

REFLECTIONS: PEACEMAKING AS SOVEREIGN ACTION AND OUTCOME

The implications these two gentlemen carry are many. Instead of a sovereignty rooted in conquest, control, power, manipulation, and wealth, we read of a sovereignty rooted in harmony and balance intrinsic in Diné traditional language, teachings, and stories.

Diné language and culture assumes that peacemaking is not just a human-to-human process of attaining harmony and balance because Diné include and embrace the so-called natural world (called Holy People or Diyin Dine'e) relatives as well. Sunlight, embodied in "Father Sky teachings," and water, embodied in "Changing Woman teachings," for example, are our relatives and partners in healing and transformation, and in the restoration of hózhǫ́.

In a colonial and assimilative framework, instead of choosing Diné harmony and balance, many of us "choose," or are forced to choose, social, political, and economic chaos and disorder engendered by colonialism's tools: capitalism, religion, education separation, consumerism, desacralized knowledge. Instead of a sovereignty rooted in and linked to healing, decolonization, transformation, mobilization, and practice, we choose an adversarial, win-lose, punishment-based sovereignty we acquired from settler colonials. Settler colonial democracy is unhealthy and dysfunctional when viewed through a traditional Diné knowledge lens. When we become blinded to settler colonial democracy, traditional Diné sovereignty can become obscured, unthinkable, and even disliked.

Many of our Diné political leaders seem to march to the orders of settler colonial versions of sovereignty, thereby helping to marginalize and obscure our potential to sustain and attain *k'é doo hózhǫ́* (e.g., kinship, harmony, and balance) sovereignty. It is precisely here that the reasons for our political, social, and economic contradiction, conflict, tension, and upheaval lie.

Indeed, thousands of discouraged Diné citizens point to the 2014–2015 elections process as illustrative of Diné confusion, inaction, contradiction, and so on. A few Diné leaders thought it OK to not speak Diné as a qualification to lead the Diné Nation. Diné youth activists point to Navajo Nation involvement in "resource colonization," or the blind, desacralized willingness of Diné political leaders to violate and contradict our beautifully ethical spiritual connection with a sacred earth to participate in what some call "the rape of Mother Earth." We are a matrilineal society, but our political decisions and research that impacts Diné law and policy are not accountable to our grandmothers.

One major law enacted in 2002 by the Navajo Nation Council is poised to reproduce, restore, revitalize, and regenerate Diné harmony and balance sovereignty. It is called the Diné Fundamental Law (DFL) (Diné Bi Beenzhaz'áanii 2002). However, the irony is that the DFL seems to stand alone against a huge and formidable Navajo Tribal Code that reproduces a confused, bipolar-like schism and political identity. The Navajo Tribal Code is largely controlled by the work and influence of foreign and alien legal concepts prized by settler colonials.

As Diné, we carry a responsibility to critically examine the violence intrinsic in colonial sovereignty to understand how it contradicts and sabotages guidelines for living embodied in hózhǫ́, k'é, and other teachings and practices found in Diné Fundamental Law. We can never understand the epistemic violence of colonial sovereignty and democracy until we exercise the use of the k'é and hózhǫ́ lens to do so, and until we relearn to practice a compassionate, loving, interdependent way of relating to each other, as well as the so-called ecosystem. A traditional Diné lens is also an inevitable critical lens that engenders a Diné critical consciousness of harmony, balance, happiness, peace, and beauty.

Today, as in the past, we have a choice of sovereignties: an assimilated and colonialized one or a Diné-rooted one. Which one do we proceed with? One way to proceed is with the non-Western, nonmodern, precolonized epistemology, pedagogy, and ontology inherent in Dinéjí hozhǫ́ǫ́ji naa'ta. It is so old, it looks new to many.

If we continue to use colonial sovereignty methodology to define and enact such policies on ourselves, we will never find ourselves in terms of our Diné identity, culture, language, history, and politics. Instead, we will hijack—or, as some say, destroy—ourselves by offering laws that only seduce and corrupt our sense of hózhǫ and k'é. We will remain imprisoned in our own lands and in our colonized mentalities.

Chili Yazzie is correct to assert that we must reject any form of self-governance that smells of colonial sovereignty. Hasten Dííl Bi Nálí is correct to recommend hozhǫ́ǫ́jí naat'á as a very appropriate and necessary methodology to understand, attain, and practice hozhǫ́ǫ́jí-based sovereignty. Harmony and balance are traditional goals of Diné lifeways. They promise sustainable, whole, natural (not denatured), happy lives for ourselves and our colonial settler neighbors. Indeed, Diné decolonization is merely to walk in beauty . . . again.

Whether our colonial settler neighbors acknowledge this or not is one huge question they must face and will continue to face. American politics is based on adversarial debate and argument, opposition to one another, crisis, and eventual hatred. It is always divisive and separational.

I like the idea of the Diné Nation acting out of its own k'é-hózhǫ sovereign matrilineal identity to engage settler colonial sovereigns and to collaborate with other Indigenous nations. This is a worthy change and transformational model to consider. It supports the idea of learning, thinking, and working together in kinship and community, of being of one mind, heart, song, and prayer. It supports the idea of using endogenous local knowledge (as opposed to outside expertise) to enact positive change.

Diné ways of knowing will help resolve the schism between the Indigenous and the Western, the colonizer and the colonized, the natured and the denatured. Diné-style justice is nonadversarial, anti-punishment and pro healing, decolonization, and transformation.

I like the idea of the Diné Nation finding ourselves in a greater whole (rooted in hozhǫ́ǫ́jí and k'é hwiindzin truths of love and compassion) interacting with settler colonials who for whatever reason remain denatured and not yet whole in the sense of k'é and hózhǫ. Why not help them out, and in doing so help each other and Mother Earth? We all must learn to inclusively and interdependently respect, love, and cherish each other.

We shouldn't give in or give up on our original selves. We come from a beautiful primordial wisdom tradition. Diné-centered decolonization is predicated on how to embody and practice sustainable, harmonious, and balanced identities. Diné epistemology is concerned with vital questions like: Who am I? Am I who I'm supposed to be? Where do I come from? How do I know what to know? If we don't take the opportunity to walk in collective harmony, beauty, and balance, we—Diné and our colonial neighbors—both lose.

Decolonization is for both the settlers and the Indigenous. In a decolonization mode, both the colonizers and colonized, the modern and nonmodern, the natured and denatured must share the same methodology. I would rather choose sovereign action implicit in Diné hozhóójí naat'á teachings and practices to embody because settler colonial processes are old paradigm, violent, oppressive, separational, and ultimately self-destructive.

Climate change, as some have written, is our next Third World War. For me, this is the truth of our global situation. We need not lose ourselves in the process of finding ourselves—too insidious. We need not enact sovereign actions that contradict and sabotage who we are to attain nationhood. Even Bilagáanas say "don't shoot yourselves in the foot" if you want to get anywhere.

To understand life through the hozhóójí anat'a, or peacemaking experience and lens, is to see sovereignty from a whole and healthy, self-organizing, self-perpetuating, and self-sustaining perspective in which interdependent and compassionate kinship and community drive and shape how we know the world. Peacemaking is about the attainment of positive self-worth, not its corruption or destruction derived from unresolved historic and intergenerational trauma. It is about healing the wounds of colonial trauma, not aggravating them. It is about Indigenous-centered decolonization and transformation that embodies the beauty and balance of earth-sky knowing, being, and becoming. It's not about the practice of violence, addiction, and ill health.

Peacemaking is a process that allows people to see choices and make decisions that positively impact individual and collective well-being. It is not based on pathologizing ourselves. Peacemaking is sovereign action at its best. It will help us see what we need to see, to know what we need to know Indigenously. It will help us find the love, peace, harmony, and balance within ourselves to, in turn, restore and regenerate positive relations with others in a good way.

It is in this space that our sense of sovereign action is best embodied and practiced. Believe it or not, like in our shoe games, we are precious, kind, playful, balanced, and loving people. Our kinship system is born of Changing Woman, who knows no harm and knows only love, compassion, and care. Why not assert and privilege Diné-centered sovereign action in this manner?

NOTES

1. Larry Emerson, *Tsénahabiłnii nishlí. Tó'aheidlíínii bashishchíín. Hoghanłání da shi nálí. Kiiyaa'áanii da shi chei. Tsédaak'áán whoyéeni shiya hoo'a'.*

2. *Bilagáana* is a term to describe white Americans. One translation of the term means "those we struggle against."

3. Historic, intergenerational trauma theory postulates that trauma and unresolved trauma can be passed from one generation to the next unless a type of intervention takes place that involves history, culture, language, identity, and politics to understand how to intervene. This theory challenges other forms of "water under the bridge" interventions that tend to obscure or eclipse historical and political (e.g., colonization) events like the Cherokee Trail of Tears of the 1830s or the Diné Long Walk of the 1860s that cause soul wounding.

4. The Nihigáál bee Iiná walkers began a yearlong journey in January 2015 to walk to each Diné sacred mountain to offer prayers of well-being for Diné and all peoples. They are focusing on Diné land use and what they call "resource colonization" to educate and sensitize Diné about the need to return to Diné ways of knowing to restore and revitalize healthy nation building.

REFERENCES

Adams, David Wallace. 1995. *Education for Extinction: American Indians and the Boarding School Experience, 1875–1928.* Lawrence: University Press of Kansas.

Alfred, Taiaiake. 1999. *Peace, Power, Righteousness: An Indigenous Manifesto.* Oxford: Oxford University Press.

———. 2005. *Wasase: Indigenous Pathways of Action and Freedom.* Peterborough, Ontario: Broadview Press.

Anaya, S. James. 2004. *Indigenous Peoples in International Law.* 2nd ed. New York: Oxford University Press.

Aronilth, Wilson, Jr. 1994. *Diné Bi Bee Óhoo'aah Bá Silá: An Introduction to Navajo Philosophy.* Tsaile, AZ: Diné College Press.

———. 1991. *Foundation of Navajo Culture.* Tsaile, AZ: Dine College Press.

Austin, Raymond D. 2009. *Navajo Courts and Navajo Common Law: A Tradition of Tribal Self-Governance.* Minneapolis: University of Minnesota Press.

Aveni, Anthony F., ed. 1975. *Archaeoastronomy in Pre-Columbian America: Native Astronomy in Mesoamerica.* Austin: University of Texas Press.

Bagley, Christopher, Loretta Young, and Anne Scully. 1993. *International and Transracial Adoptions: A Mental Health Perspective.* Brookfield, VT: Avebury.

Bailey, Garrick, and Roberta Glenn Bailey. 1999. *A History of the Navajos: The Reservation Years.* Santa Fe, NM: School of American Research Press.

Barker, Joanne, ed. 2005. *Sovereignty Matters: Locations of Contestation and Possibility in Indigenous Struggles for Self-Determination.* Lincoln: University of Nebraska Press.

Battiste, M. A. 2013. *Decolonizing Education: Nourishing the Learning Spirit*. Saskatoon, Canada: Purich Publishing.

Begay, Manley A., Jr., Stephen Cornell, Miriam Jorgensen, and Joseph P. Kalt. 2007. "Development, Governance, Culture: What Are They and What Do They Have to Do with Rebuilding Native Nations?" In *Rebuilding Native Nations: Strategies for Governance and Development*, edited by Miriam Jorgensen. Tucson: University of Arizona Press.

Beiser, M. 1974. "A Hazard to Mental Health: Indian Boarding Schools." *American Journal of Psychiatry* 31 (3): 305–6.

Benally, AnCita. 2006. "Dine' Binahat'a', Navajo Government." PhD diss., Arizona State University.

Bighorse, Tiana, Gus Bighorse, and Noel Bennett. 1990. *Bighorse the Warrior*. Tucson: University of Arizona Press.

Bitsoi, Alastair Lee. 2014. "Done Deal: Tribe Officially Owns a Coal Mine." *Navajo Times*, January 2.

Brayboy, B. M. K. J. 2005. "Toward a Tribal Critical Race Theory in Education." *Urban Review: Issues and Ideas in Public Education* 37 (5): 425–46.

———. 2012. "Postsecondary Education for American Indian and Alaska Natives: Higher Education for Nation Building and Self-Determination." *ASHE Higher Education Report* 37 (5): 1–154.

Brave Heart, Maria Yellow Horse, and L. M. DeBruyn. 1998. "The American Indian Holocaust: Healing Historical Grief." *American Indian Alaska Native Mental Health Research* 8 (2): 56–78.

Brave Heart, Maria Yellow Horse. 2011. "Welcome to Takini's Historical Trauma." http://historicaltrauma.com.

Brave Heart, Maria Yellow Horse et al. n.d. "Historical Trauma: Boarding School Trauma." http://www.nationallatinonetwork.org/images/files/Historical_trauma_Handout.pdf

Brave Heart-Jordan, Maria Yellow Horse. 1995. "The Return to the Sacred Path: Healing from Historical Trauma and Historical Unresolved Grief among the Lakota." PhD diss., Smith College.

Brooks, Catherine M. 1994. "The Indian Child Welfare Act in Nebraska: Fifteen Years: A Foundation for the Future." *Creighton Law Review* 27 (3): 661–68.

Brown, Dee. 1970. *Bury My Heart at Wounded Knee*. New York: Holt, Rinehart and Winston.

Brugge, David M., and J. Lee Correll. 1971. *The Story of the Navajo Treaties*. Window Rock, AZ: Navajo Tribe.

Bueno de Mesquita, Bruce. 2009. *Principles of International Politics*. Thousand Oaks, CA: CQ Press.

Bueno de Mesquita, Bruce, and Alastair Smith. 2011. *The Dictator's Handbook: Why Bad Behavior Is Almost Always Good Politics*. New York: Public Affairs.

Cabrera, Martha. 1995. "Living and Surviving in a Multiply Wounded Country." http://www.medico.de/download/report26/ps_cabrera_en.pdf

Cajete, Gregory A. 2000. "Indigenous Knowledge: The Pueblo Metaphor of Indigenous Education." In *Reclaiming Indigenous Voice and Vision*, edited by M. Battiste, 181–91. Vancouver: University of British Columbia Press.

Canby, William C., Jr. 1988. *American Indian Law in a Nutshell*. 5th ed. Eagan, MN: West Publishing.

Chandler, Michael J., and Christopher E. Lalonde. 1998. "Cultural Continuity as a Hedge against Suicide in Canada's First Nations." *Journal of Transcultural Psychiatry* 35 (2): 193–211.

———. forthcoming. "Cultural Continuity as a Moderator of Suicide Risk among Canada's First Nations." In *The Mental Health of Canadian Aboriginal Peoples: Transformations, Identity, and Community*, ed. L. Kirmayer and G. Valaskakis. Vancouver: University of British Columbia Press.

Cherokee Nation v. Georgia, 30 U.S. (5 Pet. 1) 1 (1831).

Coe, Michael D., and Anthony F. Aveni, eds. 1975. *Archaeoastronomy in Pre-Columbian America: Native Astronomy in Mesoamerica*. Austin: University of Texas Press.

Coffey, Wallace, and Rebecca Tsosie. 2001. "Rethinking the Tribal Sovereignty Doctrine: Cultural Sovereignty and the Collective Future of Indian Nations." *Stanford Law & Policy Review* 12 (2): 191–221.

Cornell, Stephen E., and Joseph P. Kalt. 1992. "Reloading the Dice: Improving the Chances for Economic Development on American Indian Reservations." In *What Can Tribes Do? Strategies and Institutions in American Indian Economic Development*, edited by Joseph P. Kalt and Stephen Cornell. Los Angeles: American Indian Studies Center University of California.

———. 1994. "The Redefinition of Property Rights in American Indian Reservations: A Comparative Analysis of Native American Economic Development." In *American Indian Policy: Self-Governance and Economic Development*, edited by L. H. Legters and F. J. Lyden. Westport, CT: Greenwood Press.

———. 2000. "Where's the Glue? Institutional and Cultural Foundations of American Indian Economic Development." *Journal of Socio-Economics* 29: 443–70.

————. 2007. "Two Approaches to the Development of Native Nations: One Works, the Other Doesn't." In *Rebuilding Native Nations: Strategies for Governance and Development*, edited by Miriam Jorgensen, 3–33. Tucson: University of Arizona Press.

Coronado's Report to the King of Spain Sent from Tiguex, October 20, 1541. Letters from Francisco Vazquez de Coronado to His Majesty, in Which He Gives an Account of the Discovery of the Province of Tiguex, *New Perspectives of the Southwest, Archives of the West to 1806*, Episode 1, PBS.

Cuch, Forrest, ed. 2003. *History of Utah's American Indians*. Salt Lake City: Utah's State Division of Indian Affairs.

Curriculum Guide for Diné Government: Grades 9–12. 2003. Window Rock, AZ: Office of Diné Culture, Language and Community Services, Division of Diné Education.

Deloria, Vine, Jr. 1988. *Custer Died for Your Sins: An Indian Manifesto*. Norman: University of Oklahoma Press.

Deloria, Vine, Jr., and Clifford M. Lytle. 1998. *The Nations Within: The Past and Future of American Indian Sovereignty*. Austin: University of Texas Press.

Deloria, Vine, Jr., and Daniel R. Wildcat. 1991. *Power and Place: Indian Education in America*. Golden, CO: Fulcrum Publishing.

Deloria, Vine, Jr., and David E. Wilkins. 1999. *Tribes, Treaties, and Constitutional Tribulations*. Austin: University of Texas Press.

Deloria, Vine, Jr., and Raymond J. DeMiallie. 1999. *Documents of American Indian Diplomacy: Treaties, Agreements, and Conventions, 1775–1979*. Norman: University of Oklahoma Press.

Denetdale, Jennifer. 2006. "Chairman, Presidents, and Princesses: The Navajo Nation, Gender, and the Politics of Tradition." *Wicazo Sa Review* 21 (1): 9–28.

Diné Bi Beenahaz'áanii, 1 NNC §§ 201–296 Stat. (November 8, 2002).

Diné College. 2016. http://www.dinecollege.edu/about/history.php.

Dlugokinski, E., and L. Kramer. 1974. "A System of Neglect: Indian Boarding School." *American Journal of Psychiatry* 131 (6): 670–73.

Donovan, Bill. 2011. "Census: Navajo Enrollment Tops 300,000." *Navajo Times*, July 7.

Echo-Hawk, Walter R. 2012. *In the Courts of the Conqueror, The 10 Worst Indian Law Cases Ever Decided*. Golden, CO: Fulcrum Publishing.

Emerson, Larry. 2014. "Dine Culture, Colonization, and the Politics of Hózhó." In *Diné Perspectives: Revitalizing and Reclaiming Navajo Thought*, ed. Lloyd L. Lee, 49–67. Tucson: University of Arizona Press.

Fanshel, David. 1972. *Far from the Reservation: The Transracial Adoption of American Indian Children*. Metuchen, NJ: Scarecrow Press.

Farb, Peter. 1991. *Man's Rise to Civilization: The Cultural Ascent of the Indians of North America*. New York: Penguin.

Ferrara, Peter J. 1998. *The Choctaw Revolution: Lessons for Federal Indian Policy*. Washington, DC: Americans for Federal Tax Reform Foundation.

Fletcher, M. L. M. 2008. *American Indian Education: Counternarratives in Racism, Struggle, and the Law*. New York: Routledge.

Freire, Paulo. 2000. *Pedagogy of the Oppressed*. Thirtieth anniversary ed. New York: Continuum.

Garner, Brian, ed. 1999. *Black's Law Dictionary*. 7th ed. Eagan, MN: West Publishing.

Gentry, Marcia, and C. Matthew Fugate. 2012. "Gifted Native American Students: Underperforming, Under-Identified, and Overlooked." *Psychology in the Schools* (June): 3–4.

Geortz, Gary. 2006. *Social Science Concepts: A User's Guide*. Princeton, NJ: Princeton University Press.

Getches, David H., Charles F. Wilkinson, and Robert A Williams. 2005. *Cases and Materials on Federal Indian Law*. New York: Thomson/West.

Getches, David H., Charles F. Wilkinson, Robert A. Williams Jr., and Matthew L. M. Fletcher. 2011. *Federal Indian Law*. 6th ed. Eagan, MN: West Publishing.

Gorman-Keith, T. 2004. "Sihasin—Meaning of Graduation to Navajo College Students at Northern Arizona University: An Interpretive Case Study." PhD diss., Northern Arizona University.

Graham, Lorie M. 1998. "The Past Never Vanishes: A Contextual Critique of the Existing Indian Family Doctrine." *American Indian Law Review* 23 (1): 1–54.

Guerrero, Ruben. "Economic Development at Salt River Pima-Maricopa Indian Community." Arizona State University. Tempe, AZ. 22 March 2016. Lecture.

Haile, Berard. 1943. *Soul Concepts of the Navaho*. St. Michaels, AZ: St. Michaels Press.

Hale, Michelle. 2012. "Devolution and the Navajo Nation: Strategies for Local Empowerment in Three Navajo Communities." PhD diss., University of Arizona.

Harvard Project on American Indian Economic Development. 2007. *The State of the Native Nations Conditions under U.S. Policies of Self-Determination*. New York: Oxford University Press.

Hoffman, John, and Paul Graham. 2006. *Introduction to Political Ideologies*. Harlow, UK: Pearson Longman.

Holm, Tom, J. D. Pearson, and B. Chavis. 2003. "Peoplehood: A Model for the Extension of Sovereignty in American Indian Studies." *Wicazo Sa Review* 18 (1): 7–24.

Hooker, David Anderson, and Amy Potter Czajkowski. 2013. "Transforming Historical Harms." Presented by Coming to the Table, A Project of Eastern Mennonite University's Center for Justice and Peacebuilding.

Horwitz, Sari, and Katie Zezima. 2014. "How the Stories of Native American Youths Made Obama Cry in the Oval Office." *Washington Post*, December 3.

Howard, Brian Clark. 2015. "Worst Drought in 1,000 Years Predicted for American West: Global Warming to Cause Historic "Megadrought" By Century's end." *National Geographic*, February. http://news.nationalgeographic.com/news/2015/02/150212-megadrought-southwest-water-climate-environment/.

"Indian Planner Round Table." Phoenix, AZ. 4 April 2016. Strategic planning session.

Indian Self-Determination and Education Assistance Act (PL 93-638), 1975.

Irwin, M. H., and S. Roll. 1995. "The Psychological Impact of Sexual Abuse of Native American Boarding School Children." *Journal of the American Academy of Psychoanalysis* 23 (3): 461–73.

Jacobs, D. T. 2006. *Unlearning the Language of Conquest: Scholars Expose Anti-Indianism in America: Deceptions that Influence War and Peace, Civil Liberties, Public Education, Religion and Spirituality, Democratic Ideals, the Environment, Law, Literature, Film, and Happiness*. Austin: University of Texas Press.

Jawort, Adrian. 2014. "The Declaration of Independence—Except for 'Indian Savages.'" Indian Country Today Media Network, May 1.

Jenkins, Myra Ellen, and Albert H. Schroeder. 1974. *A Brief History of New Mexico*. Albuquerque: University of New Mexico Press.

Jensen, Derrick. 2006. *Endgame: The Problem of Civilization*. Volume I. New York: Seven Stories Press.

Johns, Cliff. "Indigenous Architecture." Arizona State University. Tempe, AZ. 5 April 2016. Lecture.

Jorgensen, Miriam, ed. 2007. *Rebuilding Native Nations: Strategies for Governance and Development*. Tucson: University of Arizona Press.

Judicial Branch of the Navajo Nation. n.d. *Aspects and Perspectives of Diné Traditional Teaching*. www.navajocourts.org/indexaspects1.htm.

Kalt, Joseph P., and J. B. Taylor. 2005. *American Indians on Reservations: A Databook of Socioeconomic Change Between the 1990 and 2000 Censuses*. Cambridge, MA: Harvard Project on American Indian Economic Development.

Khachadoorian, A. A. 2010. *Inside the Eagle's Head: An American Indian College.* Tuscaloosa: University of Alabama Press.

King, Gary, Robert Keohne, and Sidney Verba. 1994. *Designing Social Inquiry: Scientific Interference in Qualitative Research.* Princeton, NJ: Princeton University Press.

Koenig, Harriet, and Seymour H. Koenig. 2005. "Acculturation in the Navajo Eden: New Mexico, 1550–1750." In *Archaeology, Language, and Religion of the Peoples of the Southwest.* New York: YBK Publishers.

Landry, Alysa. 2013. "Navajo Nation Economic Growth Creating Jobs and True Independence." Indian Country Today Media Network, August, 28.

Lansing, Danielle. 2016. "Community Connections Enhance Teacher Education at SIPI." *Tribal College Journal* 27 (3): 13–14.

Lee, Lloyd L. 2008. "Reclaiming Indigenous Intellectual, Political and Geographic Space." *American Indian Quarterly* 32 (1): 96–110.

———. 2014. "The Navajo Nation and the Declaration on the Rights of Indigenous Peoples." In *Diné Perspectives: Revitalizing and Reclaiming Navajo Thought,* edited by Lloyd L. Lee, 170–86. Tucson: University of Arizona Press.

Lee, Tiffany S. 2015. "The Significance of Self-Determination in Socially, Culturally, and Linguistically Responsive (SCLR) Education in Indigenous Contexts." *Journal of American Indian Education* 54 (1): 10–32.

Lemont, Eric D., ed. 2006. *American Indian Constitutional Reform and the Rebuilding of Native Nations.* Austin: University of Texas Press.

Lerma, Michael. 2010. "Guided by the Mountains: Traditional and Contemporary Approaches to Diné Governance." PhD diss., University of Arizona.

———. 2012. "Indigeneity and Homeland: Land, History, Ceremony, and Language," *American Indian Culture and Research Journal* 30 (3): 75–98.

———. 2014. *Indigenous Sovereignty in the 21st Century: Knowledge for the Indigenous Spring.* Gainesville: Florida Academic Press.

Linden, H. Vander. 1916. "Alexander VI and the Demarcation of the Maritime and Colonial Domains of Spain and Portugal, 1493–1494." *American Historical Review* 22 (1): 1–20.

Link, Martin A. 1968. *Treaty between the United States of America and the Navajo Tribe of Indians.* Las Vegas, NV: KC Publications.

Littlefield, Douglas R. 1999. "The History of the Rio Grande Compact of 1938." WRRI Conference Proceedings. http://wrri.nmsu.edu/publish/watcon/proc44/littlefield.pdf.

Lomawaima, K. Tsianina, and Teresa L. McCarty. 2006. *"To Remain an Indian": Lessons in Democracy from a Century of Native American Education*. New York: Teachers College Press.

Lyons, Scott Richard. 2010. *X-Marks: Native Signatures of Assent*. Minneapolis: University of Minnesota Press.

Mahoney, James. 2003. "Long-Run Development and the Legacy of Colonialism in Spanish America." *American Journal of Sociology* 109 (1): 50–106.

———. 2010. *Colonialism and Development: Spanish America in Comparative Perspective*. Cambridge: Cambridge University Press.

Mankiller, Wilma. 2008. Governance, Leadership, and the Cherokee Nation, "Leading Native Nations" interview series, Native Nations Institute for Leadership, Management, and Policy, University of Arizona, Tucson, Arizona, September 29.

Manuelito, Kathryn. 2005. "The Role of Education in American Indian Self-Determination: Lessons from the Ramah Navajo Community School." *Anthropology & Education Quarterly* 36 (1): 73–87.

Maryboy, Nancy C., and David Begay. 2010. *Sharing the Skies: Navajo Astronomy*. Tucson, AZ: Rio Nuevo Publishers.

McCarty, Teresa L. 2002. *A Place to be Navajo: Rough Rock and the Struggle for Self-Determination in Indigenous Schooling*. Mahwah, NJ: Lawrence Erlbaum Associates.

McKenzie, James, Aaron P. Jackson, Robert Yazzie, Steven P. Smith, Amber K. Crotty, D. Baum, Avery Denny, and Dana Bah'lgai Eldridge. 2013. "Career Dilemmas Among Diné (Navajo) College Graduates: An Exploration of the Dinétah (Navajo Nation Brain Drain)." *The International Indigenous Policy Journal* 4 (4). http://ir.lib.uwo.ca/iipj/vol4/iss4/5.

Michelle Kahn-John, Michelle. 2010. "Concept Analysis of Diné Hózhó: A Diné Wellness Philosophy." *Advances in Nursing Science* 33 (2): 113–25.

Mihesuah, Devon A. 2006. "Overcoming Hegemony in Native Studies Programs." In *Unlearning the Language of Conquest: Scholars Expose Anti-Indianism in America: Deceptions That Influence War and Peace, Civil Liberties, Public Education, Religion and Spirituality, Democratic Ideals, the Environment, Law, Literature, Film, and Happiness*, edited by Don T. Jacobs, 190–206. Austin: University of Texas Press.

Mill, John Stuart. 1967. *A System of Logic Ratiocinative and Inductive: Being a Connected View of the Principles of Evidence and the Methods of Scientific Investigation*. London: Longmans.

Monk, Linda R. 2001. *The Words We Live By: Your Annotated Guide to the Constitution*. New York: Hyperion.

Moore, D. L. 2013. *That Dream Shall Have a Name: Native Americans Rewriting America*. Lincoln: University of Nebraska Press.

Myhra, Laurelle L. 2011. "'It Runs in the Family': Intergenerational Transmission of Historical Trauma Among Urban American Indians and Alaska Natives in Culturally Specific Sobriety Maintenance Programs." *American Indian and Alaska Native Mental Health Research: The Journal of the National Center* 18 (2): 17–40.

Nálí, H. D. B. 2015. Diné Sovereignty and Peacemaking. Interview, April. Shiprock, NM.

Navajo Nation Council Resolutions No. CJ-9–52 (Jan. 18, 1952) and No. CMY-75–68 (May 21, 1968).

Navajo Nation Division of Community Development. Administrative Service Centers, 2016. Web. 7 April 2016.

Navajo Nation Division of Community Development. Projects, 2016. Web. 7 April 2016.

Navajo Nation Fundamental Laws of the Diné, Navajo Nation Code (2002), No. CN-69–02, Window Rock, AZ: 2003.

Navajo Nation Local Governance Act, Title 26. 1998.

Navajo Nation Office of the Auditor General. 2016. "Navajo Nation Local Governance Act Certification Process." Web. 7 April 2016.

Navajo Technical University. 2016. http://www.navajotech.edu/academics/degree-programs/master-of-arts/dine-studies.

Navajo Treaty of 1868.

Needman, Andrew. 2014. *Power Lines: Phoenix and the Marking of the Modern Southwest*. Princeton, NJ: Princeton University Press.

Neihardt, John G. 1988. *Black Elk Speaks: Being the Life Story of a Holy Man of the Oglala Sioux*. Lincoln: University of Nebraska Press.

Nevada v. Hicks, 533 U.S. 353 (2001).

Newcomb, Steven T. 2008. *Pagans in the Promised Land: Decoding the Doctrine of Christian Discovery*. Golden, CO: Fulcrum.

Nielsen, Marianne, and James Zion. 2005. *Navajo Nation Peacemaking: Living Traditional Justice*. Tucson: University of Arizona Press.

Niethammer, Carolyn J. 2001. *I'll Go and Do More: Annie Dodge Wauneka, Navajo Leader and Activist*. Lincoln: University of Nebraska Press.

Norieg, J. 1992. "American Indian Education in the United States: Indoctrination for Subordination to Colonialism." In *The State of Native America: Genocide, Colonization, and Resistance*, ed. M. A. Jaimes. Boston: South End Press.

Office of Navajo Nation Scholarship and Financial Assistance. 2016. http://www .onnsfa.org/FundingTypes/ChiefManuelito.aspx

"Official Report of the Nineteenth Annual Conference of Charities and Correction (1892)," 46–59. Reprinted in Richard H. Pratt. 1973. *"The Advantages of Mingling Indians with Whites," Americanizing the American Indians: Writings by the "Friends of the Indian" 1880–1900*. Cambridge, MA: Harvard University Press.

Oliphant v. Suquamish Tribe, 435 U.S. 191 (1978).

Parsons-Yazzie, Evangeline, Margaret Speas, Jessie Ruffenach, and Berlyn Yazzie. 2007. *Diné Bizaad Bináhoo'aah: Rediscovering the Navajo Language: An Introduction to the Navajo Language*. Flagstaff, AZ: Salina Bookshelf.

Peacemaking Program of the Navajo Nation. 2014. http://www.navajocourts.org/ indexpeacemaking.htm.

Perry, Carol, and Patricia Anne Davis. 2001. "Diné Sovereignty is Spiritual Empowerment and Self-Identity." Public hearing, Window Rock, AZ, August 16.

Pewewardy, Cornel. 2005. "Ideology, Power, and the Miseducation of the Indigenous People of the United States." In *For Indigenous Eyes Only: A Decolonization Handbook*, edited by Angela Cavendar Wilson and Michael Yellow Bird, 139–56. Santa Fe, NM: School of American Research.

Pijawka, David, James Gardner, Shaina Begay, Seneca House, Monique Reveles, Alesha Sloan, Eric Trevan, and Chandler Willie. 2013. Review and Recommendations for Updating the Community Land-Based Plans for the Navajo Nation. Navajo Nation Office of the President.

Porter, R. O. 2005. *Sovereingty, Colonialism and the Indigenous Nations*. Durham, NC: Carolina Academic Press.

Powell, Dana E., and Andrew Curley. 2009. "K'e, Hozhó, and Non-Governmental Politics on the Navajo Nation: Ontologies of Difference Manifest in Environmental Activism." *World Anthropologies Network E-Journal* 4. Guest Edited by M. de la Cadena and M. Blaser.

Quintero, Donovan. 2014. "With General Election Looming, Finality for Deschene's Chance to Remain a Presidential Candidate May Come Today." *Navajo Times*, October 17.

Ramswell, Prebble Q. 2012. "Ayali: Is It Time to Say Good-bye to American Indian Languages?" *Indigenous Policy Journal* 23 (1): 1–22.

Resolution of the Navajo Nation Council, 20th Navajo Nation Council Third Year. 2005. An Act Relating to Education, Enacting the Navajo Sovereignty in Education Act of 2005 (CJY-37–05); Amending Titles Ten and Two of the Navajo Nation Code.

Rice, Doyle. 2015. "Fla. Gov. Nans the Terms Climate Change, Global Warming." *USA Today*, March 9. http://www.usatoday.com/story/weather/2015/03/09/florida-governor-climate-change-global-warming/24660287/.

Riggs v. Estate of Attakai, No. SC-CV-39–04 (Navajo Supreme Court, June 13, 2007).

Roessel, Robert A., Jr. 1977. *Navajo Education in Action: The Rough Rock Demonstration School*. Chinle, AZ: Navajo Curriculum Center Rough Rock Demonstration School.

———. 1979. *Navajo Education, 1948–1978: Its Progress and Its Problems*. Rough Rock, AZ: Navajo Curriculum Center Rough Rock Demonstration School.

———. 1983. *Dinétah: Navajo History*. Edited by. T. L. McCarthy. Navajo Curriculum Center and Title IV-B Material Development Project. Rough Rock, AZ: Rough Rock Demonstration School.

Rosier, P., and Wayne Holm. 1980. *The Rock Point Experience: A Longitudinal Study of a Navajo School Program: (Saad naaki bee na'nitin)*. Washington, DC: Center for Applied Linguistics.

Ruggles M. Stahn, Dorothy Gohdes, and Sarah E. Valway. 1993. "Diabetes and Its Complications Among Selected Tribes in North Dakota, South Dakota, and Nebraska." *Diabetes Care* 16 (1): 244–47.

Salt River Pima-Maricopa Indian Community (SRPMIC). General Plan, "Sustainable SRPMIC: Planning for Generations." 13 December 2006. PDF file.

Santa Clara Pueblo v. Martinez, 436 U.S. 49, 56 (1978).

Sartori, Giovanni. 1970. "Concept Misinformation in Comparative Politics." *American Political Science Review* 64 (December): 1033–53.

Schenck, Ronald. 1988. "Navajo Healing." *Psychological Perspectives: A Quarterly Journal of Jungian Thought* 19 (2): 223–40.

Schilling, Vincent. 2014. "Obama Puts Native Youth Front and Center at 2014 White House Tribal Nations Conference." Indian Country Today Media Network, December 4.

Schmitt, Carl. 1985. *Political Theology*. Translated by George Schwab. Cambridge, MA: MIT Press.

"Sha' bik'ehgo As'ah Oodááłł: Living with Wellness and Health Guided by the Journey of the Sun." 2006. Navajo Health and Wellness Curriculum for Health

Promotion, Division of Public Health, Chinle Comprehensive Health Facility, Chinle, AZ.

Siebens, Julie, and Tiffany Julian. 2011. American Community Survey Briefs, Table S0601, Native North American Languages Spoken at Home in the United States and Puerto Rico: 2006–2010, United States Department of Commerce, United States Census Bureau, Economics and Statistics Administration, December.

Smith, Linda Tuhiwai. 1999. *Decolonizing Methodologies: Research and Indigenous Peoples*. London: Zed Books.

Sobralske, Mary C. 1985. "Perception of Health, Navajo Indians." *Topics of Clinical Nursing* 7 (3): 32–39.

Strate v. A-1 Contractors, 520 U.S. 438 (1997).

Szasz, Margaret Connell. 1988. *Indian Education in the American Colonies, 1607–1783*. Albuquerque: University of New Mexico Press.

Tanner, H. 1992. "A History of All the Dealings of the United States Government with the Sioux." Unpublished manuscript. Prepared for the Black Hills Land Claim by order of the United States Supreme Court, on file at the D'Arcy McNickle Center for the History of the American Indian, Newberry Library, Chicago.

Tatum, Melissa L., Miriam Jorgensen, Mary E. Guss, and Sarah Deer. 2014. *Structuring Sovereignty: Constitutions of Native Nations*. Los Angeles: American Indian Studies Center UCLA.

Terrill, Marshall. "ASU Works with Navajo Planners to Map Out Tribe's Destiny Through Training Program." *ASU Now*, 24 June 2015. Web. 5 April 2016.

Testimony by Timothy Benally, Acting Superintendent of Schools, before the U.S. Senate Committee on Indian Affairs, Navajo Nation Department of Diné Education: Hearing on Indian Education Ensuring the Bureau of Indian Education has the Tools Necessary to Improve. 113th Congress, May 21, 2014.

Thompson, Hildegard. 1975. *The Navajos' Long Walk for Education—Diné Nizaagóó Bíhoo'aah Yíkanaaskai: A History of Navajo Education—Diné Óhoołʼaahii Baa Hané*. Tsaile, AZ: Navajo Community College Press.

"United Nations Declaration on the Rights of Indigenous Peoples." 2008. United Nations, March. http://www.un.org/esa/socdev/unpfii/documents/DRIPS_en.pdf.

United States v. Wheeler, 435 U.S. 313, 323 (1978).

Walker, Ryan, Ted Jojola, and David Natcher. 2013. *Reclaiming Indigenous Planning*. Montreal: McGill-Queen's University Press.

Wall, Leon, and William Morgan. 1994. *Navajo English Dictionary*. Revised ed. New York: Hippocrene Books.

Wentzel-Fisher, Sarah. 2015. "Magic in Navajo Borderlands." *Edible Santa Fe* 37 (April/May): 50–57.

Westermeyer, Joseph. 1977. "The Ravage of Indian Families in Crisis." In *The Destruction of American Indian Families*, edited by Steven Unger. New York: Association of American Indian Affairs.

Wilkins, David E. 1987. *Diné Beehaz'áanii: A Handbook of Navajo Government*. Tsaile, AZ: Navajo Community College Press.

———. 1999. *The Navajo Political Experience*. Tsaile, AZ: Diné College Press.

———. 2002. "Governance within the Navajo Nation: Have Democratic Traditions Taken Hold?" *Wicazo Sa Review* 17 (1): 91–129.

———. 2003. *The Navajo Political Experience*. Revised ed. Lanham, MD: Rowman and Littlefield.

Williams, Robert A., Jr. 1990. *The American Indian in Western Legal Thought*. New York: Oxford University Press.

———. 2012. *Savage Anxieties: The Invention of the Western Civilization*. New York: Palgrave Macmillan.

Wilson, Angela Cavendar, and Michael Yellow Bird, eds. 2005. *For Indigenous Eyes Only: A Decolonization Handbook*. Santa Fe, NM: School of American Research.

Wolchover, Natalie. 2011. "How Many People Can the World Support?" *Live Science*, October 11. http://www.livescience.com/16493-people-planet-earth-support.html.

Yazzie, D. H. 2015. "Diné Self Governance." Unpublished manuscript. Shiprock, NM.

Yazzie, Robert, Avery Denny, Amber Crotty, Dana Eldridge, Moroni Benally, Michael Lerma, and Andrew Curley. 2011. *Recommendations for Restructuring the Navajo Nation Council*. Tsaile, AZ: Diné Policy Institute.

Yong, Amos, and Barbara Brown Zikmund. 2010. *Remembering Jamestown: Hard Questions about Christian Missions*. Eugene, OR: Wipf and Stock Publishers.

Young, Robert W. 1972. "The Rise of the Navajo Tribe" In *Plural Society in the Southwest*, ed. E. Spicer and R. Thompson. Albuquerque: University of New Mexico Press.

Young, Robert W., and William Morgan. 1987. *The Navajo Language: A Grammar and Colloquial Dictionary*. Rev. ed. Albuquerque: University of New Mexico Press.

Yurth, Cindy. 2014. "At Forum, Young Candidates Demand a Seat at the Table" *Navajo Times*, July 24.

CONTRIBUTORS

Justice Raymond D. Austin is from Chilchinbeto, Navajo Nation. Justice Austin is professor in the Department of Applied Indigenous Studies and Department of Criminology and Criminal Justice at Northern Arizona University in Flagstaff. He served as associate justice of the Navajo Nation Supreme Court from 1985 to 2001. While serving on the Navajo Nation Supreme Court, Justice Austin and his colleagues on the court took the lead on using American Indian customary law in tribal court decision-making. Justice Austin served as the Distinguished Jurist in Residence at the University of Arizona's James E. Rogers College of Law from 2007 to 2016, and was the Herman Phleger Distinguished Visiting Professor of Law at Stanford Law School in the spring semester of 1995. He has taught short courses at Harvard Law School, Arizona State University College of Law, University of Utah College of Law, and at law schools in Italy and Spain. Justice Austin thanks Professors Robert A. Williams Jr. and Robert Hershey; the James E. Rogers College of Law; and Harry Walters, Professor Emeritus, Diné College, Tsaile, Arizona, for their reviews and comments. Justice Austin also thanks his son, Joseph, JD (2014), James E. Rogers College of Law, for his review, comments, edits, and insightful discussions.

Bidtah Nellie Becker (Diné) has dedicated her professional life to the Navajo Nation and nation building. She is currently the executive director of the Navajo Nation Division of Natural Resources. President Begaye appointed her in May 2015 and the Navajo Nation Council confirmed her appointment in October 2015. She is the first woman to be confirmed by the Navajo Nation Council as the executive director. Immediately prior, Ms. Becker served as the assistant attorney general for the Navajo Nation Department of Justice Natural Resources Unit, where her practice included both environmental and natural resources matters concerning and affecting the Nation. Dedicated to tribal nation building, she helped created the Tribal In-House Counsel Association (TICA), an association dedicated to the unique issues of attorneys working in-house for tribes and their entities, and served on the TICA board until her appointment as the executive director. In 2012, President Obama appointed Ms. Becker as trustee for the Institute of American Indian Arts. She is also a member of the Navajo Studies Conference Inc. board, and its treasurer. She served many years on the Southwestern Association of Indian Arts board, which produces the Santa Fe Indian Market. She is a proud graduate of the Georgetown University School of Foreign Service and the University of New Mexico School of Law, where she was one of the founders of the online *Tribal Law Journal*. Ms. Becker and her husband, Paul Spruhan, live in Fort Defiance, Navajo Nation, and their two children attend Tséhootsooí Diné Bi'Olta', the Navajo-language immersion school.

Manley A. Begay Jr. is currently a professor in the Department of Applied Indigenous Studies, College of Social and Behavioral Sciences and Department of Educational Leadership, College of Education, at Northern Arizona University. Professor Begay is also an affiliate faculty member of the W. A. Franke College of Business at NAU. He teaches courses on Indigenous nation building, Diné history and philosophy, curriculum development, and Indigenous education. Since 1997, he has also been codirector of the Harvard Project on American Indian Economic Development at the John F. Kennedy School of Government at Harvard University. He received his master's and doctorate in administration, planning, and social policy from Harvard University, and also earned a master's in educational administration from Brigham Young University. He has also worked closely with Native nations in the United States, First Nations and Bands in Canada, Aborigines in Australia, and Maoris in New Zealand. Professor Begay has been both senior lecturer and associate social scientist in the American Indian studies program at the University of Arizona, faculty affiliate at the Institute for Environment and Society, and founding director, founding faculty chair, and faculty associate at the Native Nations

Institute for Leadership, Management, and Policy. While at Harvard, Professor Begay also served an instructor and lecturer at the Harvard Graduate School of Education.

Avery Denny is a member of the Tó dikǫzhí nisłį, Tótsohnnii bashischini, Ta'neeszą̨hnii dashicheíí, Tséníjikini dashínálí, and Hooshdodiitoii dee' eii naasa clans. Currently, he is residing in Whippoorwill, Arizona, on the Navajo Nation. He is an *Hatáałii*, a singer of the Blessingway, *Hozh—jí*, Protectionway, *Naay'ee'e ji*, and the *Tł'ééjí Hatáál*, Nightway. These are Navajo healing ceremonies consisting of two-, five-, and nine-night ceremonies, which are known as Hatáál Nahagha'. He has been teaching Diné language, culture, and history for twenty-five years. At Diné College, he has taught courses in Navajo culture, Navajo oral history, Navajo philosophy, Navajo holistic healing, Navajo herbology, and Diné educational philosophy. He speaks to schools, organizations, and Navajo Nation tribes regarding the protection of sacred sites and religious issues. Also, he has spoken on the rights and discretions of sacred sites. Avery Denny has also served as a tour guide to Dinétah (sacred sites), doing offerings and culturally educating visitors about the origin and history of the Diné people and the land. He has been an active member of the Hatáałii Association and Hatáałii Advisory Group for several years.

Larry W. Emerson is Tsénahabiłnii born for Tó'aheidlííní. His *cheis* (paternal grandparents) are Hoghanłání, and his maternal grandparents are Kiiyaa'áanii. He is a community activist, farmer, artist, and scholar, living in Tsédaak'áán, Diné Nation, east of Shiprock, New Mexico, Diné Nation. He earned his doctorate from the joint doctoral program of San Diego State University and Claremont Graduate University in 2003. His dissertation was entitled "Hozhonahazdlii: Towards a Practice of Diné Decolonization." His interests are in Indigenous studies and scholarship, social justice, decolonizing research methodologies, Diné peacemaking, education, and health.

Colleen Gorman is originally from Chinle. She is Naaneesht'ézhí Táchii'nii (Zuni/Red Running into the Charcoal Streaked Water) and born for Bįįh Bitoodniih Tódích'íi'nii (Deer Springs Bitter Water). Kinłíchíí'nii (Red House) and Dibé Łízhin (Black Sheep) are her maternal and paternal grandparents. Colleen lives in Albuquerque with Carlos Barros and their blended family. Their children are Táchii'nii Gorman, Phillip Bailey, and Salvador Barros. She is a multimedia artist, muralist, poet, visionary entrepreneur, charter school founder and teacher.

Michelle Hale is Navajo, Laguna, Chippewa, and Odawa from Oak Springs, Arizona. She is of the Laguna Sun clan born for Todichiinii (Bitterwater). She is an assistant professor of American Indian studies (AIS) at Arizona State University, where she teaches courses in tribal government, reservation economic development, tribal planning, and federal Indian policy, along with the introductory course to AIS. Dr. Hale's current research on Navajo community development stems from dissertation work done on Navajo local governance and chapter-driven initiatives for greater control and ownership of decision-making, administrative process, and outcomes.

Michael Lerma (P'urhépecha) is an assistant professor of politics and international affairs and applied Indigenous studies at Northern Arizona University. His recent research has explored the efficacy of traditional Diné institutions of governance. Michael also contributes to research conducted by the Diné Policy Institute. He teaches courses on international relations, tribal government, Native American politics, and research methods. Michael's research generally advocates for future Native nation building via consolidation of Indigenous interests and expansion of Native nation control of norms within the international political economy.

Leola Tsinnajinnie is Filipino and Diné, born for the Táchii'nii (Red Running Into the Water) clan. She is also married into Tamaya (Santa Ana Pueblo). She is a member of the Torreon/Star Lake Chapter of the Navajo Nation where she was raised. She earned her bachelor's degree in sociology and her master's degree in American Indian studies from the University of Arizona. Her doctorate concentration is in educational thought and sociocultural studies from the University of New Mexico's College of Education. Her areas of focus are Indigenous education, decolonization, and Native student conceptions of nation building. She is an assistant professor and faculty member in the Native American Studies Department at the University of New Mexico.

INDEX